Letting
Stories
Breathe

what a great book —enjoy

Letting Stories Breathe

A Socio-Narratology

Arthur W. Frank

THE UNIVERSITY

OF CHICAGO PRESS

Chicago and London

ARTHUR FRANK is
professor of sociology
at the University of
Calgary. His books
include *At the Will of
the Body: Reflections on
Illness*; *The Wounded
Storyteller: Body,
Illness, and Ethics*;
and *The Renewal of
Generosity: Illness,
Medicine, and How to
Live*, the latter two
published by the
University of Chicago
Press.

The University of Chicago Press, Chicago 60637
The University of Chicago Press, Ltd., London
© 2010 by The University of Chicago
All rights reserved. Published 2010
Printed in the United States of America

19 18 17 16 15 14 13   12 11 10   1 2 3 4 5

ISBN-13: 978-0-226-26013-6 (cloth)
ISBN-10: 0-226-26013-5 (cloth)

Library of Congress Cataloging-in-Publication Data
Frank, Arthur W.
    Letting stories breathe : a socio-narratology / Arthur W. Frank.
       p. cm.
    Includes bibliographical references and index.
    ISBN-13: 978-0-226-26013-6 (hardcover : alk. paper)
    ISBN-10: 0-226-26013-5 (hardcover : alk. paper) .
    1. Discourse analysis, Narrative—Social aspects.   2. Narration
(Rhetoric)—Social aspects.   3. Dialogue analysis—Social
aspects.   4. Storytelling—Social aspects.   I. Title.
    P302.7.F73 2010
    808.3'93—dc22

                                                  2009053092

♾ The paper used in this publication meets the minimum
requirements of the American National Standard for Information
Sciences—Permanence of Paper for Printed Library Materials,
ANSI Z39.48-1992.

To my daughters,

Kate and Stewart,

and telling stories

together.

Contents

prologue

"Mabel, people want to know about things in your life in a way they can understand. You know, how you got to be who you are. There has to be a theme."

"I don't know about no theme."

I squirmed in my seat. Her hands didn't move. "A theme is a point that connects all the dots, ties up all the stories . . ."

"That's funny. Tying up all the stories. Why somebody want to do that?"

"When you write a book there has to be a story or idea, a theme . . ."

"Well, theme I don't know nothing about. That's somebody else's rule. You just do the best way you know how. What you know from me."—Greg Sarris, Mabel McKay: Weaving the Dream

None of us can ever retrieve the innocence before all theory when art knew no need to justify itself, when one did not ask of a work of art what it said because one knew (or thought one knew) what it did.—Susan Sontag, Against Interpretation

I can only answer the question "What am I to do?" if I can answer the prior question "Of what story or stories do I find myself a part?"—Alasdair MacIntyre, After Virtue

We are all the victims of stories in one way or another, even if we are not in them, even if we are not born yet.—Iphigeneia in Barry Unsworth, The Songs of the Kings

This book proposes ways to think about and study stories so that we can learn to live better with the stories that surround and circulate through our lives. The book is also about dialogue, which can begin by hearing each of these epigraphs talking to the others.

Greg Sarris reports a conversation in which he is thinking like the graduate student he is at that time, working to produce an ethnographic narrative analysis for his dissertation.[1] He believes he needs a theme that connects the stories told by the subject of his dissertation, Mabel McKay, a world-renown Native American artisan. The woven baskets for which she is most famous are part of her practice as a traditional healer. And in all she does, Mabel McKay is a storyteller. She finds the idea of "tying up all the stories" to be funny. Thinking about stories that way is "somebody else's rule." She knows that stories are too lively and too wild to be tied up.

Mabel McKay is a living exemplar of the world that Susan Sontag laments as being lost.[2] Mabel McKay does not need to ask what artworks *say*, because what stories *do* is immanent in her life and being. The baskets she weaves and the stories she tells are less things she produces than vital forces she works with to affect the lives of those around her, from her family to strangers who view her work in museums. In her practices, stories do things that most people would think of as good.

Iphigeneia speaks as a character in the retelling of an ancient story, and that story casts her as its victim.[3] Her plight represents the dark side of Alasdair MacIntyre's observation:[4] Iphigeneia knows what story she is in, and what it requires her to do is terrible. The story takes place at the beginning of the Trojan War. The Greek army is assembled and ready to sail for Troy, but the seas are becalmed. The gods require a sacrifice before the winds will blow, and as Agamemnon's daughter, Iphigeneia must be that sacrifice. The family story of which this moment is part extends back through generations of betrayals and murders, and the story will continue after her death to include more betrayals and murders, including that of Agamemnon. Iphigeneia knows she must become a sacrifice, because of the story that everyone is caught up in. That story is less her choice than her fate.

The title of this book, *Letting Stories Breathe*, proposes a trope that contrasts with the goal that Sarris has been taught and Mabel McKay deprecates: tying up stories. The problem of studying stories is how to avoid, so far as possible, imposing on them what Mabel McKay calls "somebody else's rule." To do that, I pay attention as carefully as I can to what storytellers say about stories, which complements what many social scientists say. The study of stories I propose is less about finding themes and more about asking what stories do, which is to inform human life. Stories inform in the sense of providing information, but more significantly, stories give form—temporal and spatial orientation, coherence, meaning, intention, and especially boundaries—to lives that inherently lack form. How stories inform lives can be a gift or a danger.

If MacIntyre is right that people derive at least some of their sense of what they must do from stories, then the stakes on studying stories are high. Mabel McKay stands for all who use stories to heal. Iphigeneia stands for all whose lives are imperiled by stories.

Stories make life good, but they also make life dangerous. They bring people together, and they keep them apart. This book is about humans' necessary, inescapable, sometimes beneficial but too often imperfect companionship with stories. Its goal is to improve the terms of that companionship.

Introduction: Six Stories about Stories

Trust in the tale is old.
—Virgil, *The Aeneid* (9.92, Robert Fagles, trans.)

Stories may not actually breathe, but they can animate. The breath imputed by this book's title is the breath of a god in creation stories, as that god gives life to the lump that will become human. Stories animate human life; that is their work. Stories work with people, for people, and always stories work *on* people, affecting what people are able to see as real, as possible, and as worth doing or best avoided. What is it about stories—what are their particularities—that enables them to work as they do? More than mere curiosity is at stake in this question, because human life depends on the stories we tell: the sense of self that those stories impart, the relationships constructed around shared stories, and the sense of purpose that stories both propose and foreclose.

Stories breathe life not only into individuals, but also into groups that assemble around telling and believing certain stories. After stories animate, they instigate. In the outer circle of Dante's *Inferno*, the lovers Paolo and Francesca claim that their shared reading of a story of courtly love instigated their illicit affair. Contemporary sociologists argue that stories mobilize social movements, and stories send nations off to war. In Dante's account as well as that of sociology, a good life requires living well with stories. When life goes badly, a story is often behind that too.

SIX STORIES

A commitment to letting stories breathe means that stories should have the first word. Here are six or maybe seven (because it is not always clear when a story deserves to be called different from another story) short stories that all reflect on storytelling. Each is a story about becoming caught up in stories. I will return to these stories throughout later chapters and offer them here with only enough commentary to introduce significant arguments in this book.

Like any storyteller, I hope that readers will find themselves as engaged in these stories as I do. But not all stories engage all people; stories reflect and generate differences. Readers who do not find themselves caught up in any or all of these stories are invited to understand their lack of engagement as a first lesson about stories: any particular person will respond to the call of only some stories among the many that call out to people. A first difference between narrative analysis and either everyday or performance storytelling is that analysts ask how people's lives are defined as much by the stories they overlook as by those they do become caught up in. Analysis begins in moments of interrupting either of these processes. Analysis interprets not only the story, but also its reception and continuing transmission: who is caught up in which story, and who tells that story again?

Fifteen years ago I became caught up in a story that I have told on numerous public occasions, sometimes reading it, sometimes telling it from memory. The story is by the South American writer Eduardo Galeano, and it is titled "Christmas Eve."

> Fernando Silva ran the children's hospital in Managua. On Christmas Eve, he worked late into the night. Firecrackers were exploding and fireworks lit up the sky when Fernando decided it was time to leave. They were expecting him at home to celebrate the holiday.
>
> He took one last look around, checking to see that everything was in order, when he heard cottony footsteps behind him. He turned to find one of the sick children walking after him. In the half light he recognized the lonely, doomed child. Fernando recognized the face already lined with death and those eyes asking for forgiveness, or perhaps permission.
>
> Fernando walked over to him and the boy gave him his hand.
> *"Tell someone, . . ."* the child whispered. *"Tell someone I'm here."*[1]

In the last lines, the dying child is fading into a story about himself. With his closing plea, the story we have been hearing begins. Fernando Silva is asked to tell a story. From Fernando Silva the story reaches Eduardo Galeano, who puts it in his book, from which I now retell it, and so on, as those who retell the story become *part of* the story that includes all responses to the child's plea. That plea becomes the story's volition, as the story speaks so much more forcefully than the child who speaks so softly. But while retelling "Christmas Eve" is a response to the child's suffering, that retelling cannot in itself claim much moral superiority. As often as I have told this story, I remain all too capable of passing over many other stories that call for my engagement in even more compelling terms. Perhaps this story, which leaves so much unsaid and asks only to be retold, is as much as I can handle.

Galeano's story belongs at the beginning of this book because it is about events morphing into a story in which those events continue. The chaining of stories goes backward to the Christmas Eve of the Christian gospel, as well as forward to the future acts of telling that the story requests. "Christmas Eve" also exemplifies the difficulty of distinguishing fiction from non-fiction. It occurs in a book of short writings that vary from clearly imaginative retellings of folk tales to equally obvious political journalism, with no markers as to which is which. The storyteller refuses to tell his readers whether "Christmas Eve" is a report, retold from what a real person named Fernando Silva told the author, or whether it is a fable spun from the author's imagination—but imagination based on what lived experiences, and true to what? Stories always pose that question: what kind of truth is being told? Stories never resolve that question; their work is to remind us that we have to live with complicated truths.

The next two stories-about-stories are a pair. Both begin with an earlier story that works to hold people to a particular understanding of their lives. That story is then incorporated into a later one, the telling of which is an act of breaking free from the first story, or at least instigating new possibilities for what that story will be allowed to do. These stories work across generations within a family, connecting family members but also separating them.

The first of this pair is from Sharon O'Brien's memoir *The Family Silver*.[2] The story is about the set of silver—place settings of dinner utensils—that gives the memoir its title. The silver was purchased by O'Brien's grandfather, Dan Quinlan, an actor and vaudeville performer whom she calls, with irony bordering on derision, "Handsome Dan." O'Brien first tells what might be called the family-authorized version of the story:

Ever since I came to remember stories I had heard about the Repoussé [the style of engraving that became the family's name for the silver]. Handsome Dan had bought the fabulous, beyond-price silver set during one of his flush periods. "It was exquisite," my mother would say, as she told and retold the story. "Simply exquisite. Shipped from Paris to Baltimore, and then by rail to Elmira [New York]." When my mother described the Repoussé's odyssey she seemed to be still marveling that anything French could have found its way to Elmira. After she died I discovered that the Repoussé was not French at all: the Paris purchase must have been one of Handsome Dan's stories. (56)

In O'Brien's opening sentence, *stories* sound good: childhood memories that are part of a trajectory leading to her present book. By the last sentence, stories have become suspect, potentially dangerous; they participate in what emerges as a pattern of deceit. The family silver becomes a consequential actor in the story of O'Brien's family. After O'Brien's grandmother's death, her mother and aunts sever contact with one another after disputing the inheritance of the silver.

The story about the original story begins when O'Brien's mother, who throughout her life remains dazzled by how "exquisite" the Paris purchase is, tells O'Brien how Dan's wife reacted to the arrival of the silver:

When the silver set arrived in Elmira, my grandmother wept. "She sat at the kitchen table," my mother said, "just sat there and cried."
"Why?"
"They didn't have the money," she said. "My mother was scrimping and saving, and His Nibs goes and spends it all on the silver."
"Why didn't she send it back?"
"She couldn't. Every piece was monogrammed with a Q."
When that wooden crate arrived, unbidden and unannounced, my grandmother would have seen Handsome Dan's love of display, rather than his love of her. Now she had all those glorious place settings, and not enough money to buy the meat and vegetables she would have wanted to spread out on the kitchen table, right there where she was crying. (57)

How, O'Brien's multigenerational story asks, can her mother describe O'Brien's grandmother sitting and crying, yet still glorify the Paris origins and the "exquisite" design of the silver? How can she not see the story as her daughter sees it and as the memoir draws its readers into understanding what happened? For O'Brien, the foreground that represents the truth of the story is her grandmother crying. For her mother, those tears remain part of the background to what really counts, which has more to do with the silver's Parisian origins: "She would evoke the Repoussé lingeringly, worshipping its excess," an excess that O'Brien then elaborates as she often heard her mother elaborate it: the number of each type of utensil, fish knives to runcible spoons. *The Family Silver* belongs at the beginning of this book for many reasons—one is because it demonstrates how stories and material objects work together, each informing the other—but most of all because the story shows how deeply people become caught up in one version of a story, even though the same events could be told to a very different effect. In memoirs, old stories are constantly being reframed to have new effects.

A second family-memoir story complements O'Brien's family-silver story. This story is told as the beginning of Maxine Hong Kingston's *The Warrior Woman*.[3] Like O'Brien, Kingston seeks to understand what stories transmit from one generation to the next. Her memoir opens with her mother telling her a story. Unlike Galeano's story that asks to be retold, Kingston's mother begins her story with the opposite injunction. Her daughter must not tell the story she is about to be told, but she is to keep this story with her to guide her, informing her actions and sense of who she is:

> "You must not tell anyone," my mother said, "what I am about to tell you. In China your father had a sister who killed herself. She jumped into the family well. We say that your father has all brothers because it is as if she had never been born." (3)

The story tells how the Chinese men emigrated, found work if they were lucky, and sent money home to their families. The aunt became pregnant "long after the time when it could have been possible" after her husband's departure. "The village had also been counting. On the night the baby was to be born the villagers raided our house. Some were crying. Like a great saw, teeth strung with lights, files of people walked zigzag across our land, tearing the rice" (3–4). The villagers kill the family's livestock, rip up clothing, break crockery, and steal what is not destroyed. "Your aunt gave birth in the pigsty that night. The next morning when I went for water, I found her and the baby plugging up the family well" (5). The point is unambiguous: "Don't humiliate us. You wouldn't like to be forgotten as if you had never been born. The villagers are watchful" (ibid.). Kingston writes that this story was not unusual in her childhood: "Whenever she had to warn us about life, my mother told stories that ran like this one, a story to grow up on" (ibid.).

That phrase, "a story to grow up on," could be the title of this book. People grow up being cast into stories, as actors are cast into their parts in a play—but that is too deterministic a metaphor. People are like actors cast into multiple scripts that are all unfinished. From all the stories that people hear while they are growing up, they remain caught up in some, forget many others, and adapt a few to fit adult perceptions and aspirations. O'Brien and Kingston both engage in an adaptation of stories each grew up on, telling a story about the telling of that story and thereby changing how they remain caught up in the story. A different adaptation is evident in the fourth story.

This story is clearly fictional, taken from Leo Tolstoy's novel *War and Peace*.[4] It concerns a minor character named Mademoiselle Bourienne, who carries with her a story she has grown up on, and that story guides her powerfully but not well. Mademoiselle Bourienne is employed as the companion to Princess Marya. Mademoiselle is educated, gentile, and poor. The princess is also educated, very rich, and—at least at this point in the novel—a woman whose looks do not immediately draw men to her. Mademoiselle is considered very attractive, and she attracts Prince Anatole. Anatole is noble but poor and has been brought by his father to court Princess Marya, with hopes of a marriage that will restore their family's fortunes. Anatole prefers to imagine a future in which he marries the rich princess but enjoys her pretty companion on the side. Mademoiselle allows him to kiss her when they are alone. The princess discovers them, dismisses Anatole, and forgives Mademoiselle.

Tolstoy gives his most detailed attention to what leads Mademoiselle to imagine the future that will unfold when she reciprocates Anatole's attentions. A story from her past compels her toward this future:

Mademoiselle Bourienne has also been roused by Anatole's arrival into a state of high excitement, but her thoughts were of a different order [than those of Princess Marya]. Naturally, a beautiful young girl with no fixed position in society, with no friends or relations, not even a country of her own, was not looking forward to a life spent waiting on Prince Nikolay Bolkonsky [Princess Marya's father], reading to him and being a good friend to Princess Marya. Mademoiselle Bourienne had long been looking forward to the day when a Russian prince sensitive enough to see her as superior to all those ugly, dowdy, clumsy, Russian princesses would fall in love with her and carry her off. Now he had come. Mademoiselle Bourienne remembered a favorite story of her aunt's which she had adapted and loved to run over in her imagination. It was about a young girl who had been seduced, and her poor mother had appeared to her and reproached her for giving herself to a man without getting married. Mademoiselle was often moved to tears when she imagined herself telling *him*, her would-be seducer, this story. Now *he* was here—a real Russian prince. He would carry her off, then "my poor mother" would come on the scene, and they would be married. This future history of hers had been unfolding in Mademoiselle Bourienne's mind all the time they were talking about Paris. Mademoiselle Bourienne was not a scheming woman (she certainly never planned ahead), but everything had been prepared within her long before this and it had suddenly focused on Anatole the moment he appeared, after which she longed to please him and tried as hard as she could. (240)

Mademoiselle's story belongs early in this book because it shows how a story can guide someone's perception and action. Mademoiselle has grown up on a story her aunt told her, adapting it until the story may have little resemblance to what her aunt once told—her aunt might well be appalled at the story that guides Mademoiselle's flirtation with Anatole. What is called *the story* here is a process that in this instance unfolds over years. The effect of the story her aunt once told her does not depend on a single instance of telling and hearing. If, according to Heraclitus's maxim, a person can never step into the same river twice, so also the same story is never told twice, no matter how many times it is told.

Tolstoy emphasizes that Mademoiselle "never planned ahead." Her actions in responding to Anatole, purposeful as they are, are not "scheming." Rather, Mademoiselle's actions are the result of being caught up in a situation that fits a preexisting plot, and that plot then leads her onward—it conducts her. The story her aunt once told her, as she has adapted it, conducts Mademoiselle, and she believes in the part she plays. She trusts the story.

Telling Mademoiselle's story at the beginning of this book recognizes literary stories as being within its purview. One reason for doing so is a core premise of this book: to learn about stories and the effects of storytelling, *trust the storytellers*. Tolstoy knows what stories can do. But there is more. I find myself caught up in the story of Mademoiselle Bourienne, and I accept Tolstoy's fiction as presenting a subtle psychological truth about stories and human consciousness, because I recognize in the story what has too often been my own position: how I have repeated in my imagination some story that I have, as Tolstoy writes, "adapted" and then found myself in a situation that makes possible the future imaged in that story. Like Mademoiselle, I too have then felt compelled to act out what the story requires. If I do not repeat the stories that I have adapted and gone over in my imagination, that is because I, like Mademoiselle, eventually was embarrassed by what the story led me to do. This form of thinking with stories is all too human, which is part of why Princess Marya forgives her companion for seducing her suitor.

From Mademoiselle Bourienne we learn that stories do not simply report past events. Stories project possible futures, and those projections affect what comes to be, although this will rarely be the future projected by the story. Stories do not just have plots. Stories work to *emplot* lives: they offer a plot that makes some particular future not only plausible but also compelling.[5] That EMPLOTMENT[6] is the extensive meaning of Kingston's metaphor of a story *to grow up on*. Stories learned early in life have an especially compelling force, but growing up never ends. We humans spend our lives like Mademoiselle Bourienne, adapting stories we were once told, although O'Brien and Kingston adapt the stories they grew up on to a very different effect from Mademoiselle's adaptations. Not least among human freedoms is the ability to tell the story differently and to begin to live according to that different story.

Next are twin stories, each the mirror image of the other. So perhaps this introduction tells seven stories, not six. The anthropologist Allen Feldman describes how indoctrination and training classes of Republican and Loyalist paramilitary groups in Northern Ireland during the conflicts of the 1970s each told an origin story of Ireland.[7] Each story "gives birth to a particular temporality" that serves a political purpose. "The origin," Feldman writes, "beyond the time it has engendered, is immutable and not open to discussion. In its permanence and remoteness, the origin guarantees all subsequent bifurcations, all repetitions of itself" (14).

The origin story told by Republican paramilitaries—those who wanted to free Northern Ireland from British rule—describes "the prehistoric geological division of the island of Ireland from the European land mass," which is more the assertion of a primal reality than it is a story. The prehistoric reality of Ireland's separation might be called a narrative insofar as it establishes the plot of future stories of particular contests hinging on that prehistoric division. The core narrative of separation foretells the eventual outcome of all such stories. Feldman continues, describing these stories:

> The course of instruction treated subsequent historical conflict as the rift between a geographically inspired cultural-economic separatism and outside forces such as Christianity, British colonialism, and capitalism. These interlopers were depicted as undoing what geography had created. (17)

This origin story casts the paramilitary recruits as the protagonists in future stories of resistance to the interlopers. The eventual success of that resistance is assured by the prehistoric origins of the cause.

The complementary Loyalist (to Britain) origin story "traces the origins and ethnicity of Ulster Protestants back to the ten lost tribes of Israel. Here too the motifs of separation and demarcated territory predominate" (18).

This origin story more clearly is a story, with characters that act in a plot. But it also functions as a narrative, under the auspices of which a course of instruction can tell the same stories that the Republicans tell, but here the "interlopers" are destined to assume their rightful place in Ireland.

Feldman offers a view of the dark side of stories. A story leads Mademoiselle Bourienne into indiscretion and embarrassment. The paramilitaries are going to kill people, and stories will lead them. I place the indoctrination stories at this book's beginning to exemplify narrative dangers, but living without stories is not an option. Another storyteller worth trusting, Joan Didion, offers what might be the definitive testimonial to the importance of stories: "We tell ourselves stories in order to live."[8] Many stories can be dangerous, but an analogy is that stopping eating is no solution to the recognition that some food will poison us. We need stories to live.

A final story about stories is told by Frederick Douglass, the nineteenth-century American escaped slave, political advocate, and, perhaps most memorably, autobiographer. Here Douglass describes his experiences after his escape, when he was beginning to speak at abolitionist meetings:

> During the first three or four months, my speeches were almost exclusively made up of narrations of my own personal experience as a slave. "Let us have the facts," said the people. So also said my friend George Foster, who always wished to pin me down to my simple narrative. "Give us the facts," said Collins, "and we will take care of the philosophy." Just here arose some embarrassment. It was impossible for me to repeat the same old story month after month, and to keep up my interest in it. It was new to the people, it is true, but it was an old story to me; and to go through with it night after night was a task altogether too mechanical for my nature. "Tell your story, Frederick," would whisper my then revered friend, William Lloyd Garrison, as I stepped upon the platform. I could not always obey, for I was now reading and thinking . . . It did not entirely satisfy me to *narrate* wrongs; I felt like *denouncing* them.[9]

The dilemmas inherent in performing a story of personal experience— what might be called dilemmas of *narrative authenticity*—may never have been expressed more clearly. Douglass is troubled by how a story that is his—hard-won through suffering he has experienced and witnessed—is beginning to do its work independently of the person he is now becoming. He expresses how vital yet precarious the relation is between stories as expressions of AUTHENTICITY and stories as works of witness and advocacy.

Douglass's appraisal of the location of his storytelling is acute: "Fugitive slaves, at that time, were not so plentiful as now; and as a fugitive slave lecturer, I had the advantage of being a *'brand new fact'*—the first one out" (366).[10] People are cast into stories, but storytellers invent themselves in the stories they tell, and some storytellers have to do more invention than others. Not only must Douglass invent himself as a "brand new fact," but more than any other storyteller in this chapter, he must create an audience capable of comprehending this new self he brings into being in his stories.

Douglass's situation is complex because he feels used by those to whom he is also grateful. The abolitionists want him to limit himself to being the embodied representation of his story, and Douglass supports the ends to which they use him. Yet he is caught in a paradox. "Be yourself," he is coached, but this is followed by the advice that it's "better to have a *little* of the plantation manner of speech than not; 'tis not best that you seem too learned" (367). Douglass acknowledges that his friends are probably right, so far as advancing the cause of abolition is concerned. But he adds: "Still I must speak just the word that seemed to *me* the word to be spoken *by* me" (367; original italics). That statement could be the epigraph of narrative authenticity.

The issue is more consequential than Douglass being bored with telling the same story "night after night." The story he tells is no longer authentic to the person who is "now reading and thinking" and who no longer expresses himself in "the plantation manner of speech" that would make him sound authentic in the ears of his audience—*authenticity* always being a dialogue, and sometimes a contest, between storyteller and listeners.[11] Douglass's story exemplifies the demands for authenticity in storytelling and the dilemmas of achieving that authenticity. His story is as much a trap he must escape as it is a truth to which he is responsible.

* * *

These stories will return, especially in the next two chapters. Having given stories the first word, I conclude this introduction with a brief summary of how this book will proceed.

INTRODUCING SOCIO-NARRATOLOGY
SOCIO-NARRATOLOGY expands the study of literary narratives—NARRATOLOGY—to consider the fullest range of storytelling, from folklore to everyday conversation.[12] Among the many definitions of narratology, David Herman's is especially useful for understanding the nature of socionarratology:

> Narratology's basic premise is that a common, more or less implicit, model of narrative explains people's ability to understand communica-

tive performances and types of artifacts as stories. In turn . . . the goal of narratology is to develop an explicit characterization of the model underlying people's intuitive knowledge about stories, in effect providing an account of what constitutes humans' narrative competence.[13]

Herman proceeds to point out that this narratological project, heavily dependent on structural linguistics, emerged just when "its deficiencies were becoming apparent in the domain of linguistic theory itself" (14). My use of *narratology* dispenses with the baggage of seeking any formal underlying model of competence, while holding on to the recognition that being human, and especially being social, requires the competence to tell and understand stories. When that competence is diminished, which happens to many people, opportunities for participation in collective life contract. As MIKHAIL BAKHTIN observes: "A given consciousness is richer or poorer in genres [that is, its ability to understand different types of stories], depending on its ideological environment."[14]

Not least important in this quotation is Bakhtin putting the onus for lesser competence on people's environment, not individuals. People's access to narrative resources depends on their social location: what stories are told where they live and work, which stories do they take seriously or not, and especially what stories they exchange as tokens of membership, with jokes being the most frequent among these.[15]

Socio-narratology shares particular affinities with at least two other projects for understanding stories. Wayne Booth proposed "ethical criticism" as "any effort to show how the virtues of narratives relate to the virtues of selves and societies, or how the ethos of any story affects or is affected by the ethos—the collection of virtues—of any given reader."[16] The title of one of his books, *The Company We Keep*, anticipates my understanding (developed at the end of chapter 1) of stories as good or bad companions, although I took that metaphor not from Booth but from Donna Haraway.[17] Socio-narratology also shares much with Brian Boyd's claim for "evocriticism"—*evo* as in evolutionary—insofar as this seeks to "connect literature . . . with ongoing research of various kinds that can refine and challenge our understanding of human nature and thought."[18] Like Boyd, I seek to use narratology to understand how life becomes social. Unlike him, I am less interested in explaining origins, either of stories or of human consciousness.

What, then, are the claims and operating premises of socio-narratology?

First and primary, socio-narratology attends to stories as *actors*, studying what the story does, rather than understanding the story as a portal into the mind of a storyteller. Of course socio-narratology is interested in storytellers and story listeners, but they are understood as being enabled to be who they are because of stories. Those stories are never *theirs* except as reassemblies of fragments on loan. These fragments include standard motivational schemes for characters, plot occurrences, and recognizable styles, such as the "plantation manner of speech" that Douglass is encouraged to use in his storytelling to validate its authenticity.

Stories *act* in human consciousness, with individuals sometimes being aware of what story is acting and sometimes not. The anthropologist Claude Levi-Strauss, one of the great scholars of myth, wrote that "myths get thought in man unbeknownst to him."[19] People have often forgotten the stories that think in them; they overestimate the personal originality of what Douglass, quoted above, calls "the word to be spoken *by* me." Two axioms of socio-narratology are that no one ever thinks a story that is wholly original to that person, and no one ever thinks a story alone.

People tell stories that are very much their own, but they do not make up these stories by themselves.[20] In my earlier work I proposed a distinction between stories that people tell about their own lives and commonly available narratives that are the resources people use to construct their own stories.[21] More recently, the medical historian Anne Harrington organizes her history of mind-body medicine around five narratives that she distinguishes from stories.[22] The specific narratives that Harrington presents will be discussed in chapter 5; here my concern is her terminology, which establishes the NARRATIVE / STORY DISTINCTION. Harrington understands *stories* as "living, local, and specific," referring "to immediate, concrete events, people, scientific findings, and more" (24). *Narratives* are the resources from which people construct the stories they tell and the intelligibility of stories they hear. Narratives

> are templates: they provide us with tropes and plotlines that help us understand the larger import of specific stories we hear, or see in action. They also help us construct specific stories of our own . . . We learn these narrative templates from our culture, . . . in the way we might unconsciously learn the rules of grammar at home—by being exposed to multiple individual examples of living stories that rely on them. (24–25)

What Harrington calls culture is a more generalized version of Bakhtin's "ideological environment." The point of general scholarly agreement is that people's stories, however personal they are, depend on shared narrative resources. Although, as I noted in 1995, a consistent distinction between narrative and story is difficult to sustain in usage.

As actors, stories and narratives are resources for people, and they conduct people, as a conductor conducts an orchestra; they set a tempo, indicate emphases, and instigate performance options. The orchestra conductor's silence would not be understood as the absence of his or her effect on the music. Booth goes further, writing: "We all live our lives in a surrender to stories about our lives, and about other possible lives; we live more or less *in* stories, depending on how strongly we resist surrendering to what is 'only' imagined."[23] Mademoiselle Bourienne exemplifies those who surrender most easily. O'Brien and Kingston exemplify those who resist surrendering to the stories they grew up on, choosing instead to live what Booth calls other possible lives.

Second, stories are crucial actors not only in the making of narrative selves—selves that, as Booth says, live more or less in stories—but also in making life social. Stories connect people into collectivities, and they coordinate actions among people who share the expectation that life will unfold according to certain plots. The selves and collectivities animated by stories then animate further stories: revising old stories and creating new ones—though whether any story is ever truly new is always contestable. Stories and humans work together, in symbiotic dependency, *creating the social* that comprises all human relationships, collectivities, mutual dependencies, and exclusions. That symbiotic work of stories and humans creating the social is the scope of socio-narratology.

This conception of *social* as a process, not a state, and far more a verb than a noun, is developed by Bruno Latour in *Reassembling the Social*.[24] Although Latour's title reflects the impossibility of avoiding reference to "the social," his point is that *social* is not a substantive entity but rather a collection of practices, among which I include storytelling. Life has to be made social through constant work of reassembling.[25] The social as perpetual reassembly is usefully imagined by recalling the philosopher Otto Neurath's famous simile: "We are like sailors who have to rebuild their ship on the open sea, without ever being able to dismantle it and reconstruct it from the best components."[26] Like those sailors, people have to tell stories about lives that are always in progress, using whatever narrative components are at hand. Those stories then become one of the bases around which collectives assemble, from couples to social movements.

Third, the *narratology* part of socio-narratology pays attention to what *makes stories distinct* as a form of narration; what *capacities* enable stories to do the work they do? Chapter 1 will elaborate the multiple capacities of stories. Stories do not do everything. The question is, what do they have the capacity to do best?

Fourth, socio-narratology considers a *continuum of stories* including literature, folklore, journalistic reports, and interludes in everyday conversation. My premise is that each of these GENRES of storytelling depends on the others, because people learn to be storytellers and story listeners from all the stories they hear. Each form of storytelling—fiction or nonfiction, folklore or journalism—teaches people how to make sense of stories in other forms, how to perform and how to respond. Each form does its own distinct kind of work, but those works depend on each other. "If the border is fuzzy between life and narrative," Booth writes, "the distinction between narratives that are true and those that are fictions is even fuzzier."[27]

Fifth, socio-narratology recommends a mode of interpretation that is DIALOGICAL in the sense defined by Bakhtin. The crucial principles are that no voice is ever singular—every voice contains multiple other voices—and that in the interpretation of a story, as in the telling of stories, no speaker should ever be FINALIZED. As Bakhtin put it, no "last word" should ever be pronounced that forecloses what another person might become.[28]

Sixth, socio-narratology is practiced by way of *dialogical narrative analysis*.[29] In the background of that analytic practice—my preference for that term over *method* will be discussed in chapter 3—is the recognition that people are constantly doing their own narrative analyses, making sense of the stories they hear. One reason I draw a disproportionate number of examples from memoirs is that this genre formalizes what happens constantly in everyday talk: people retell stories to an effect different from an earlier telling, sometimes reflecting explicitly on that earlier telling and sometimes adapting the story as if it were being told for the first time. Everyone is a memoirist in the stories we each adapt and retell, and memoir may be the most self-conscious work of nonacademic narrative analysis. What distinguishes academic narrative analysis from everyday interpretation begins with the practitioner having the leisure to take more time at it, and especially having the advantage of being able to delay responses to stories in both time and space.[30]

My version of narrative analysis is qualified as *dialogical* as a reminder that analysis is always about the relationship between *at least two* and most often three elements: a story, a storyteller, and a listener. None of these could be what it is without the others. What is analyzed is how *each allows the other to be*: the story animates some individual or collective entity or process, and someone tells the story, thereby reanimating it.[31] Indisputable as it is that people tell stories, that does not relegate stories to being the mere products of human telling. Socio-narratology, although always relational in recognizing that all parties act, pays most attention to stories acting. It analyzes how stories breathe as they animate, assemble, entertain, and enlighten, and also deceive and divide people. Narratology in its early structuralist versions cuts stories up into small pieces in order to formulate principles of how those pieces are assembled. Stories became patients on the narratological dissecting table.[32] Socio-narratology, then, lets stories breathe by studying how they can do what they can do.

Seventh, dialogical narrative analysis takes particular interest in *learning from storytellers*. A preeminent example of such learning is the anthropologist Julie Cruikshank's description of the Yukon master storyteller Angela Sidney: "Her great skill came not just from remembering and knowing the stories, but from knowing how to use them appropriately in different situations to *produce the effect* she knew good stories can create."[33] I understand Cruikshank as meaning exactly what she says. Angela Sidney's skill is knowing how to use stories, but this skill depends on recognizing that "stories can create." Which echoes my primary claim of socio-narratology, that stories act. The primary lesson from storytellers is that they learn to work with stories that are not *theirs* but *there*, as realities. Master storytellers know that stories breathe.

A QUALIFIED APOLOGY AND A CHAPTER SUMMARY

This book began in workshops on narrative analysis that I have presented for almost a decade. Those workshops taught me at least two humbling truths. First, no one will ever read everything that has been written about stories and storytelling. And as corollary to that: any book on narrative that seeks to deploy all the definitional distinctions that fill the literature on narrative will find itself unable to get out of the thicket in which it has embedded itself. Socio-narratology also has to breathe, which means leaving much behind for others to reintroduce, if they can make the case for that reintroduction.

In the course of my reading, I began to play what I called the footnote game. I see a footnote and before I read it, I guess what book or article will be cited. I am usually wrong, at least about what the author cites. I am correct in that what I guessed makes the same argument and could have been cited, but the author has learned the same thing from a book or article I have not read. But then, I seem to have read something that the author has not. The point of the footnote game is not only to prove that no one has read everything; it is to demonstrate that no one needs to read everything.

My other humbling realization is that no one can ever say anything new about stories or storytelling. Academics value original contribution. But, as the gateway to Dante's inferno warns those who pass through it to abandon all hope, so the gateway to narrative analysis should caution scholars to abandon all pretense of saying anything original. That does not mean abandoning the hope of saying something useful and interesting that leads people to imagine different possibilities for how their lives are formed and informed—much as a story leads people to imagine different possible lives.

Humility aside, I believe that social scientists and various researchers using social scientific methods have been too exclusively concerned with stories as self-reports that provide more or less valid information about people's lives, and have neglected storytelling as a pervasive and crucially important form of human activity. Incomplete as any single book on storytelling necessarily is, this one attempts to bring together voices that are not yet in dialogue with each other, in order to provide greater theoretical and methodological coherence to narrative research. Perhaps the apology for this book and its aspiration is best expressed in a maxim quoted by Pierre Hadot: "A rather new and rather original book would be the one that would make one love old truths."[34] If I have few new truths to offer, I hope this book enhances the love of old ones, and some old stories too.

The exposition of socio-narratology proceeds as follows:

Chapter 1 is about what *capacities* stories have that other forms of narration do not. Those capacities enable stories to do what they are best able to do—in particular, how they get both tellers and listeners so intensely caught up in what stories tell. How do stories elicit such a high level of engagement, and what does that enable stories to do?

Chapter 2 considers the work that stories do: first, how stories give people a sense of subjectivity, and then how groups assemble around shared understandings of particular stories. These forms of work are not, in themselves, especially newsworthy. The interest lies in how the capacities of stories that have been elaborated in chapter 1 enable stories to play their part in doing this work. This chapter's conclusion introduces the ethical issue that the final chapter returns to: how can people live well with stories?

Chapters 3, 4, and 5 shift to practices of dialogical narrative analysis. My argument throughout this book is that narrative analysis has no method in the sense of a canonical sequence of steps that, if followed properly, produce an analysis.[35] But that lack of procedure does not mean that each researcher is starting from scratch. Unlike Frederick Douglass's self-description quoted earlier in this introduction, none of us is "the first one out." Exemplars provide guides to what form research can take. Chapter 3 presents five specific questions that can orient analytic interest. Chapter 4 addresses the core issue of interpretation, beginning with various suspicions about interpretation. Narrative analysis interprets stories, but its primary interest might be called meta-interpretive: studying how people interpret as they do, and how interpretations mediate the effects that stories have. This chapter also suggests what is distinct about a commitment to *dialogical* interpretation. Chapter 5 presents six exemplary forms of narrative research that can be called dialogical. These forms are not intended to be exhaustive, but do present a sufficient range of possibilities.

Finally, chapter 6 asks what a *good* companionship with stories might be. A bias that sets me apart from some colleagues in social science but makes me comfortable among bioethicists is my belief that any analysis ought to contribute something to humans' understanding of how to live—not just how living is done, but how it *ought* to be done. The contemporary popularity of stories—sometimes bordering on exaltation—whether in academia, journalism and electronic media, or various clinical and therapeutic practices, often obscures the reality that people do not always live well with stories.[36] If narrative analysis does not improve the quality of companionship between humans and stories, then it has failed. The work of improving companionship will always be unfinalized, but the last chapter tries to play some part in that process.

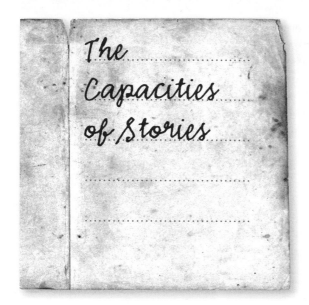

The **Capacities of Stories**

1

The aim here is to look at the varieties of animation or vitality that are attributed to images, the agency, motivation, autonomy, aura, fecundity, or other symptoms that make pictures into "vital signs," by which I mean not merely signs for living things *but signs as* living things. —W. J. T. Mitchell, *What Do Pictures Want?*

Every narrative tale—from the Iliad *to the latest Pulitzer Prize–winning newspaper serial—has the same narrative structure . . . : A central character encounters a problem, struggles with it, and, in the end, overcomes it or is defeated by it or is changed in some way. If the story . . . lacks one of those elements, you should not write it as a narrative.* —Bruce DeSilva, "Endings"

In the beginning is a story—if only because the idea of a *beginning* presupposes a sense of narrative. But what is a story, how do stories breathe, and what capacities enable stories to have the effects they do?

A response can begin with the question raised by this chapter's epigraph by W. J. T. Mitchell: in what sense are stories vital *living things*?[1] I then turn to what stories are, an issue most usefully approached by describing the capacities of stories, because these capacities give stories their vitality. Stories' capacities begin as the familiar stuff of literary narratology: characters, plot, POINT OF VIEW, and so forth, but the interest is not in discovering some underlying structure of narrative; the question is, *what enables stories to have their effects*? By thinking about stories' *capacities*, socio-narratology focuses on how stories act to make life social. A story, I propose, exists when *enough* of the capacities of stories are at play. Or, to paraphrase Bruce

DeSilva in the second epigraph, if the material does not sufficiently utilize these capacities, then that material is not appropriate for dialogical narrative analysis—however important it may be otherwise.[2]

I make no attempt to define stories.[3] The emphasis is on watching them act, not seeking their essence. In place of a definition, this chapter's final section does offer a descriptive phrase that I find most useful for keeping in mind what socio-narratology recognizes about stories.

HOW STORIES BREATHE

Tolstoy's pathetic story of Mademoiselle Bourienne (introduction) has a curious effect, the longer it is contemplated. The story upsets the commonsense temporal relation between stories and experience. According to the conventional understanding, people have experiences—something happens—and then they tell stories that represent those experiences. This temporal sequence of event preceding narration understands stories as *mimetic*: stories imitate life that has already happened and now is being represented in the story.[4] The anthropologist Cheryl Mattingly rejects the mimetic understanding of stories most clearly, reversing the temporality to put stories before experience: "There is no reality without narrative. Because we have stories, we believe we are having experiences. Experience is, at best, an enactment of pre-given stories."[5]

Tolstoy places a story at the beginning; that story will shape the action that becomes the event. His authorial intrusion into Mademoiselle's processes of thought discovers a complex relation of mutual MIMESIS. Mademoiselle *first* knows a story—the story she has adapted from what her aunt told her—and *then* that story conducts her action. She sees the people and possibilities around her *according to a story* that she has received and adapted. The story sets her course of action and is her moral compass in this action. Mimesis happens, but as a reciprocal process. Life and story imitate each other, ceaselessly and seamlessly, but neither enjoys either temporal or causal precedence. Mademoiselle's story sets in motion a future course of action, which Tolstoy's story represents; and his story of Mademoiselle becomes someone else's companion, possibly reshaped as it is retold in that person's imagination.

Tolstoy is not alone in reversing the temporality between stories and experience. Brian Boyd, in his study of the evolutionary advantages conferred by art and especially by stories, suggests how stories refine the human capacity to simulate possible futures:

> Stories employ words and conventions, but long before most narrative conventions emerged, we evolved a capacity not only for reexperiencing

the past in memory but also for flexibly reconfiguring it to offer concrete simulations of future situations.[6]

Which is exactly what Mademoiselle does with her story in the process of adapting it until the simulation could become reality. The historian Georges Duby describes how the stories known by medieval knights offered simulations of the futures they would enact: "Their ardor was focused entirely upon fulfilling the obligations of chivalry, upon respecting the rules of an ethic inculcated during adolescence and kept alive in their minds by all the stories and songs they listened to."[7] In anthropology, Renato Rosaldo observes this process in his ethnographic work among the Ilongots: "Huntsmen in fact seek out experiences that can be told as stories. In other words, stories often shape, rather than simply reflect, human conduct."[8] Rosaldo's conclusion—that stories often shape human conduct—is the core premise of socio-narratology.

An especially articulate testimonial of stories preceding the expression of experience is offered by the novelist Eric Ormsby, quoted by Alberto Manguel in his treatise on stories:

> Sometimes I have a feeling that words lead a private existence of their own, apart from us, and that when we speak or write, especially in moments of strong emotion, we do little more than hitch a ride on some obliging syllable or accommodating phrase.[9]

Mademoiselle Bourienne seems to hitch a ride less than she is taken for a ride, and that makes Ormsby's point all the more strongly. People not only "hitch a ride" when they tell stories. More pervasively, what people know as experience hitches a ride on stories those people know; the stories shape what becomes the experience.[10]

Jerome Bruner tells an autobiographical story of hitching a ride on a story when he returned from Europe on the eve of World War II. On his ship, most of his fellow passengers were fleeing the Nazis:

> The Book of Exodus shaped my way of telling myself the story of those fleeing souls on the *Shawnee*, and telling myself that story shaped my very experience of that transatlantic crossing. And so it is with classic narrative plights. They become templates for experience.[11]

Mademoiselle's plight is that her story is not a very good template for her experience, serving her not nearly as well as the story from the Bible serves Bruner.

This reversal of event-experience-story temporality underpins Mitchell's epigraph and its proposal to understand images as "living things."[12] But even Mitchell does not mean quite *living*. Posing to himself the question, "Do you really *believe* that images want things?" he responds: "My answer is, no, I don't believe it. But we cannot ignore that human beings (including myself) insist on talking and behaving as if they *did* believe it" (11). Do human beings actually talk and behave as if they believe that stories are living things, acting with a volition that seems to be their own? Tolstoy did, Cervantes did in *Don Quixote*, and the passage just quoted from Eric Ormsby speaks of words leading "a private existence of their own." The literary critic Wayne Booth states the case in its fullest version:

> Even the life we think of as primary experience—that is, events like birth, copulation, death, plowing and planting, getting and spending— is rarely experienced without some sort of mediation in narrative; one of the chief arguments for an ethical criticism of narrative is that narratives make and remake what in realist views are considered more primary experiences—and thus make and remake ourselves. The transition from what we think of as more primary (because "real") to the experience of stories about it is so automatic and frequent that we risk losing our sense of just how astonishing our story worlds are, in their power to add "life" upon "life"—for good or ill.[13]

Booth expresses little doubt that stories breathe, as he writes that "teachers should concern themselves with what a novel might *do* to a student" (4). Here are four other examples of people talking as if stories are living things. The examples are chosen because each writer—none is a writer of fiction— is a serious student of stories, and they offer a disparity of perspectives.

The linguist Charlotte Linde titles one of her articles "The Acquisition of a Speaker by a Story."[14] The article, discussed in greater detail in chapter 2, is an ethnography of an American insurance company. The story of the company's founder, Mr. McBee, figures prominently not only in the training of new employees, but as an everyday reference in company talk. Certainly the story is a resource that speakers use. But Linde's title emphasizes how the living story *acquires* its speakers, making them its own, even when they define themselves in distinction from the story. Linde elaborates: "If a story can acquire new tellers, it can break free of the lifetime of its participants and witnesses and develop what is potentially an indefinitely long lifetime."[15]

A second example is provided by Jo-ann Archibald, a Canadian Indigenous educator.[16] Archibald describes her first experience giving a workshop for Native student teachers in which "the story took on a 'life' and became the teacher."[17] Her phrasing—describing the story not as a teaching tool, but rather as the teacher—is more than a figure of speech. Archibald quotes from course journals that several students kept: "We didn't know what was going to happen," one student writes; "I remember [one of the participants] was hurting [emotionally, spiritually] and somehow it [the story] took care of her and [then] all of us . . . I'd say [this story] had a life of its own" (97, all brackets in original).

Archibald then quotes a long story that one of her students tells about an encounter on a busy urban street. The writer, who might or might not have read Tolstoy, sounds remarkably like Mademoiselle Bourienne if she had offered an account of what it was like to be caught up in the story her aunt had once told her. "The bird story" refers to one of Archibald's teaching fables.

> Both my friend and I were thinking of your story, totally. It was like we were inside the story . . . It was like being an actor in the story . . . all of a sudden [there] was silence . . . It was like that same [story] space opened up. We could say to each other, it was exactly like Jo-ann's story . . . I hadn't actually connected to that part of the bird story before . . . I can't articulate it well, [but] it was like living out that story. (99, some ellipses and all brackets in original)

My third example of people talking as if stories are living things is from Rita Charon, physician and teacher of humanities in medicine, whose book *Narrative Medicine* presents a narratology appropriate to medical practice.[18] Charon writes that the practitioner of narrative medicine "conceptualizes the narrative itself as a dynamic partner in their intercourse, able of its own to alter what happens between them" (108; compare with 110). Charon understands stories not as tools but as *partners*, with the story "able of its own" to have effects.

My fourth example is from the *New York Times* columnist David Brooks, editorializing on how people are "born into" a particular history and culture, yet individuals retain a responsibility for "selecting and constantly revising the master narrative we tell about ourselves."[19] Brooks then speaks of the other side of the coin, the power of stories:

> The stories we select help us, in turn, to interpret the world. They guide us to pay attention to certain things and ignore other things. They lead us to see certain things as sacred and other things as disgusting. They are the frameworks that shape our desires and goals.

If writers like Ormsby and critics like Booth are most inclined to talk about stories as living things, the quotations from Linde, Archibald, Charon, and Brooks show that this way of talking and thinking is not restricted to artists. The point, following Mitchell's qualification of the sense in which stories are living, is to take seriously that people seem unable to resist talking as if stories were living things, probably because people have fairly regular experiences of stories acting on their own. Claude Levi-Strauss acknowledges his contention that "myths get thought in man unbeknownst to him" is regarded by some critics as "utterly meaningless," yet this understanding of myths remains what Levi-Strauss calls "a lived experience."[20] I do not believe that stories breathe because Tolstoy so clearly depicts it in his story of Mademoiselle Bourienne. Instead, I believe Tolstoy's story because it expresses what is already my own lived experience, and at the beginning of that experience as I can know it are stories.

A final objection might point out that people alone are able to tell stories; stories cannot tell on their own. Which is true, but the complexity of the relationship between story and teller is best expressed by Archibald, reporting her extensive work with Indigenous storytellers. "A synergistic action happens between the storyteller and the story," she writes, "but it is the storyteller who ultimately gives breath, or life, to the story."[21] The storyteller gives breath to the story, but the story is already there, waiting. Archibald quotes a storyteller, Ellen White: "Storytellers have to be very responsible. They are setting the pace of breathing. A story is, and has, breath. Storytellers learn to let that happen" (112). People are responsible for telling stories, but as White says, the story has breath; telling is letting the story happen. Archibald's conclusion reiterates "the power of the story to 'be the teacher'" (ibid.). The storyteller speaks, but the story teaches—a complex synergy.

Thinking of the story as the teacher leads in the direction indicated by Pierre Bourdieu's descriptive phrase: "unchosen choices."[22] The stories that people grow up on are unchosen, and as templates for experience—or, what we hitch a ride on—these stories lead people into choices that are unchosen. People choose stories, but they have less choice about the principles that set their choosing. The idea that people make unchosen choices is a core of modern social science—Marx, Freud, and Durkheim each built his theoretical edifice on a version of this idea. That destabilizing of the sovereignty of consciousness remains disturbing. Dialogical narrative analysis elaborates that disturbance. The stories that animate people are as often unchosen as they are chosen.

link with digital choices.

WHAT IS A STORY?

My working understanding—not a definition—of *narrative* is simply this: *one thing happens in consequence of another.*[23] In one of the finest metaphors in literary narratology, Frank Kermode compared the structure of narration to the ticking of a clock: each *tick* creates an expectation for the corresponding *tock* to follow.[24] Consider one of the world's shortest stories, exhaustively analyzed by the sociologist Harvey Sacks. A child says: "The baby cried. The mommy picked it up."[25] The crying baby is the tick, and the mommy picking it up is the tock. In narratives, things happen *tick tock*.

If narratives begin as *tick tock*, they soon become more complicated. William Labov, originally in collaboration with Joshua Waletzky, proposes what is probably the most commonly cited narrative structure of stories.[26] The telling of a story begins with an *abstract*, which puts listeners on notice that a story is about to be told and may suggest the story's genre: a joke, a news report, a personal confession, a family anecdote, and so forth. Next is the *orientation*, in which the time, place, and main characters of the story are specified. The plot begins with what Labov calls a *complicating event*. Stories are told because something out of the ordinary has happened. This out-of-the-ordinary complication may or may not be troublesome in the sense of presenting difficulties, but it requires some response. The story moves toward an ending when the complicating event has an eventual *resolution*, which is where the story will leave things, although the action described in the story may continue. The penultimate stage of the narration is its *evaluation*, in which the storyteller expresses some attitude toward what happened—it was funny, wonderful, inexcusable, disgusting. The evaluation may express a lesson learned—fables are the genre in which the evaluation is explicit as a moral principle—and the listeners are usually expected to share this evaluative stance. The narration ends with a *coda*, in which the turn-at-talk is returned to other speakers.

All six components, which are stages because they occur in sequence, make up what Labov calls "fully formed" narratives. Most actual stories, although built from this narrative structure, are not fully formed narratives: some stages are missing and others are out of order. Further complicating the *tick tock*, one story is often embedded within another. As Maxine Hong Kingston's mother tells her story, the aunt's pregnancy is the complicating event. In Kingston's memoir, her mother telling her the story is the complicating event.

Eduardo Galeano's "Christmas Eve," with which this book began, has no abstract; the reader's act of opening Galeano's book serves as the story's abstract. The orientation gives Fernando Silva's profession and when and where the story takes place, and it tells us that Fernando has plans for the evening. When he hears the footsteps behind him, those come as a complication to his plans—he will not be joining his family as soon as he had planned. What is complicated is also suspenseful: we readers share Fernando's uncertainty about what the child wants or needs, and what may be within Fernando's capacity to provide. Their handshake is one kind of resolution, but the significant resolution occurs when the child states what he wants: the haunting plea, "Tell someone I'm here." Any evaluation is implicit, and there need be no coda, because on the printed page the end of the story is graphically clear. When "Christmas Eve" is told orally, the storyteller has to sustain a silence after the child's plea.

Labov's stages do more than simply describe the narrative structure of "Christmas Eve," that is, how the telling of the story unfolds in time. They are helpful for thinking about why this story deserves to be called haunting. The dying child's plea may be a resolution in formal linguistic terms, but the plea becomes the complicating action of other stories told as responses to that plea. The child's plea becomes the complicating action in the story of the rest of Fernando Silva's life and potentially in the life story of anyone who reads "Christmas Eve." The story haunts because each ending becomes another beginning.

Labov's stages can be usefully thought of as the horizontal dimension of a story, its unfolding in time: both time within the story itself and the time of the story's telling. But compare Labov's stages to the description of stories offered in Bruce DeSilva's epigraph to this chapter. To fill in Labov's stages with content—and make the story more than a structure—stories must utilize distinct capacities. Most of all, stories must have the capacity to attract and hold listeners, as Boyd emphasizes repeatedly: "Art's effects on human minds depend on its power to compel attention."[27] Boyd writes specifically of art, but everyday stories are people's art. As Ben-Ami Scharfstein argues in his magisterial study of human aesthetic practices. "The broadening of the idea of art is justified because nothing made by human minds or hands, nor any human act, is without its aesthetic origin and aura . . . everything we make is on the verge of art, an expression of its maker's characteristic skill, imagination, and aesthetic sensibility."[28] Like the boundary between the aesthetic and the everyday, the boundaries of what stories are should remain fuzzy. But when a child asks to be told a story, not any kind of narration will do. The child wants to be affected in a certain way, and as little as children could specify what that impression should be, they can express clearly when a story fails. I thus turn to the capacities that equip stories to have the effects they can have.

CAPACITIES OF STORIES

This section might be called *stories' narrative equipment.*[29] I present these capacities beginning with recognizable concerns of narratology and moving to issues that are more distinctly social scientific, although the entire schema depends on blurring boundaries of academic turf. As I elaborate different capacities, the emphasis shifts from how stories work—what they consist of—to how stories do their work for people and on people.

Just as most stories are not fully formed narratives in Labov's sense, specific stories rarely if ever draw on all the capacities discussed in this chapter, and many stories exhibit capacities not discussed here. Nor does any threshold number of these capacities mark qualification for being a story. Stories, to be stories, must have a *sufficient* number of these capacities, and sufficiency depends on how the capacities are used, as well as the tolerances of those who receive the story. This listing of stories' capacities is both incomplete—I hope others will add to it—and simply suggested. Each capacity has an immense literature behind it. I endeavor to engage that literature in the most selective way, to pursue my point of specifying how stories need these capacities if they are to make life social.

Trouble. Stories have the capacity to deal with human troubles, but also the capacity to make TROUBLE for humans.

"Everybody agrees," Bruner writes, "that a story begins with some breach in the expected state of things—Aristotle's peripeteia. Something goes awry, otherwise there's nothing to tell about. The story concerns efforts to cope or come to terms with the breach and its consequences."[30] In presenting Trouble as the core aspect of stories, Bruner follows not only Aristotle but also Kenneth Burke, who wrote Trouble with the capital *T*. Trouble is a more direct name for Labov's complicating event. A story becomes recognizable as a story when, in Bruner's phrase, something goes awry.

Socio-narratology's interest in Trouble is twofold: first, how do stories present models of dealing with different kinds of trouble, and second, how do stories themselves make Trouble? Kingston's story (told in this book's introduction) begins with double Trouble. There is the trouble in the story: the illicit pregnancy precipitating the attack on the household. But as the story of the aunt's pregnancy opens Kingston's memoir, the memoirist's trouble is that she was told this story as one of those she should grow up on. The mother's storytelling is indicative of a childhood that was troubled, or at least confused. "The emigrants confused the gods by diverting their curses," Kingston writes; "They must try to confuse their offspring as well, who, I suppose, threaten them in similar ways—always trying to get things straight, always trying to name the unspeakable."[31] Kingston thus sets her memoir's agenda: to set things straight, although she realizes that if nothing is unspeakable, *straight* does not, cannot, mean linear truth telling. One way to deal with a troublesome story is to resituate it within a different story—the memoir—in which the force of the original story is transformed. Kingston sets things straight by embedding one story within another.

The set of silver in Sharon O'Brien's story (told in the introduction) seems to be the Trouble, but exactly whom it troubles and how it troubles different family members continue to shift throughout the memoir. If Kingston's mother is deeply troubled by the aunt's pregnancy, O'Brien's mother does not consider herself at all troubled by the silver. Quite the opposite: she loves to enumerate the different kinds of knives, forks, and spoons. The memoirist's trouble is how her mother can tell the story of her mother's tears yet be remarkably untroubled by those tears. O'Brien's memoir is, at least in part, a story about the contrasts between who is troubled by something, who ought to be troubled, and who has what narrative resources to tell what kind of story about being troubled.

Allen Feldman's paramilitary stories (introduction) present a third variation on narrating Trouble. If the Republican geological origin story were told in a geology class, it would be understood as a technical account and might raise questions of good or bad science, but not political trouble.[32] The narration becomes a story when it is told in political indoctrination classes, where it is heard as a fable explaining what the Irish would call The Troubles. The origin story will then cause all manner of Troubles for both those whom it calls to act and those against whom this story justifies violence.

Socio-narratology begins with Trouble that swirls through stories: it is their occasion, their content, and too often their outcome.

Character. Stories have the capacity to display and test people's character.

Charles Tilly argues that what makes stories unique among other forms of narrative is that they are character driven.[33] A story's characters are those who, to return to Bruner, exert efforts to come to terms with whatever the Trouble is. The story tells the success or failure of those efforts, or in a more philosophical tale, the difficulty of evaluating success or failure. Stories have a singular capacity to delve the *character of the characters* who deal with trouble. Stories incite and guide reflection on *who* these people are and the significance of being that kind of person. Many stories, if not most and possibly *all*, involve some test of character: a decisive moment at which a character's response declares what sort of person she or he is. This test can be as simple as whether the mommy will pick up the crying baby, but such a short story provides little scope for the formation of the character that is tested.

All the characters in the stories from the introduction have been *cast* as who they are, in senses of both theatrical casting and also of being thrown into the world by some force beyond themselves.[34] The stories' interest lies in what the character does with that casting. The child in "Christmas Eve" is cast into dying in that hospital, and Fernando Silva is cast to encounter him there. They accept their casting by undertaking the work to discover their character's possibilities. Mademoiselle Bourienne wants a new casting as wife of a Russian prince, rather than as companion to a princess. Kingston and O'Brien are cast into families, and their memoirs are stories of how they resist that casting. Feldman's paramilitaries want to change how their country has been cast in its historical story; they seek to restore what they understand as its true casting. Frederick Douglass has been cast horribly as a slave, and in his life after escape, he is cast into a role that offers few guidelines or models: he casts himself as "the first one out."[35] All stories— here I risk the universal *all*—are about characters resisting or embracing or perhaps failing to recognize the character into which they have been cast, as that character must respond to some Trouble.

Socio-narratology is interested in how stories work to make characters available as generalizable resources that listeners use to engage in work on their own character. Stories form character by evaluating different expressions of it as possibilities for action and as possible identities. For dialogical narrative analysis, at least four questions can be specified.

First, how does the story cast its characters—and thus teach listeners to regard themselves—with respect to the interplay between collective responsibility and individual fulfillment? Kingston, O'Brien, and Douglass write memoirs in order to take a more flexible stance toward a collective story of which each finds him- or herself part. Each understands him- or herself as always necessarily part of some collective, but each finds that this collective imposes a story that resists individual stylistic variation, elaboration, or play. Each memoirist seeks greater possibility to breathe within a story that can be constricting. That dilemma seems universal, and stories have the capacity to deal with it, even though the stories are part of what must be dealt with.

Second, socio-narratology is interested in how stories' characters represent variations on the typical motivational schemes within groups in which those stories have currency.[36] Stories explore not only what characters do, but also their reasons for acting. Any group's parameters for acceptable reasons for acting are expressed in that group's corpus of stories. Stories teach good reasons for acting, and stories can be appealed to as supports for claims that an action was acceptable. ACCOUNTS make actions at least recognizable and understandable to third parties, if not necessarily legitimate and acceptable.[37] Most stories are interpretable as accounts, but accounting may not be what is going on for the storyteller and listeners.[38] Many stories are told simply to pass the time, to reaffirm relationships, and for the pure pleasure that storytelling provides, with its capacities for suspense and imagination. But even those stories prepare for future accounts by making motivational schemes recognizable, if not typical.

√ Third is the dialogical issue: how far does the story claim to know the character's motives and fix those motives to the character, like the white or black hat that identifies heroes and villains in silent-film Westerns? How much room does the story grant its characters for multiple, conflicting, and changing expressions of their character? Stories seem fully capable of doing either kind of work: identifying people as fixed to a single motivation line that defines their character, or alternatively, showing the complexity and fluidity of people's motives. Stories that formulate an enemy against whom war is the only option exemplify the former capacity.[39] The hero in literary tragedy and romance—King Lear and Parzifal, respectively—exemplifies the latter: she or he makes mistakes, even terrible ones, but comes to profound realizations.

Finally, how does human character express itself in relation to nonhuman things that act like characters? This question requires a distinction between *characters* and *actors* in a story. Most characters are actors (except those who simply pass by as part of the scenery), but not all actors are characters. In O'Brien's story, the silver is certainly an actor: it causes other actors to act, and in a stronger sense, it enables other actors to be who they are.[40] O'Brien is enabled to be a memoirist by the silver, very differently but no less significantly than the silver enabled her great-grandfather, Handsome Dan, to perpetuate the persona that was his character.

The difference between characters and actors is their respective capacities for motive. The silver acts, but it cannot be motivated; any motives are projected on it by humans. Only characters have motives, so for nonhumans to be characters, they must be anthropomorphized, like talking animals in folktales (who often turn out to be humans under a spell). Between characters and actors, only characters have character, and the distinctive capacity of stories is to question character: its formation and deformations, its enactments or refusals, its decisive effects, and how it perhaps ought to be other than what it is.

Point of view. Stories have the capacity to make one particular perspective not only plausible but compelling.

Brian Boyd, building his case that stories confer an evolutionary advantage to species that can tell them, contends that "fiction cultivates our sympathetic imagination by prompting us to see from the perspective of character after character," which most narrative scholars would agree with, the only argument being over whether fiction enhances the sympathetic imagination more than journalism or ethnography, among other genres of storytelling.[41] Yet stories can also limit people's sympathetic imagination by making the perspective of one character too compelling.

I become caught up in Frederick Douglass's story because as I read it, I feel the tension of Douglass sitting in his seat in an auditorium, being introduced, knowing he is expected to tell his story one way (just "the facts") but compelled to show the audience he is more than someone who has lived that story: he has been reading and thinking. Douglass reminds his readers that the demands made by his abolitionist sponsors were not unreasonable; how they wanted him to appear made good strategic sense. But the more I become caught up in Douglass's point of view, the more any other perspective becomes impossible for me to take seriously. As soon as I begin to weigh different interests, the story pulls me back into the tension of Douglass's body, waiting to get up and hear what he can bring himself to say.

That is the power and the danger of stories. As listeners progress from story to story—or *if* they progress—they see from the perspective of character after character, and their sympathetic imagination is enhanced. But when listeners become caught up in one story, that story can claim the validity of one person's or group's point of view, sometimes wisely but sometimes far too well.

Suspense. Stories make life dramatic and remind people that endings are never assured.

Until suspense is felt, words may narrate a sequence of events, but they cannot be much of a story. Cheryl Mattingly states one of the most indispensable capacities of stories:

> If narrative offers an intimate relation to lived experience, the dominant formal feature that connects the two is not narrative coherence but narrative drama . . . We follow narrative suspensefully, always reminded of the fragility of events, for things might have turned out differently.[42]

Suspense depends on a tension between different possible outcomes—some to be hoped for and others to be feared. Sharpening this tension, suspense, perhaps more than any other capacity, enables stories to elicit engagement: stories *work* because people get *caught up* in a story. But more than enhancing engagement in stories, suspense expresses a central moral truth of stories. The last part of the quotation, Mattingly's "might have turned out differently," reminds us of stories' capacity to express and to deal with life's indeterminacy—especially the indeterminacy of actions. Things not only might turn out otherwise in the future; they might, in the past, have happened otherwise than we suppose. Much of the power of stories is their ability to express life's "might have turned out differently" quality and to discover means to live with that openness.

Even "The baby cried. The mommy picked it up" has a minimal element of suspense, which may be not so minimal for the child who considers this story worth telling. Suspense requires that listeners care about the characters in the story (another aspect of why Tilly seems right—stories are character driven) and that something significant be at stake for those characters. In the child's story, the immediate stake is the plight of the crying baby, and the greater stake is a moral principle that crying children ought to be cared for. The story does not build suspense; its minimalism assumes that listeners already care for the crying baby. The fact of crying is sufficiently suspenseful for the child storyteller.

Although Galeano's "Christmas Eve" is only slightly longer than "the baby cried," it ramps up the reader's caring and suspense. The character type that is invoked, the dying child, arouses caring. But perhaps I begin to care about this dying child with the word "cottony." The child is not quite barefoot but not fully shod. The cotton is soft in texture as well as sound, and the feet within it are vulnerable. My caring is not fully sealed until the child's plea, with its imputation that this child has knowledge most adults lack: he knows where *here* is. The suspense of the story is less how soon the child will die. The greater suspense is whether the adults, who begin with Fernando Silva and extend to whoever now reads the story, will be willing and able to respond to the dying child's plea: will his story live on? And, will the telling of that story spread recognition of the *here* of that hospital, in that country, at that time?

Frederick Douglass's story generates suspense over whether he will say what his sponsors want, but another level of suspense is that Douglass is telling his story in public at a time when he could have been sent back to his master; legally, he remains a slave. Here is stories' capacity for suspense at its fullest. Reading that episode in Douglass's *Autobiography*, I know what will happen. Douglass will not be captured, and he will develop his thoughts and his denunciations. He will become one of Abraham Lincoln's most respected friends and a leading public figure for half a century. Most readers begin his *Autobiography* knowing that. But as I read the early episode in Douglass's life, I still feel suspense. This suspense seems to hinge on my knowing that the story *could have* turned out differently, and that is the narrative drama, as Mattingly says. Even knowing full well the outcome of a story long finished, as I read Douglass's *Autobiography* the possibility that it could have turned out differently makes me suspenseful.

Interpretive openness. Stories have the capacity to narrate events in ways that leave open the interpretation of what exactly happened and how to respond to it.

Homer's *Odyssey* ends with a curious object. Near the end of his journey, Odysseus visits Tiresias, the seer, in the Underworld and learns how he will return to his home in Ithaca and kill his wife's suitors, who infest his house. Tiresias tells Odysseus that he must then make one last journey, taking an oar and walking inland until he reaches a place where people know nothing of the sea and think that what he carries is a winnowing fan (or shovel) for sifting grain. Having arrived there, he must sacrifice to the gods; then he can go home in peace.[43] The object Odysseus carries is both things: by the sea, it is an oar; inland, it is a winnowing fan. Stories are full of such objects that defy any single specification.[44] Stories *are* such objects that defy specification. Stories are good at being several things at once, and they are good at equipping humans to live in a world that not only is open to multiple interpretive understandings but requires understandings in the plural.[45]

Stories' most distinct and useful capacity to work with and on humans may be their openness to multiple understandings. People's multiple interpretations make stories available for multiple uses; or, people's different responses to the same story reflect that story's interpretive openness. The Canadian storyteller Thomas King offers a gentle reminder of stories' openness in his series of lectures published as *The Truth about Stories*—a title that I interpret as ironic but others could understand differently, or maybe King's editor wrote it. In each chapter of his book, King tells several stories, with one being prominent. He ends each chapter with a kind of refrain. The refrain at the end of the first chapter refers to a creation story King has told about a character named Charm, who is the Mother of human creation. Charm's story returns in the last chapter of this book. For now, our interest is solely in King's refrain:

> Take Charm's story, for instance. It's yours. Do with it what you will. Tell it to friends. Turn it into a television movie. Forget it. But don't say in the years to come that you would have lived your life differently if only you had heard this story.
>   You've heard it now.[46]

In different versions of this refrain, King suggests different things people can do with stories; his lists become a cumulative elaboration of stories' openness to multiple use, with each use involving a different shading of interpretive understanding. What does not change among these refrains are the lines saying that once a story is told, those who have received it have it as theirs and will use it as they will, with the story lending itself to each of these uses but also shaping each use.

King knows that also, a story has those who receive it, which is why he always reminds his audience that they cannot claim not to have heard it. He knows that whatever people think they are doing with stories—telling them to friends, turning them into a movie, forgetting them—stories are doing things with people. King knows that stories are *out of control*.

Out of control. Stories are like the magic spell that Mickey Mouse creates in the "Sorcerer's Apprentice" segment of the film *Fantasia*, when the enchanted broom keeps on bringing more and more water until the place is flooding.[47] Stories have a capacity to act in ways their tellers did not anticipate.

King's refrain does more than give his audience, eventually his readers, permission to do what they want with the story he has told. He recognizes that once a story has been put into play, it will have effects that neither he as storyteller nor they as listeners can control. King retells a version of a story told in Leslie Marmon Silko's novel, *Ceremony*, about how evil comes into the world. Some witches are having a contest over who can scare the others. Finally one witch tells a story prophesying the violence and destruction that white people will bring when they come. The story goes beyond the boundaries of the contest; the other witches ask the storyteller to take it back. "But, of course, it was too late," King writes. "For once a story is told, it cannot be called back. Once told, it is loose in the world." He concludes: "So you have to be careful with the stories you tell" (10).

Going back to King's metaphor—if it is a metaphor—about stories being "loose in the world," how loose are stories? This question is akin to asking in what sense stories breathe. Socio-narratology cannot answer this question, but it can shift the inquiry and usefully describe a continuum of storytellers' varying levels of willingness to let their stories loose; or, how far storytellers are willing to admit that stories are out of control. At one extreme is King telling his listeners and readers they can do what they want with his stories, except claim they never heard them. At another extreme are those who tell the origin stories that Feldman heard in paramilitary indoctrination sessions. Those indoctrinators, who I imagine would have been content to be called that, do not invite their listeners to do whatever they want with the origin stories. The stories are supposed to have one interpretation only; no discussion. King's approach can be called dialogical, or multivoiced. The indoctrination approach is MONOLOGICAL.

Dialogical narrative analysis has particular interest in which situations are defined by monological or by dialogical storytelling. Dialogical storytellers like King know their stories are interpretively open and out of control, and dialogical listeners respond with interpretive openness. Monological storytellers have an illusion of controlling the stories they tell, limiting interpretation, and monological listeners hear the story as being closed to their interpretive play. Those who tell stories and those who receive these stories are not necessarily on the same side of the divide between dialogic and monologic interpretation; four permutations can be observed. But any such typology is always limited in its predictive force, because stories are tricksters. As often as stories are conscripted to advance some cause, they do that work only for a while and then turn against those who conscripted them. They can always be told to a different effect. Stories readily take sides; they just refuse to stay on the same side, and stories conduct both tellers and listeners to take different sides.

Inherent morality. Stories inform people's sense of what counts as good and bad, of how to act and how not to act.

Stories depend on a principle of *response*, operating both in the story and in the storytelling scene. Characters in stories respond to Trouble, both their own and one another's. Those who tell and receive stories respond to each other as well as to the content of the story that is told. Stories are literally *responsible*.[48] People are able to respond because stories have taught them how.

Stories most evidently teach what counts as good and bad by linking characters' actions to consequences that listeners *feel* are good or bad. Children need not be told explicitly that Cinderella's stepmother is acting badly or that Cinderella marrying the prince is good. Good and bad are embodied feelings experienced before they can be learned as moral principles. Thomas King understands this when he cautions us to be careful what stories we tell. King tells about a friend of his, Louis Owens, a Native novelist and critic who, like too many of King's friends, commits suicide. "We both knew that stories were medicine," King writes of their friendship, "that a story told one way could cure, that the same story told another way could injure."[49] The inherent morality of stories is in the relation between their content and the process of their telling. The storyteller aspires to know the way to tell that can cure, but storytelling is never without risk.

Although Feldman's paramilitary indoctrinators use stories with short-term success, that monological use denies what stories are best at doing, which is to open up moral complexity. In stories, characters could always do otherwise, and in many stories there would be good reason for doing otherwise. Stories work well at depicting the necessity, the difficulty, and often the danger of choosing how to live. Most stories show people that they must declare themselves, but only some stories make the virtues of commitment seem straightforward, and then only so long as the story is kept in control. Fernando Silva is lucky in at least this sense: what he must do is clear. The story could be told differently, so that Fernando Silva had a dozen dying children who wanted to spend a moment with him, and instead of being expected at home he was expected in surgery. The focal incidents in memoirs often occur when the memoirist as character has to declare him- or herself. Memoirists make storytelling a medium to create a moral clarity that life-in-flux rarely provides; thus clarity is never quite the same as certainty. The value of stories is to offer sufficient clarity without betraying the complexity of life-in-flux.

Resonance. Stories echo other stories, with those echoes adding force to the present story. Stories are also told to be echoed in future stories. Stories summon up whole cultures.

Poststructuralist narratologists use the term INTERTEXTUAL to describe how any text is dependent on other texts, but I prefer Northrop Frye's term RESONANCE.[50] In literature, resonances are called allusions, but Frye realizes that as stories fill life, the resonances in most stories are unintended by the storytellers. No one ever makes up a story by him- or herself, and no one ever tells or hears a story all by itself, dissociated from any other stories. Any story is shaped by the other stories that the storyteller and listeners know. The critic and psychoanalyst Pierre Bayard expresses this idea with particular clarity, writing specifically about books but referring equally to stories: "Thus it is that in truth we never talk about a book unto itself; a whole set of books always enters the discussion through the portal of a single title, which serves as a temporary symbol of a complete conception of culture."[51] Any one story is, in Bayard's excellent metaphor, a portal. This book talks about single stories as if they stand alone. However convenient such talk may be, Frye and Bayard remind us of the falseness of thinking about any story in the singular. Stories are textures of resonances.

Symbiotic. Stories work with other things—first with people, but also with objects and with places.

The most evident SYMBIOSIS is between stories and the people who tell them. Stories and people need each other. I quote again Joan Didion's eloquent testimonial to stories: "We tell ourselves stories in order to live."[52] The complementary or symbiotic side is equally true: Stories live in being told. I find it significant that Didion, on whose choice of words it is fair to place considerable weight, does not say that we *make up* stories in order to live. The stories are somehow already there, waiting to be told. We are born into stories that we depend on for our identities and that depend on us to perpetuate them. As I will now do.

When I was a boy and spent much time with my grandparents, I was fascinated by a silver pitcher that was covered with dents. My grandparents had older things in their home, but these had been well cared for. The pitcher drew me to it because it obviously had been knocked about. Therein lay a story, which I enjoyed having my grandfather tell me. As I retell the story, I am amazed what a short and simple story it is. As a child I heard it as a much longer story, because it was a portal through which I saw so many imaginative possibilities about my family, who they were, and who I was or might be.

During the American Civil War, my maternal grandparents' family lived in Tennessee. I have learned since that my great-great-grandfather converted his factory to arms manufacturing for the Confederate army, and that suggests why the family home might have been a particular target for pillaging by Union troops when they moved through the area around Nashville. The simple story I knew as a child, almost as simple as "The baby cried. The mommy picked it up," was that when the Union troops were approaching the house, my great-grandfather (a boy about the age I was, when I was so fascinated with the silver pitcher) threw much of the family silver down the well so that the Yankees would not plunder it. The pitcher was retrieved from the well and eventually ended up in my grandparents' home in Hartford, Connecticut, where they had come to live among those Yankees, and where their family, including me, grew up as New Englanders.

When I reflect now on the story, part of its attraction was doubtless its carnivalesque reversal of norms: under the circumstances, what is disallowed becomes praiseworthy. Another part of the attraction was the tactile reality of the pitcher itself, giving the story a tangible presence. But also, the story is a reflection on place, or the juxtaposition of two places: Tennessee, the place of origin where the story's action occurs, and Connecticut, where the story is told. By connecting those places, the story opened up for me the idea, which can be a revelation to some children, that my family had not always lived where I had always known them to be living, nor had they always lived how I knew them to be living.

Stories work with places as well as objects. The anthropologist Keith Basso studied the stories embedded in Apache place-names in New Mexico. He describes the symbiotic relation between stories and place: "Annie Peaches's claim—that the land occupied by Western Apaches 'makes the people live right'—becomes understandable as a proposition about the moral significance of geographical locations as this has been established by historical tales with which the locations are associated."[53] The tales establish the moral significance of locations, which in turn remind people of the stories.

Stories always work with something: with storytellers, with antecedent stories, with places, and with material objects like the dented pitcher. Greg Sarris tells a story about Mabel McKay (introduced in the prologue) using this symbiosis as part of one of her healings: "Then Mabel . . . handed him a small green stone. 'Keep this with you at all times,' she said. 'It has my song on it.'"[54] When people are not telling stories, those stories live in objects, at least for a while.

Shape-shifting. Stories change plots and characters to fit multiple circumstances, allowing many different people to locate themselves in the characters in those plots.

Jo-ann Archibald quotes Native storyteller Shirley Sterling, describing stories' shape-shifting: "So the story takes on a life of its own and it travels from person to person and it . . . takes a different shape, but there's something the same. Each person interprets slightly differently and yet it's really amazing how some stories will persist . . ."[55]

Archibald herself provides a fine example of a shape-shifting story. She tells the story of "Coyote Searching for the Bone Needle," respectfully thanking Eber Hampton, who told her the story, for his permission to retell it (35). Coyote finds a hole in the toe of his favorite moccasins after a long day hunting. He searches for his special bone needle to sew them, crawling around the fire as he tries to find it. Owl sees him and comes to help. After Owl can't find the needle, he asks Coyote where he last used it. Coyote says he last used it "over in the bushes" to mend his jacket. Owl asks Coyote why he's looking around the campfire, instead of in the bushes. "Well, it's easier to look for the needle here because the fire gives off such good light, and I can see better here" (36).

That was not the first time I heard this story. I first heard it as a joke about a drunk crawling around in the gutter; Google readily provides several versions. A policeman comes by and asks the drunk what he's doing. He's looking for his car keys; he dropped them opening the car door. The policeman says he doesn't see any car. The drunk says his car is parked up the block. The policeman asks why he isn't looking there, and the drunk says he can see better here under the streetlight.

Coyote's singular power is his capacity to shape-shift; stories have that power.

Performative. Stories are not only performed; they perform. Basso quotes an informant, Benson Lewis, saying: "Stories go to work on you like arrows."[56] Stories *do* things; they *act*.

PERFORMATIVE is a word that is used with different emphases in the jargon of several academic disciplines.[57] Whatever else storytellers are doing—reporting, convincing, instructing, indoctrinating, recruiting, amusing, generating sympathy or antipathy, or simply passing the time—they are always performing, and how they do whatever else they do is affected by the needs of the performance. These needs are, again most simply, anticipating the response of those who receive the story and shaping the story in anticipation of that response. In oral storytelling, reshaping occurs throughout the course of the telling, as listeners' responses are perceived.

Performative also implies that something is brought about by the performance; the storytelling does something. Of all that the dying child in "Christmas Eve" could ask of Fernando Silva, that child asks him to tell a story: "Tell someone I'm here." That request presents storytelling as moral action. Telling the child's story is *acting*, just as surely as if the dying child had made a request to build a new hospital. In one sense, Fernando Silva agreeing to tell the child's story (which we are not told explicitly but assume) changes nothing—the child will still die—but in another sense it changes everything about that death. When Silva accepts becoming a witness to the child's death, he gives that death . . . what? We could say that he elevates solitary and contingent suffering and makes it both universal and *responsible*. Telling the child's death becomes a way of responding. The story helps those who hear it out of their helplessness as surely as it helps the child out of his.

Stories do not cease to perform when they are not being told, after any specific performance ends. They remain *resonant* even when they are not consciously remembered. The easy location of that resonance is in humans' memory traces; stories are held deep in memory. But I prefer what Mabel McKay seems to mean when she gives the man a small green stone and tells him that her song is on it.[58] Or in it.

Truth telling. Stories' capacity to report truths that have been enacted elsewhere is always morphing into their more distinct capacity to *enact* truths. These truths are not copies of an original. They are enactments in which something original comes to be, as if for the first time, in the full significance that the story gives it.

The performativity of stories is crucial to what is particular about their claim to truth.[59] Consider again Charles Tilly's distinction between stories and technical accounts as two different kinds of narrative. Technical accounts claim to be true whether or not the accounts are told and whether or not people believe them. Unlike technical accounts, stories *become true* as they are told. Whatever claims a story makes to represent realities outside itself—and many stories do make such mimetic claims—the core truth of the story is not correspondence but performance.[60]

Frederick Douglass attempts to tell truths about slavery that most of those in his audiences are deeply predisposed either to disbelieve as fabrication or to dismiss as unfortunate incidents that are no reason to change what is otherwise a legal, economically viable system. Douglass reports slavery as it is, but his story counts because he also performs himself as a new species of embodied witness. What Alberto Manguel writes about the relation between stories and reality catches the sense in which Douglass's stories are both mimetic and creative:

> They can't be fictional inventions, in the sense of forgeries or misrepresentations; they need to be invented fictions, in the sense of discovering historical truths that can be granted reality in narrative words. They must, in a deeply literary sense, ring true.[61]

Douglass's speeches are discoveries of historical truths that can be granted reality only in his narrative words. He balances the need to make the words "ring true" against his own need to present himself as he truly is, not as the enactment of the audience's imagination of a plantation slave—an imagination that Douglass never fit. His performative truths are not forgeries or misrepresentations, but they are artful self-presentations.

Stories have the capacity to balance multiple truths that have respective claims to expression. The more *dialogical* the truth—or the more POLY-PHONIC, in Bakhtin's sense of blending multiple voices into a harmony in which they never entirely merge but retain some distinctiveness—the greater the capacity of stories to tell the truth that there are multiple truths.

Finally but perhaps most significant, **Imagination.** Stories have the capacity to arouse people's imaginations; they make the unseen not only visible but compelling. Through imagination, stories arouse emotions.

My simplest way to determine what is a story is the bedtime test. If a self-respecting six- or eight-year-old asks for a story before bedtime, would she or he accept *this* as a story? Some narrations that are surprisingly close to Tilly's technical accounts might pass the bedtime test. My younger daughter used to ask for a story about how dinosaurs became extinct; what she expected were two competing geological theories of extinction. These narrations were not driven by characters. I did not anthropomorphize the dinosaurs; as I described the extinction theories, dinosaurs made no choices. My best guess is that the narrations qualified as bedtime stories because they aroused a sufficient degree of imagination. My daughter could imagine the earth growing darker after being struck by a meteor, dust filling the air, food growing scarce.

Even if a story has characters and a plot, if it does not arouse imagination, it will not be much of a story. Suspense depends on imagination, because it requires imagination to recognize what Mattingly calls "the fragility of events," the recognition "that things might have turned out differently."[62] Stories create imaginations of how the past might have gone differently and the future is open to any possibility. The imagination instigated by stories can lead people into trouble—Mademoiselle Bourienne—or it can be their road to greatness, as it is for Frederick Douglass. The capacity of stories is to arouse people's imaginations concerning how their lives might have been different, and the possibilities that still lie open to them.

STORIES AS MATERIAL SEMIOTIC COMPANIONS

This chapter has not offered a formal definition of stories. Instead, I have elaborated a number of the capacities of stories. My emphasis on capacities follows Donna Haraway: "One must think not in terms of essential properties, but in terms of strategies of design."[63]

But how to think about what a story is, for socio-narratology? In one sense, a story is any narration that has sufficient capacities of stories—or that passes the bedtime test. Something more succinct seems called for, however. Definitions risk privileging some essential quality of stories, and stories are always *more*. My descriptive phrase is a point of departure and return: a good place to begin inquiry, and a good place to come back to, when the way seems lost. I combine two evocative phrases from John Law and Donna Haraway: for socio-narratology, stories are best thought of as *material SEMIOTIC companions*.

The explanation of this phrase begins with a statement by Law that needs to be quoted at length, because it seems so crucial to the objectives of a socio-narratology:

> Donna Haraway and Sharon Traweek teach us that when we tell stories these are performative. This is because they also make a difference, or at any rate might make a difference, or hope to make a difference. Applied to technoscience, the argument goes further: in fact, it is quite radical. It is that *there is no important difference between stories and materials*. Or, to put it a little differently: stories, effective stories, perform themselves into the material world—yes, in the form of social relations, but also in the form of machines, architectural arrangements, bodies, and all the

rest. This means that one way of imagining the world is that it is a set of (pretty disorderly) stories that intersect and interfere with one another. It means also that these are, however, not simply narrations in the standard linguistic sense of the term.[64]

The performativity of stories is emphasized here, and my discussion of the shape-shifting capacity of stories is given extended force. In Law's version, stories' capacity for symbiosis becomes literal shape-shifting: stories not only work with objects; stories take the form of objects, which are known as materialized stories. Thus we get to Law's law (italics in the original): "*There is no important difference between stories and materials.*"

Stories are made up of signs—their semiotic being—and they are material not only as they do things, including inciting love affairs and wars, but also in their capacity to take the material forms that Law specifies: machines, bodies, and buildings. In my notes on stories I have a wonderful phrase, the source of which I regret having lost. Stories are "made of air but leave their mark."[65]

These material-semiotic beings become humans' companions. My usage of *companion* is suggested by Donna Haraway's writing on what she calls *companion species*.[66] From Haraway's rich development of this trope I take two crucial ideas. First, companion species shape each other in their progressive coevolution.[67] Second and more basic, good companions take care of each other, although "taking care" always involves each shaping the other. In both respects, each companion enables the other to be.

The stories about stories with which this book began can now be understood as representing a variety of companion relations. Fernando Silva is not only a character in "Christmas Eve." That story tells how it becomes Fernando Silva's companion, and it offers to become the companion of anyone who receives it. The story that Maxine Hong Kingston's mother makes her companion is one of the ghosts that Kingston grows up among. *Haunted* would pretty well describe Sharon O'Brien's relation to the family silver and its story. Kingston and O'Brien both consider their respective haunting stories to be a bad companion, until they contain it within another story that is the companion each chooses to live with. Mademoiselle Bourienne does not seem to contain the story that she has adapted from her aunt, despite its having led her into mischief; it may continue to be her bad companion. Frederick Douglass's story of being a slave is a companion that he not only needs—it gives him his place on the lecture tour—but also resents, because the story requires him to fit a "plantation" image that others expect as part of that story. Finally, the paramilitary indoctrinators whom Feldman describes work to insinuate a companion in their recruits' lives. The indoctrinators intend that their recruits will evolve as paramilitaries with those stories shaping how they perceive the necessity and legitimacy of their actions.

Stories are material-semiotic in their double embodiment. Ben-Ami Scharfstein, reflecting on the human impulse to create art, of which stories are one form, writes: "A work of art is the imagined and then created body that is meant to satisfy an inner demand or hunger for direct experience."[68] Whether the story tells what has happened or imagines some happening, the body of the storyteller must create the body of the story so that experience can be—or more accurately, so that a human body's experience can be—materialized in the body of the story. "This gratification," Scharfstein continues, "is direct because it consists of the inherently pleasurable acts of the sensory, muscular, and imaginative processes by which the embodiment is consummated" (60). Consummated, that is, in the use of voice and hearing, in the use of the body to gesture and vision to see those gestures, or perhaps imagine them. In storytelling, the body embodies the story, which consummates the experience of the bodies participating in the storytelling. "When the absorbing directness of the process is great enough," Scharfstein concludes, "it makes the artist momentarily whole" (60–61). In storytelling, the teller's momentary wholeness is shared with a listener who experiences the story's "absorbing directness" in his or her body. Stories are always semiotic as words, images, and gestures that signify. But storytelling materializes the semiotic. Here is no abstract code but rather Scharfstein's "acts of the sensory, muscular, and imaginative processes by which the embodiment is consummated."

When Haraway says, "There's no place to be in the world outside of stories," at least part of what she means is that there is no existing as a human outside a companionship with stories that are semiotic in their being and material in the effects they bring about.[69] The capacity of stories is to allow us humans to be.

Stories
at Work

The trickster in the narrative is the narrative itself.
It creates and inhabits ambivalent space.
—Lewis Hyde, *Trickster Makes This World*

Tricksters help to understand the fundamental question, why do people need stories as companions?[1] Reading Lewis Hyde convinced me that tricksters are more than just another character type that shows up regularly in stories. Trickster stories are told for many reasons—especially for pleasure and moral education—but as Hyde's epigraph to this chapter says,[2] tricksters—whether Hermes, Loki, Jacob, Raven, or, at the fringes, Prometheus—embody aspects of what stories are. This chapter is dominated by trickster stories, from Coyote to Samson, who is less often thought of as a trickster. How these tricksters act mirrors how stories use their capacities to do the kinds of work they are best equipped to do. The title of Hyde's book is, I believe, exactly right: tricksters do make the human world, which is also to say that stories make the world human.

Tricksters often bring a gift that is crucial to the possibility of people becoming fully human, but the gift is shaded—tricksters also make life dangerous for humans. Raven brings the light that he has stolen; Hermes does not invent music but he significantly advances it, thus making peace with Apollo, whose cattle he has stolen; Prometheus gives humans fire. Tricksters' less clearly defined gifts—the kind of gifts Coyote brings—fall into the general category of teaching what it is to be human in a world that requires adaptation. Stories are among those less clearly defined gifts. Not all stories are gifts that people want. Hyde quotes the preeminent scholar of tricksters, Paul Radin, writing that the trickster is "at one and the same time creator and destroyer, giver and negator . . . [who] knows neither good nor evil yet . . . is responsible for both" (158). The complexity of trickster gifts is how they embody what people *need*, wanted or not.

To return to the question of why people need stories as companions, Hyde puts it best:

> It might be right to say that trickster, like the psychopath, has a "rudderless intelligence," but if so it is a useful intelligence, for it continues to function when normal guidance systems have failed, as they periodically will. Finally, for all his failings and all the grief he authors, trickster is also a culture hero, inventor of fish traps, bringer of fire, the one who turned his own destroyed intestines into foodstuffs for the New People . . . Trickster is among other things the gatekeeper who opens the door into the next world; those who mistake him for a psychopath never even know such a door exists. (158–59)

In human lives, stories precede normal guidance systems, and stories continue to function when normal guidance systems have failed. Stories bring their share of grief; companionship with them is by no means entirely benign, and those who ignore their dangers will probably end badly. But stories also reenchant what becomes disenchanted; in Hyde's lovely phrase, they open a door to the next world. Those who seek to banish stories because of their dangers will never know that reenchantment is possible.

STORIES' PRIMARY WORK: MAKING THE EARTH HABITABLE

Frank Kermode, whom I quoted in chapter 1, writes that when narrative contains time within the sequence of *tick tock*, narrative *humanizes* time.[3] I understand this to mean: narrative makes this earth habitable for human beings. Narrative takes duration that is inherently without order and imposes the sequential and predictable order of *tick tock*. *Tick tock* is habitable time.

Stories' primary or primal work is to provide people with a guidance system that directs attention within what William James famously called the "blooming, buzzing confusion" of the world that humans are cast into.[4] People need terms of *selection*—what to pay attention to—and following immediately is the need for *evaluation*, or what to think about what has been selected. Stories work as people's *selection/evaluation* guidance system. I write selection/evaluation with a hash mark, because to select is already to evaluate; the processes are continuous, separable only upon reflection.[5]

This guidance system functions not as rules, though some stories come close to setting principles. Stories are better imagined—and this is an imagination—as a tacit system of associations that makes particular aspects of the world seem worth attending to and suggests default evaluations of what is selected. Selections and evaluations are constantly being overridden by other, often more conscious considerations; they are, I emphasize, a *default* system. Nevertheless, as nondetermining as this selection/evaluation guidance system is, it processes a large proportion of what might be called candidate-experience: what happens to a person that, if attended to, becomes that person's experience. Candidate-experience becomes experience because it fits stories people know; as examples, recall Mademoiselle Bourienne and also Jerome Bruner crossing the Atlantic on the *Shawnee*, as the book of Exodus shaped what he saw and how he evaluated it.

Bruner does not think *about* the book of Exodus so much as he thinks *with* that story guiding his thoughts. People not only think *about* stories; far more consequentially, people think *with* stories. Or, stories give people their first system for thinking. Julie Cruikshank writes about the master storyteller Angela Sidney:

> During the years we have worked together recording the events of her life, she has repeatedly demonstrated that she thinks and processes information with reference to the narratives she learned as a young woman. She has shown that she organizes, stores, and transmits her insights and knowledge of the world through narratives and songs describing the human condition.[6]

The longer I have quoted this description and thought about the difference between Angela Sidney and those mythical but often invoked creatures, *most people*, the more I believe that this difference is mostly one of self-reflection, which is a considerable difference. Angela Sidney is consciously using her stories, working with them, and she is better aware of what they can do. To understand how Angela Sidney works with stories, an analogy to dogs is useful, because dogs are Donna Haraway's paradigm of a companion species.[7] Some dogs work with their owners to track or to herd; other dogs, lacking outlets for what they do best, pull their owners around on their leashes. Haraway argues at length that people who train their dogs well are careful to respect them as dogs; that is, to respect the specificity of the dog's particular breed and the otherness of the species. Similarly, Angela Sidney respects her stories' specific genres and their otherness. She knows that she can tell the stories, but they are not hers in any possessive sense. She respects that stories have lives of their own, and she is participating in those lives. That reflective respect seems prerequisite to whatever control she has over these stories.

Another way of expressing this difference between a master storyteller and most people is to quote again John Law from the preceding chapter: "This means that one way of imagining the world is that it is a set of (pretty disorderly) stories that intersect and interfere with one another."[8] Angela Sidney, Mabel McKay, and memoirists like Sharon O'Brien and Maxine Hong Kingston have worked hard to order how their stories intersect and reinforce one another. The rest of us live with stories as Law describes: in a pretty disorderly way. Yet we muddle through. Even unruly companions take care of us.

Stories can do all this because among different types of narrations and accounts, among different speech genres, stories have the singular capacity to generate the most intense, focused engagement among listeners and readers. People do not simply listen to stories. They become *caught up*, a phrase that can be explained only by another metaphor: stories get under people's skin. Once stories are under people's skin, they affect the terms in which people think, know, and perceive. Stories teach people what to look for and what can be ignored; they teach what to value and what to hold in contempt.

FINE-TUNING HABITABILITY

The primary work of stories is making the "blooming, buzzing confusion" habitable by ordering it into foregrounds and backgrounds of attention and value. The more fine-tuned work of stories as a default guidance system involves two axes. One axis traces how stories help people to understand who they are, and how stories connect them to affiliations. On the complementary axis, stories show people what can be good about themselves and about life, but stories also make life dangerous; they get people into trouble. As Radin says about tricksters, stories are creators and destroyers, responsible for both good and evil.[9]

I call these *works* of stories to emphasize that what happens is a process.[10] In work as in stories, certain ends are hoped for and anticipated, but things always might turn out differently. Useful as it can be to distinguish four works of stories—self, affiliation, goodness, and danger—these four are all one work, because selves are always affiliated, and goodness is never separable from danger. Any breathing, vital story does multiple kinds of work, often in the same situation at the same time. Distinguishing different types of work is nothing more or less than analytic convenience. As categories, these types of work are so general that they have little interest in themselves. It is hardly news that humans learn to become selves, that they affiliate into groups, or that life can be good and is often dangerous. The interesting questions are *how* these commonplaces happen in particular lives and situations, and how might they happen not just differently but better. Dialogical narrative analysis takes seriously what Thomas King says, that stories can cure and stories can injure.[11] The work of dialogical narrative analysis is to increase the rate of cure and minimize injury.

How Stories Teach People Who They Are

The idea of NARRATIVE IDENTITY has had such broad usage during the last several decades that even a perfunctory review would require a full chapter.[12] Instead of the term *narrative identity*, I find it more useful to think of *narrative identifying*, emphasizing that sustaining an identity is never final and also suggesting the reciprocal processes of narratives making available possible identities and people identifying themselves through narratives.

How stories teach people who they are begins with what is called INTER-PELLATION, a term given currency by the philosopher Louis Althusser.[13] Interpellation most simply means calling on a person to acknowledge and act on a particular identity; a crying baby calls on the person who may have slipped out of the parental identity to start assuming that identity. To use Althusser's preferred verb, the baby *hails* the person to be a parent. Or in medical offices, the waiting-room administrator calls out the name of the next patient, hailing the person to become all that being a patient involves.[14] Interpellation in storytelling proceeds on two levels: the story calls on its characters to be particular sorts of selves, and it calls on listeners to recognize themselves in particular characters.

The question is why certain interpellations have force; why do people take up the identities they are called to assume? This section's pursuit of that question leads to the idea of NARRATIVE HABITUS, or the collection of stories in which a life is formed and that continue to shape lives. Beyond narrative habitus is the *inner library* of stories, which is the deepest point of psychological descent in this book. Interpellation is then briefly revisited, before moving to a brief consideration of how stories connect but also disconnect people from each other. Getting back out of the inner library requires a bit of creative disorder, which I call narrative ambush.

A STORY INTERPELLATES COYOTE. One of the saddest Coyote stories, "Coyote and the Shadow People," is a shape-shifted variant of the Greek myth of Orpheus and Eurydice.[15] Coyote's wife has died and he journeys to the other world, the shadow world, to bring her back. Unlike Orpheus, Coyote stays awhile in that world, meets many old friends, and enjoys himself. People there are visible only during the hours of darkness; they fade away during daylight. Finally and after some prodding, Coyote, his wife, and his guide—the Hermes character, ominously called "the death spirit" but quite friendly—leave for the world of the living. Orpheus was instructed that if he turned and looked at Eurydice, he would lose her forever. Coyote must not touch his wife until she is fully returned to life. As their journey progresses, she becomes more and more visibly solid. Coyote cannot resist touching her too soon; she vanishes. Then comes my favorite line in all the Coyote stories, when the angry guide shouts at Coyote: "You inveterate doer of this kind of thing!"[16] The archaic phrasing of the translation somehow enhances the power of that line, which I shout regularly at myself, ever since hearing the story.

The "you inveterate doer" line is an overt instance of what stories always do, but usually do more quietly: stories *interpellate* characters. In every story I can think of, at least one character is interpellated, or hailed, or cast, or called to be a certain identity. The death spirit hails Coyote, naming him and requiring him to recognize and acknowledge himself as having the identity to which he is hailed. The guide does not judge Coyote's action, as in, "You have chosen badly." His message is: *You are in your essence*. Coyote is called on by the story to know himself as one who will inevitably do what he has done in the story. But while Coyote is hailed most directly, those who listen to the story are also being interpellated, at least in potential identities that they might share with Coyote.

In more complex stories, the interpellation crosses the boundary between the story's content and its telling. In "Christmas Eve," Fernando Silva is hailed to be witness to the child's dying, and that interpellation immediately extends to the reader of the story, who is also called to respond to the child's plea. Mademoiselle Bourienne is hailed *by* her aunt's story to follow the example of the woman *in* her story and win a husband. In the memoir stories of Maxine Hong Kingston, Sharon O'Brien, and Frederick Douglass, the memoirist is first hailed by a story in her or his life. By retelling that story within the memoir, the storyteller achieves as close to a self-hailing as possible. No such self-hailing is possible in Allen Feldman's ethnography of Irish paramilitaries. Recruits are hailed by their respective origin stories to set history back on its preordained path. Their place in the story is not optional.

Althusser, as a Marxist concerned with ideology, presents interpellations as virtually nonrefusable: the "Hey, you" demands acknowledgment. The interpellations of stories are powerful, yet people do refuse these: memoirs are often acts of refusal. Kingston will not remain the fearful, shamed girl that her mother's story calls her to be; O'Brien will not be part of another generation of women subjected to Handsome Dan's insecurity and neediness; Douglass will not be only the person whom the politics of abolition require him to be. Refusal of interpellation is possible, but this refusal is achieved only through the effort of fashioning a story that can contain the original interpellating story.

Stories that interpellate the character or listener into a deprecated identity are hard to walk away from, because at least they offer some identity. If Coyote were not in the story being the inveterate doer that the story casts him to be, who would he be? To say "anyone he wants" misses how much the sense of self is tied to stories into which the self is cast. To be as interpellated by the story or not to be at all   that seems to be Coyote's question and the question posed by all the stories told in this book's introduction. The power of this dilemma is best illustrated by the child in "Christmas Eve" who hovers on the verge of literal disappearance as he dies. He absolutely needs a story that will allow him to gain both self-recognition and recognition by others, and thus become able *to be*, before he dies. The all too human dilemma is that by accepting being in a story, a person at least provisionally accepts being what the story casts him or her to be, its interpellation.[17] Coyote may not be human in many respects, but in accepting his interpellation in the story of bringing back his wife, he is at his most human.[18]

Coyote's story aspires to tragedy, because Coyote always knows what story he is in and what that story will require him to do. He knows before he touches his wife that he is an inveterate doer of that kind of thing, because his nature is the nature of the character he is cast to play in this kind of story. Coyote, Orpheus, Bluebeard's wife, and Adam and Eve are all also cast into stories that are instances of the injunction-that-must-be-violated narrative. This casting is my socio-narratological version of the term SUBJECT POSITION: the character's more or less reflective awareness of who the type of narrative requires him or her to be, and what being that character requires him or her to do. The subject, both in the story and hearing the story, feels a tension between hitching a ride on the immanent volition of the story and being carried where such a story usually goes, versus the possibility that this time things could turn out differently: either the story might have changed, or the protagonist might this time, through some act of will, rewrite the story by acting differently from what the old story required.[19]

"Coyote and the Shadow People" presents a character unable to choose but also responsible for his choices. We who tell or hear the story are left with the truth of Bourdieu's oxymoron, *unchosen choices*.[20] Coyote, Orpheus, Bluebeard's wife, and Adam and Eve all make such choices. Whoever hears those stories is interpellated as one who, like these characters, will make unchosen choices. We are all inveterate doers of *that* kind of thing. The

did you choose, or were u chosen??

escape clause is that most of us are fortunate enough to be cast into multiple stories, and most of the time, the interpellations of those stories play against each other, softening if never negating the force of any single interpellation. Here we begin to see the general solution to many of the problems that attend stories: increase the number of stories that are allowed to act. That idea will be developed especially in this book's final chapter.

NARRATIVE HABITUS. The collection of stories that interpellate a person is his or her narrative habitus. What I call *narrative habitus* adapts Pierre Bourdieu's concept of HABITUS.[21] I follow Bourdieu in leaving *habitus* untranslated, but the most adequate translations would be "dispositions" or "second nature," as one might speak of doing a familiar task as second nature. A person's *habitus* is her or his disposition to recognize something as familiar or to it find strange and obscure; to like or dislike; to feel comfortable or uncomfortable either doing something or in the presence of something. Disposition suggests not what people are determined to feel, want, think, choose, or act to bring into being, but rather how they feel *conducted* to do what they do; as they undertake their lives, the course that seems to flow most naturally.

Tolstoy provides a fine instance of habitus in another of his authorial intrusions into a character's consciousness. The character is one of the main protagonists in *War and Peace*, Prince Andre. Tolstoy describes Andre, then an adjutant to the commanding general, surveying what will be the field for the battle of Austerlitz. He sees potential troop movements, he thinks about artillery placement, he plans and emplots the battle as a series of chess moves. "This was his way of thinking," Tolstoy writes.[22] Tolstoy might also have written of Prince Andre's way of eating, or dressing, or understanding his place in his family, as well as doing his work. Yet people do, in the course of their lives with changing circumstances and relationships, come to see differently, eat differently, and so forth; Prince Andre himself will change. Habitus does change, but to chart changes in characters' habitus requires a story the length of *War and Peace*.

Narrative habitus is the embedding of stories in bodies. People are disposed to certain stories just as they are disposed to particular foods. Food to which I am disposed not only tastes good; such food tastes *right* in the sense that eating that food affirms who I am and ought to be. Because of my embodied history of eating—who has fed me what, within what relationships and in what circumstances—certain foods bring a sense of comfort that exceeds what they actually taste like, or their nutritional value, or their level of culinary prestige. As it is of food, so it is also for narrative and stories. Jo-ann Archibald, trying to articulate how becoming a storyteller affected her way of doing narrative research, expresses habitus when she writes: "It was as though these stories became embedded in my body."[23] "Sometimes a person needs a story more than food to stay alive," says Badger Woman in Barry Lopez's fable, *Crow and Weasel*. "That is why we put these stories in each other's memory."[24]

Some stories are heard, immediately and intuitively, as *belonging* under one's skin. Narrative habitus is a disposition to hear some stories as those that one ought to listen to, ought to repeat on appropriate occasions, and ought to be guided by. Narrative habitus describes the embodied sense of attraction, indifference, or repulsion people feel in response to stories; the intuitive, usually tacit sense that some story is *for us* or not for us; that it expresses possibilities of which we are or can be part, or that it represents a world in which we have no stake. If, like most concepts, narrative habitus glosses too neatly the complexity of *all* that disposes a person to become caught up in a story or not, at least it focuses attention on this issue.

Narrative habitus is the unchosen force in any choice to be interpellated by a story, and the complementary rejection of the interpellation that other stories would effect if a person were caught up in them. The complexity of narrative habitus might never be specified, but it can be broken down for more adequate description. I offer four components. Each suggests why habitus is both individual and collective, always holding subjectivity as a feature of membership.

First, narrative habitus involves a *repertoire* of stories that a person at least recognizes and that a group shares. These stories are known against an unseen background of all the stories that person does not know and stories that do not circulate within any particular group.

Second, narrative habitus provides the *competence* to use this repertoire as embodied and mostly tacit knowledge. Narrative habitus is the feel for what story makes a good follow-up to a previous story; what story fits which occasion; who wants to hear what story when. A person's narrative habitus enables knowing how to react when a story is told, according to what kind of story it is. Complementary to that competence, narrative habitus enables prediction of how others will react to a story that might be told.

These first two considerations are anything but trivial in people's lives. People fit into groups or not, they are recognized as appropriate for membership or they are regarded as perpetual outsiders, depending on what stories they know and their knowledge of how to react to these stories.

Third, narrative habitus disposes a person's *taste* in stories, with taste predicting which future stories a person will be open to. When readers of this book see that the next story is Coyote folklore or a social scientific study of MidWest Insurance, do they anticipate that story with interest, or do they roll their eyes at its inclusion and skip several pages, hoping to find what counts as a real story? Which call of stories do people answer, among all the stories that call, each day? Again, most human responses to stories are tacit, embodied, and predisposed.

4 (Fourth, narrative habitus predisposes a sense of the right and fitting resolution toward which a half-told story should progress; it is the feel for what kind of narrative move leads to what next kind of move. Narrative habitus is how most readers know, as soon as Coyote is told that he must not touch his wife or he will lose her, that he will touch his wife and lose her. I describe this tacit knowledge as *predictable plot completions*: if people are told an incomplete story, how will they complete the plot? Plot completions will cluster for several significant reasons. One is that plots are finite in their possibilities. A second reason is that to be a member of a group is to grow up on stories shared within that group. *We*, that densest of pronouns, are those who expect Coyote to touch his wife too soon and lose her; we *know* that will happen, and the story interpellates us as those who share that narrative habitus. People's sense of how plots will probably go reflects and generates their everyday common sense of which actions lead to which consequences, whether in stories or in life. People's habitus of expected plot completions is nothing less than their sense of life's possibilities.

After I had been thinking about narrative *habitus* for some time, using the concept to understand how stories get under some people's skin yet make no impression on other people, I encountered Pierre Bayard's strange idea of the *inner library*, which proposes the odd-sounding possibility of being influenced by stories that have not been heard.

INTO THE INNER LIBRARY. "For a true reader," writes Pierre Bayard, "it is not any specific book that counts, but the totality of all books."[25] As important as specific stories are to people, any one story has meaning only in relation to all the others. What Bayard calls the inner library is the organization of all the stories a person can be influenced by; and on Bayard's account, this *all* includes stories the person could not actually tell but nevertheless knows, preconsciously or unconsciously. In simplest terms, the inner library is the organization of narrative habitus; less simply, it is the dynamic principle by which stories have their effects.

Bayard is a psychoanalyst as well as a literary critic, and the inner library requires more inferences about the depths of mental life than dialogical narrative analysis usually engages in. Yet, the inner library seems a necessary complement to and elaboration of narrative habitus. Bayard's almost commonsensical premise is that just as a librarian knows a book by knowing where it belongs among other books, people make sense of a story by placing it among similar stories. Bayard distinguishes between knowing the *content* of a book, or a story for our purposes, and knowing its *location*, maintaining that the latter is the more important knowledge (11).

People have an inner library of the stories they know, including stories they might have heard, or that are resonant in stories they once heard. This inner library predisposes attention to those stories that can be readily located; they sound like familiar stories. And conversely, the inner library predisposes disregard for stories that have no apparent location. The general principle of reception is reluctance to create new sections of the inner library. At the extreme, stories not readily locatable in the listener's inner library will be off the radar of comprehension, disregarded as noise. Yet as I will discuss later in this chapter, some stories bid successfully for the creation of new inner-library sections, thus expanding narrative habitus.

Bayard's distinction between content and location poses nicely the problem of hearing a story like Kingston's at a distance from the scene in which the story was told—first-generation immigration and Chinese culture. To someone living outside this context, the story's content is readily accessible, and that may be the problem: non-Chinese readers-at-a-distance all too readily locate the story in *their* inner libraries, but that location is different from where the listeners-on-the-scene would locate the story. The same story has significantly different meaning when located in different sections of different inner libraries.[26]

Bayard cites the anthropologist Laura Bohannan's report of reading a summary of Shakespeare's *Hamlet* to the Tiv, a people who have no familiarity with Shakespeare or any other aspect of Western culture. Bayard's description of their response says much about how stories interpellate listeners who have no location for those stories in their inner library:

> It is not, then, the story of *Hamlet* that they [the Tiv] hear, but whatever in that story conforms to their notions of the family and the status of the dead and might serve to comfort them . . . The alarming passages are either ignored, or they undergo a transformation that allows the largest possible overlap between their inner book and *Hamlet*. (83)

The anthropologists Linda Garro and Cheryl Mattingly comment: "A coconstructed narrative emerges through the push and pull between Bohannan's telling of a story world and the world where the story is told."[27] This description of the Tiv implies limits to mutual understanding: people are not hearing the same story when they locate that story in respectively different inner libraries. But it also implies people's potential to retell a story—or "co-construct" it, in Garro and Mattingly's terms—to fit their inner library. Whether that co-construction represents an expanded understanding or a misunderstanding can be a very fine line.

Bayard's description of the Tiv's reaction to *Hamlet* refers not to the inner library, but to a more specific concept, the *inner book*. At this point his argument turns distinctly psychoanalytic. Bayard's several complementary definitions of the inner book are worth quoting in full, because they sharpen the distinction between what is heard, depending on the inner book through which a listener does hear a story, and what could be heard if the listener were hearing through a different inner book. As psychoanalytic as the argument is, it is important for socio-narratology, because no one creates an inner book from anything other than shared cultural resources. Where Bayard refers to *book*, please substitute *story*.

> I propose the term *inner book* to designate the set of mythic representations, be they collective or individual, that come between the reader and any new piece of writing, shaping his reading without his realizing it. Largely unconscious, this imaginary book acts as a filter and determines the reception of new texts by selecting which of its elements will be retained and how they will be interpreted. (82–83)

> Like collective inner books, individual inner books create a system for receiving other texts and participate both in their reception and their reorganization. In this sense, they form a grid through which we read the world, and books in particular, organizing the way we perceive these texts while producing the illusion of transparency. (85)

> Woven from the fantasies and private mythologies particular to each person, the individual inner book is at work in our desire to read—that is, in the way we seek out and read books. It is that phantasmagorical object that every reader lives to pursue, of which the best books he encounters in his life will be but imperfect fragments, compelling him to continue reading. (85)

I quote these passages in part because of the importance of Bayard's *filter* or grid through which people organize what they perceive. Bayard expresses a crucial aspect of habitus: its deceptive transparency. Looking out through that filter or grid, there seems to be only the world as it is, appearing as if unfiltered. Adapting Bayard, we can imagine the inner story as the set of representations that come between the listener and any new story, determining which elements of that new story will be selected and interpreted, which will not be heard at all, and which will be changed to make them fit the inner story (as Mademoiselle Bourienne has adapted whatever story her aunt once told her, making it her inner story). And, the inner story predisposes which future stories a person will seek out, feel comfortable with, be able to learn from, and remember. That much of Bayard's argument seems to elaborate Bourdieu's habitus.

According to the psychoanalytic aspect of Bayard's argument, people spend their lives seeking a story that can match the inner story. This search will never end, because each actually encountered story will necessarily be an imperfect representation of the inner story, or chimerical imagination of a story. Seeking stories becomes a process of displacement—each next story displacing the imperfect one before, seeking what can never be found. The Holy Grail—the mythic cup that caught Christ's blood and is the object of quests by King Arthur's knights in medieval romances—symbolizes the perfect inner story. Grail stories can be read reflexively as stories about the quest for the ideal story, which will effect all final healing and reconciliation. Or, the story that, once told, will quench desire for any other stories. The attraction of Grail stories is tied to the hope that all this questing—or displacement in psychoanalytic terms—might someday end; that there is a telos, a finish line, a homecoming after which no travel is necessary. Psychic reality is closer to the end of Homer's *Odyssey*: having finally returned home, Odysseus is sent off on another journey, and only the reader's need for an ending suggests that this next journey will be any shorter than that from which he has just returned.

When Bayard writes that this inner book is "largely unconscious," he does not mean that the listener is *simply* unaware of what filters reception; it's not that simple. For Bayard, "the books that we talk about . . . are often no more than screen books. Or, if you prefer, what we talk about is not the books themselves, but substitute objects we create for the occasion" (46). The injunction that begins Kingston's mother's story, *You must not tell anyone*, marks a rare occasion when the screen is spoken. The story of the aunt's pregnancy is never to be told again, and it might even be forgotten. But all stories that are told will henceforth be substitute objects for that story. Each other story will be a screen behind which the story of the pregnant aunt lurks, affecting how that story is heard. That original story need never be spoken, but it will always be heard by the one whose consciousness operates with or through that screen. Other people will be baffled why she reacts to stories as she does, as she herself may be, until the original story is brought back to full awareness, freeing new stories to be what they are, not a reflection that both conceals and perpetuates the original story.

Bayard is clear that this whole process of inner libraries, inner books, and screen books is both durable and open to change, like habitus: "For if our inner books, like our fantasies, are relatively stable, the screen books about which we speak are endlessly being modified, as we shall see, and it is futile to imagine we can put a stop to their metamorphoses" (108–9). Bayard seems useful here in explaining an apparent paradox that Bourdieu spent his career seeking to clarify: how habitus can be predisposing, but predisposition is never determination.

Bayard's final contribution to socio-narratology is to correct a tendency of habitus to seem unified, coherent, and consistent:

> The *reading subject* . . . is not a unified and self-assured figure but an uncertain one, lost among fragments of texts he can barely identify. For this figure, no longer able to distinguish his own texts from those of others, each encounter with a book becomes terrifying, for it threatens to bring him face-to-face with his own madness. (56)

If we are tempted to dismiss Bayard's usage of *madness* as hyperbole, perhaps that reaction defends the vital human illusion that our encounters with new stories are transparent, and we are open to the world as it actually is. It is mad to realize that the stories to which we feel attracted—the stories we apparently choose to tell and retell—are screen stories, substitute objects created for the occasion, screening us from the phantasmagorical untellable story that is the principle of the screening. But perhaps such a realization is also a path toward freedom from displacements that repeat unhappiness.

This whole line of argument is psychoanalytic in the best and worst senses. At worst, it is undeniable (and undialogical), because the more you deny it, the more your denials affirm the principle of your investment in maintaining the unconscious reality that is threatened with being brought into the sunlight and crumbling. At best, Bayard explains why the Tiv's incomprehension of *Hamlet* is a fine example of people's general inability to understand each other's stories. Whatever readers make of Bayard's explanation, the problem he addresses is undeniable: when two inner libraries do not overlap, "the dialogue of the deaf arises" (73). If the world were not so full of those dialogues of the deaf, and if so much real damage did not result, then it might be possible to take Bayard less seriously.

OUT OF THE INNER LIBRARY: NARRATIVE AMBUSH. Bayard seems to place all the action on the side of consciousness, often unconsciousness, whereas I want to let stories breathe. Sometimes, stories that have no place in people's inner library still teach those people who they can be; stories have a capacity for *narrative ambush*. The abolitionists who toured Frederick Douglass hoped that some Americans living in the northeastern states in the 1850s would be ambushed by his stories of the brutalities of slavery. Many in the audience would attend the event out of curiosity or to express hostility, but they would be moved by what Douglass told them. Postings on Amazon.com responding to Douglass's *Autobiography* suggest that contemporary readers are still being ambushed by his stories.

Vital, breathing stories can break through the filters and grids. Stories can make themselves heard whether or not they fit a narrative habitus, inspiring listeners to create new sections in their inner library. An objection is that this apparently new inner-library section has been there all along. Long-forgotten stories have already prepared a location for these only-apparently-new stories, and what seems like an epiphany is only the conscious realization of a shift that had been taking place in small increments for some time. That objection cannot be decided: reports of narrative ambush—religious conversion narratives are paradigmatic—can always be dismissed as failure to notice what predisposed the person to be ambushed. Any person knows so many stories that any new story always has antecedents. Narrative habitus can affect what stories will be heard and taken seriously next, but people can also be responsive to new stories. (face-to-face with murders)

The South African psychologist Pumla Gobodo-Madikizela tells a story of her own narrative ambush.[28] Gobodo-Madikizela was the sole psychologist on Bishop Desmond Tutu's Truth and Reconciliation Commission (TRC), and one of her jobs was to interview a primary witness at the commission hearings, Eugene de Kock. De Kock is an infamous character in South Africa, having been a covert hit man for the apartheid regime and regarded as having done more killing than any other state agent. As a black South African, Gobodo-Madikizela approaches de Kock as the incarnation of pure evil.

When Gobodo-Madikizela interviews de Kock, he denies nothing, but as he tells her the story of his life, she perceives a human being who has done terrible things but who was led to those things as life leads all of us: one step at a time, each step making the next seem necessary. De Kock lived in dangerous times and succumbed to the worst impulses of those times; but in dangerous times, people do terrible things. Further complicating her judgment is de Kock's testimony before the TRC, which proves crucial in forcing other former government officials to testify. His testimony embodies truthfulness. At the book's end, Gobodo-Madikizela is profoundly ambivalent about the justice of de Kock remaining in prison.

Part of Gobodo-Madikizela's ambivalence stems from her awareness of the inherent unfairness of the TRC process: some defendants were never charged or were given amnesty, and others were punished. Another part stems from her having heard de Kock tell his story—and that whole story, including his testimony at the TRC, is a good deal more than his murders. Gobodo-Madikizela wonders if de Kock's capacity to solicit sympathy is part of his pathology; her friends and associates accuse her of being seduced. She rejects that as too simple. The evil and the good are not reconciled. But evil is *not final*.

De Kock emerges from the book as an exemplar of a character who cannot be finalized in any single judgment, and Gobodo-Madikizela's refusal to render a finalizing judgment makes her book profoundly dialogical. She allows herself to be in relation to de Kock as Bakhtin argues Dostoevsky places himself in relation to his characters: not controlling them or seeking to know their innermost thoughts and motives.[29] Gobodo-Madikizela listens to de Kock, observing both his terrible mistakes *and* his redemptive acts. She accepts the human capacity for both and the reality that neither may be that far from the other.

"We are the sum of these accumulated books" (73), Bayard writes, in a good epigraph for narrative identity. I agree, but if what counts is narrative *identifying*, then this accumulation is never fixed and the sum is never finalized. The gestalt of attention and inattention, memory and forgetting, valuation and devaluing, has to be relatively stable, but relatively stable is still open. We humans are the sum of perpetually *accumulating* stories, because often enough stories break into the inner library, reshaping the new accumulation.

How Stories Connect People

Stories will not leave people alone. Stories call individuals into groups, and they call on groups to assert common identities. Coyote stories connect those who grow up on them, but showing how stories connect requires a story about people whose group identity has to be created and remains tenuous. I return to Charlotte Linde's ethnographic study, mentioned in chapter 1, of an American insurance company she calls MidWest Insurance, a company that definitely has a story.[30] Actually, the company has many stories revolving around one shared story. "Agents tell stories about their early days, and the course of building their business," Linde writes. "Managers tell stories about changes in the company. And everyone tells stories about the founder of the company" (612). Linde's concern is with the importance of memory in reaffirming identity, and how personal identity forms within collective identities. In particular, she asks "what it means for a person to remember something that she did not experience, or indeed, to be encouraged or exhorted to remember it as a national or religious duty" (608). Or at MidWest, a corporate duty, a sense of being affiliated within a company that has inherent problems of sustaining collective identity, because each agent—Linde describes them as "independent contractors" (611)—has his or her own clients and runs a quasi-autonomous franchise within the parent corporate structure.

MidWest achieves collective identity by what Linde describes as "narrative induction": "the social work that an institution performs to make one person's story everyone's story: relevant to everyone and available to everyone as a role model" (613). The role-modeling story is that of the founder in the 1920s, Mr. McBee. His authorized biography was written in the 1950s and, like all stories, does not do its work alone. Mr. McBee's life story is "embedded within a matrix of American stories that help to shape its structure, just as this story helps to structure the stories of its members" (614). Mr. McBee's story is also symbiotic, working with the small museum in the lobby of the corporate headquarters. The museum includes such material objects as "a Model A Ford in pristine condition, built in the year the company was founded; a gleaming fire engine from the same period; the first rate chart drawn up by the founder on a piece of brown paper; posters of radio and television programs sponsored by the company" (611); and so on through clothing, plaques and gifts given to recognize agents' performance, and photographs that are visually continuous with photographs in individual offices. Memory work pervades the company, merging material artifact and story as each informs the other.

Members of the company are not unified in how they identify with Mr. McBee's story, nor is the whole story ever told on any single occasion (622). Rather, as Linde says, "pieces of it are told as possibilities."[31] "Not all careers fit the paradigm," she writes (621–22), "and not all stories form part of the paradigmatic narrative."

Yet all those who hear the company story are interpellated: they are called to be those whose story this *somehow* is, however differently individual members relate to the paradigmatic narrative. As Linde puts it: "The paradigmatic narrative represents the work of an entire institution to create such relevance for particular narratives" (622). Those who receive the story are called to make themselves knowable not only to themselves, but also to one another with respect to the story that all share as a common reference. The story works as the ground of individual unchosen choices, because it is a collective unchosen choice. Someone once was the author of the bound volume that is Mr. McBee's authorized biography, but Linde points out that no one person wrote the paradigmatic narrative: "It was a joint creation, and its shape was only fully understood in retrospect" (626). I would add that as most paradigmatic narratives do their work, *retrospect* is a moving target, a sequence of changing retrospective understandings, never a fixture.

Stories connect so effectively because their interpretive openness allows individuals to fashion their own variations, which more or less shift the shape of the paradigm. "The paradigmatic narrative was not just told to agents" (623), but also was used by them to define their own progress and success. The richness of Linde's narrative analysis lies in her descriptions of how individual agents played with and off the paradigmatic narrative. Collective narrative identifying is effective because it engages and develops individual narrative identifying.

Yet significant questions remain: what would predispose someone to undertake management training at MidWest in the first place, and would such a person already be predisposed to becoming caught up in Mr. McBee's story? Those issues take us back to *narrative habitus* and even into the psychic depths of Bayard's *inner library*. Bourdieu's theory suggests that new agents become caught up in Mr. McBee's story because they perceive something valuable to be at stake in the story; they are able to take the story seriously—not everyone could—and they are serious about pursuing its stakes. Mr. McBee's story resonates with stories in their narrative habitus; it articulates (in the sense of *fits*) with those stories, and it articulates (in the sense of *expresses*) other aspects of the habitus, including what counts as employment.

Bayard suggests an interpretation of why, as Linde notes, MidWest has such a remarkable record of retaining its agents, compared with turnover at comparable companies. Mr. McBee's story gets under agents' skin. The story works as an inner story that company agents feel *compelled*, to use Bayard's strong verb, to seek to approximate in stories of their own careers. Mr. McBee does not necessarily become a role model; agents may make fun of the story. But to adapt Thomas King's phrase from chapter 1, they cannot act as if they never heard it.

If the understanding of the company story derived from Bourdieu and Bayard seems tautological—the company's memory work is effective because employees are disposed to such stories—it remains useful, for example, as the basis for studying high attrition rates in many equity-hiring programs. The problem may be neither the clarity with which the company story is told, nor the attentiveness of candidate employees. Instead, the problem is that the story being told has no location in the candidate's inner library; it fails to resonate with any inner story. All of us, when we fail to connect with groups and organizations, are like the Tiv hearing *Hamlet*. To make such connections, we would need to remodel our inner library—and people do that. But it is not easy work.

How Stories Make Life Good but Also Dangerous

After stories have taught people who they are and provided a basis for their affiliation into groups, stories help them live in a world that is both good and dangerous. Stories help separate what is good from what is dangerous, and stories do their share in creating good and danger. In sacred texts, in literature, and in everyday conversation—especially jokes—humans work with stories to explore what is good and what is dangerous. That stories actively make the world good and also make it dangerous is less evident.

I began by imagining separate and opposite works of making good and making dangerous involving different stories told in different ways. The more I thought with and about supposedly good stories and supposedly dangerous stories, the more I understood that most stories do both: to point toward the good often instigates danger, and from what is dangerous there is often an emergence of good. What forced my recognition of this duality was Lewis Hyde's discussion of the Norse myth of Loki's killing of Baldur.[32]

As I had always understood the story, the duality could not have been clearer between the good represented by Baldur, the Shining One, the gods' hope for the future, and evil represented by Loki, sometimes a humorous trickster but here a jealous, scheming god of destruction. Frigg, the mother of Baldur, seeks to protect her son, so she solicits a pledge from everything in the world—every plant, mineral, and creature—that it will not harm him. Those pledges having been made, the gods celebrate the invulnerability of Baldur by having a festival, the centerpiece of which is a spectacle of gods throwing things at Baldur. Nothing will harm him, so whatever is thrown deflects before touching him. It's fine sport, but it annoys Loki, who is jealous of Baldur.

Loki tricks Frigg into telling him that there is one thing—the tiny mistletoe plant—from which she did not bother to get a pledge. Loki collects some mistletoe and attaches it to a spear. He asks the blind god Hod why he stands on the sidelines, not honoring Baldur by joining in the sport and throwing something. Hod demurs, citing his blindness. Loki offers to guide him, giving him the spear tipped with mistletoe. Hod throws the spear, and Baldur is killed. The gods retaliate by binding Loki to a rock, over which a serpent drips venom. Loki's faithful wife collects the venom in a cup, but when the cup must be emptied, venom drips on Loki. His agonized movements cause the earth to rumble.

This story always represented what I understood as the darkest side of the trickster figure. Loki is pure evil. Angry as Apollo is at Hermes for stealing his cattle, even he has to admit that the baby Hermes is cute, and they reconcile. Hermes becomes a faithful servant of the gods, and his act of theft recedes into the background. Coyote causes plenty of collateral damage, but the damaged characters seem to get over it readily enough, and there is usually something funny about what Coyote is doing, in part because he often ends up damaging himself more than others. The death of Baldur is not collateral damage, and there is nothing funny involved. It's just evil. Or so I thought. Lewis Hyde offers a different way of understanding the story.

Hyde points out that the version of the story as we know it reflects the Christian influence that was becoming pervasive when the story moved from oral telling to written form. The Christian narrative required a duality between the contrasting poles of good and evil. The trickster character is co-opted to play the devil, and the nuance of the trickster's acts is lost in the retold version. Hyde then imagines the pre-Christian version of the story. Here, Frigg initiates the cycle of wrongdoing when she tries to obstruct the natural order of things. In an agricultural society, seasonal change is especially important; disruption of this cycle is trouble—or Trouble—of the sort that stories begin with.

Frigg upsets the natural order of vulnerability to death. She commits the cardinal mythic sin of seeking to institute permanence. The trickster's role—his assigned work in the order of things—is to restore movement when stagnation threatens. Loki does just that. The killing of Baldur is not about evil that is jealous of good, destroying what is hopeful. The killing is a restoration of the necessary cyclical change that Frigg disrupts when she makes Baldur into something unnatural, even for a god (at least a Norse god). Loki causes damage, as tricksters usually do, but the story teaches the creative necessity of what is damaging.

The last word can be given to the anthropologist most associated with trickster stories, Paul Radin. Radin writes of the trickster: "Yet through his actions all values come into being."[33] That is not to imagine either Loki or Eugene de Kock—who has more than a few trickster qualities—as being good. Rather, Radin points out that values derive from stories. Values name types of actions first exemplified in stories, and understanding those values begins with returning to stories to make sense of what it means, in practice, to act according to a value. In the mythology of the Indigenous people of the British Columbia coast, Raven, their trickster, brings light to the world. Like Hermes, Raven is a thief; he steals the light. Stealing is not good; light is good. Stories enable humans to live with this paradox, embodied in the trickster.

DANGERS OF STORIES THAT ARE ALSO GOOD. My discussion has focused on interpretation of what happens in a story. The complementary aspect is what happens as an effect of a story being told. Here I turn to a different story, the tale of Samson from the Hebrew Bible, as interpreted by David Grossman.[34] The story is one of the longest in the Hebrew Bible, found in Judges 13–16. Grossman, who is also a novelist, brings a storyteller's sensibility to his study of Samson, pointing out numerous points at which the narrator makes odd or unpredictable choices. I will return to Grossman's interpretive style in chapter 4. Of concern here is a minor but significant part of Grossman's book, in which he talks about how the story of Samson has been appropriated in contemporary Israeli iconography. If we today can only guess at the effects of the story when it first was told, we can observe how the story continues to affect understandings and actions, and perhaps to effect understandings and actions.

Like most oral folktales, the story of Samson has a simple structure: a birth, three repetition cycles of Samson being betrayed by a woman, and a death. Other things happen, including Samson killing a lion and later finding a beehive with honey in the lion's carcass, but the narrative structure is birth, betrayals, and death. The birth of the hero is never straightforward. A heavenly messenger announces Samson's imminent arrival to his mother, who has been judged "barren." A marginal interpretation holds that this messenger is Samson's biological father. The child is to be dedicated as a Nazirite, which Grossman glosses as "a person who puts a partition between himself and life," adding that the word combines "the root *ndr*, meaning 'vow,' and the word *zar*, 'stranger'" (22). In practical terms, a Nazirite is not to drink alcohol, approach a dead body, or cut his hair, but is permitted to have relations with women.

Samson is born in the tribe of Dan, living in the borderlands between the Israelites and the Philistines, whose military advantage lay in their development of iron weapons (42). Grossman points out that Samson's weapons are entirely natural, most famously the jawbone of an ass with which he slays a thousand Philistines. The biblical text and subsequent rabbinical commentary are clear that "Samson was called," but Grossman notes that it is not clear exactly to what he is called, except kill Philistines, which he does without any particular plan or strategic objective. The killings are ad hoc, solitary, and without follow-up; Samson never attempts to rally the Israelites to organized resistance. The story is complicated further by Samson's choices of Philistine women as his sexual partners. He either kills Philistines or has sex with them. Which brings us to the three betrayals.

The first betrayal occurs when Samson is marrying a Philistine and, in one of his trickster moments, poses a poetic riddle to the wedding guests, with a considerable wager attached. Unable to solve the riddle, the Philistines press Samson's wife to get him to tell her, as she eventually does, passing on the answer. In response to the guests solving the riddle, Samson abandons the marriage. Then he travels to a city further within Philistine territory, and, in Grossman's description, "he cuts down thirty innocent people, who had the bad luck to run into him in the streets of their city" (80). He steals these people's clothes and uses them to pay off his wager to the wedding guests.

The second betrayal is by a Philistine prostitute whom Samson visits after he has killed the thousand with a jawbone. She betrays him, but he kills those who come to capture him and walks off carrying the gates of the city, which Grossman neatly interprets as "the barrier that creates the distinction between the locals and outsiders or enemies" (109). That counts as another trickster moment, as tricksters are boundary crossers. Grossman also notes with regard to Samson what I suggested earlier in this chapter about Coyote touching his wife and losing her because the story he is in casts him as a character who will do that. Samson is explicitly destined either by God or by the story, depending on the listener's beliefs. But destiny is not wholly determining, as Grossman observes: "even if Samson's great mission of battling the Philistines has been imposed on him from above, and if his whole life is a journey determined in advance, here [in choosing the gates as the object of his wreckage] Samson manages to muster a few sparks of free will, as yet again he finds a uniquely self-expressive mode of carrying out his task" (109–10).

The third betrayal is the one immortalized in high art and popular culture: Samson telling Delilah that the secret of his strength lies in his hair. He tells her only after giving her several wrong answers, which mirror earlier wrong answers he has given others who have tried to learn this secret. What Grossman says about Samson's first betrayal by his wife seems equally true of his later betrayal by Delilah: he effectively "'invited' her betrayal, condemning her to betray him. And thus arises the troubling suspicion that this is just what he wanted" (75). Grossman makes suggestive proposals as to why Samson might want to be betrayed, most of them referencing *stranger* as one of the root words in *Nazirite*. To simplify an elegantly complex if nondialogically intrapsychic argument, betrayal is the only way Samson can imagine overcoming the alienation that is one dark side of how he was dedicated before his birth. When he tells his true secret to Delilah, he says that if his hair is cut, "I shall become weak, and be like any other man" (Judges 16:17). Being like any other man, Grossman argues, is what Samson most wants. Many heroes end up being betrayed, but Samson's betrayal, coming after two rounds of what seem like rehearsals, has an unmistakable sense of being what he intends.

The story of Samson ends with his famous death, when after an undefined period of captivity and now blinded, he is brought before the Philistines as an amusement at a festival. After asking God to restore his strength (his hair has grown again), he breaks the two central pillars supporting the temple, "so that the dead which he slew at his death were more than they which he slew in his life" (Judges 16:30). Grossman observes that Samson may be the "first suicide-killer," adding that "although the circumstances of his deed were different from those familiar to us from the daily reality of the streets of Israel, it may be that the act itself established in human consciousness a mode of murder and revenge directed at innocent victims, which has been perfected in recent years" (143). His footnotes point out that rabbinical commentary, while generally accepting of Samson, has not been blind to the troubling aspects of his destructive aggression.

Within the narrative frame of the story, Samson is a character who is interpellated before his birth: he is called to be a Nazirite. This interpellation works as a disconnection, not a connection. Samson is set apart from everyone. At one point the submissively colonized Jews respectfully ask Samson if they can bind him and turn him over to the Philistines. He consents, and when he is being handed over, he breaks the ropes, picks up the jawbone of an ass, and massacres the enemy. If anything, Samson seems less connected to his own people than to the Philistines, among whom he chooses to live and attempts to love. Grossman's conclusion seems inevitable: from before his birth, Samson "will always lack the capacity for simple human contact that comes so naturally to most people" (22). Samson does not even have any particular contact with God, who does not speak to him but seems only to use him as an instrument of destruction.

But what of the effect of telling Samson's story: what work does the story do? It interpellates those who hear it to take Samson as a model. "Jews throughout the ages took pride in the tales of his heroism and yearned for the physical strength, bravery, and manliness that he represented," Grossman writes. "They esteemed, no less, his ability to apply force without any restraints or moral inhibitions" (87). The story of Samson thus connects through the institutionalization of this one facet. Grossman points out that "elite combat units have been named after him, from 'Samson's Foxes' of the 1948 War of Independence to the 'Samson' unit created during the first Palestinian *intifada* in the late 1980s" (88). On a more popular level, there is also "a chain of body-building clubs called the 'Samson Institute,' set up in the 1960s, by a muscle-bound rabbi named Rafael Halperin" (ibid.).

Grossman, who is Israeli, offers a nuanced interpretation of the subjectivity that Samson's story offers to both individuals and collectives, and how this sense of self can lead toward something that could be good but also can be dangerous. He is worth quoting at length for the care with which he blends the good and the dangerous in what the story brings about:

> Yet there is a certain problematic quality to Israeli sovereignty that is also embodied in Samson's relationship to his own power. As in the case of Samson, it sometimes seems that Israel's considerable military might is an asset that becomes a liability. For it would seem, without taking lightly the dangers facing Israel, that the reality of being immensely powerful has not really been internalized in the Israeli consciousness, not assimilated in a natural way, over many generations; and this, perhaps, is why the attitude toward this power, whose acquisition has often been regarded as truly miraculous, is prone to distortion.
>
> Such distortion may lead, for example, to ascribing an exaggerated value to the power that one has attained; to making power an end in itself; and to using it excessively; and also to a tendency to turn almost automatically to the use of force instead of weighing other means of action—these are all, in the end, characteristically "Samsonian" modes of behaviour. (88–89)

Samson is the paradigm of a story that offers a subjectivity that can become a basis of connection; it enchants a hostile world by making God's presence immanent. It shows possibilities of overcoming adversity. But the story also creates its own dangers. As Grossman writes about Samson's death: "the act itself established in human consciousness a mode of murder and revenge directed at innocent victims" (quoted earlier, 143). The story as a whole is one of many that establishes in human consciousness a mode of understanding other people as first, hostile, scheming, and brutal; second, because of those qualities, deserving to die; and third, faceless in those deaths. The story speaks of death only as quantities: in Samson's first killing, thirty; then a thousand; and then more than all the others combined.[35]

Samson's story can be heard as a universal fable of dedication to a higher purpose, making dreadful mistakes in pursuit of that purpose, and finally regaining the fullest sense of purpose in a summative act of self-sacrifice. That hearing teaches the good. Or it can be understood as a dangerous story: dangerous to Israel by being a model of the poorly considered reliance on force, and dangerous to all those who fit the mold of "Philistines" and thus can be killed without discrimination or specific purpose. Nor can the qualities that make the story elevating be separated from those that make it murderous. The story performs the human confrontation with the inextricability of seeking a higher purpose and the danger of falling into evil. Perhaps when both sides of the story are seen for what they are, then a story like Samson's that so easily goes out of control can be tamed to become a better companion to the humans who live with it, so that it no longer divides those who hold it as their own story from those whom the story casts as the objects of divine wrath.

LIVING RIGHT, JUST LIKE A STORY

Native Elder Angela Sidney is quoted by her scholar-apprentice, Julie Cruik-shank, as saying: "I want to live my life right, just like a story."[36] Looking at a photograph of Angela Sidney's weathered face, to me she seems to be the source of all values, and I believe that her stories will lead people to live their lives right. But what about Mademoiselle Bourienne, who thinks she is right when she lives like her reworked version of her aunt's story; what about Maxine Hong Kingston's mother, who believes that her daughter will live her life right if guided by the story of her pregnant aunt; what about Allen Feldman's paramilitaries, who believe their origin stories show them what is right; and what about the story of Samson and the complexities of internalizing the power that the story not only describes in its content but also inscribes as it is told? Many people are living "just like a story," and their lives are anything but right—at least according to those whom their story casts in the role of the Philistines or, in Feldman's term, the interlopers.

The power of stories is the problem with stories: they are far too good at doing what they do, which is being the source of all values. But having observed this problem, stories *are* the source of all values. Calling stories the source of all values echoes Radin's statement quoted earlier, that through the trickster's actions "all values come into being," the equation completed by Hyde when he writes: "the trickster in the narrative is the narrative itself."[37] The problem of living right with stories is no easy problem, whether we say that humans are cast into stories, or if we say that stories cast humans into their lives.

To repeat Thomas King's refrain, you can do whatever you like with a story, except say you haven't heard it.[38] Following King's refrain, say what you will about Samson's story, believe it or be appalled by it (it already has been turned into a movie), it keeps Samson company, even if the terms imposed by the story make it impossible for him to keep any other company for very long. Samson's story is his companion, and like the etymology of *Nazirite*, this company is part vow and part stranger. The story of Samson continues to keep many people company, binding them to different vows and estranging them from whomever their Philistines are, possibly even estranging them from themselves.

The story of Samson can be a good companion or a dangerous one, depending on what is made of the boundaries that the story alternately upholds—Jew seeming to be eternally separated from Philistine—but then effaces, especially in Samson's sexual liaisons with Philistines. The moral issue is what a person's responsibilities are toward people on either side of the boundary and toward the boundary itself. In the course of teaching narrative for enough years, I have asked myself if stories are *always* about boundaries. Some boundaries are evident in the content of the story: the gates that Samson pulls down and carries away are an evident boundary. The stories told in this book's introduction assert boundaries between the living and the soon-to-be dead; between the rich princess and her paid companion without independent means; between the chaste and those who are pregnant outside marriage; between those who buy into a version of a family myth and those who perceive the destructive aspects of that myth; between Irish Protestant and Irish Catholic. If stories make selection/evaluation possible, that selecting and evaluating requires that stories also be boundary creators.

Finally, an even grander question: does the fate of the world depend on the balance between boundary maintenance, which humanizes time and space, and boundary crossing, as the dynamic force of keeping life in motion? To be human is to confront a sequence of questions throughout a life, of which boundaries to respect, which to cross, and how to know the rules of crossing. Stories create the boundaries, yet they also are humans' companions in living with—though not necessarily within—these boundaries.

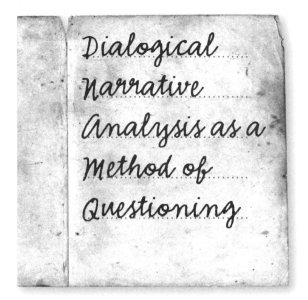

Dialogical narrative Analysis as a Method of Questioning

3

Oedipus the King *is a story about the awful danger of storytelling.*
Storytelling in this case makes something happen with a vengeance. It
leads the storyteller to condemn, blind, and exile himself, and it leads
his mother-wife, Jocasta, to kill herself. —Hillis Miller

The story develops together with the plot: the event being narrated
and the event of narration itself merge in the single event of the artistic
work. —Mikhail Bakhtin

"Fine," a colleague once asked me, after I had described stories
as vital actors that make life social, "but what do we study?" The previous
chapter began to answer that question: socio-narratology studies the work
that stories do as material-semiotic companions. It studies how stories give
people the resources to figure out who they are, and how stories both connect and disconnect people. It studies how stories inspire people toward the
good—an aspiration that stories have singular capacities to instigate and
articulate—and it studies how stories make life dangerous, often by casting
other people as suitable objects of aggression. It studies how stories create and play with boundaries: who defends which boundaries, who crosses
boundaries, and what effects those boundaries have.

This chapter shifts to a method of socio-narratology—dialogical narrative analysis. If socio-narratology is the theory, dialogical narrative analysis
is the practice; it is as close to being a method as I can justify. Dialogical narrative analysis studies the mirroring between what is told in the
story—the story's content—and what happens as a result of telling that

story—its effects. Or as Bakhtin writes in this chapter's epigraph, the relation between the events being narrated and the event of narration.[1] The balance between story content and effects is rarely even; some analyses lend themselves more to one side or the other. But the mutual dependence of content and effects can never be forgotten, whichever is foreground or background.

This chapter and the two that follow suggest ways of doing dialogical narrative analysis. These chapters are pervaded by a sense of the limitations of standardizing methods in social science (the next section in this chapter) and by a suspicion of interpretation (especially in chapter 4). This chapter begins by asking what a *method* can or should be, concluding that some methods are more useful for the questions they offer than for any procedures they prescribe. Taking that observation seriously, the chapter then presents a set of questions that can orient a dialogical narrative analysis.

A METHOD FOR THE MOVEMENT OF THOUGHT

I follow Catherine Riessman in believing that there is not, nor should there be, any method of narrative analysis, if *method* is understood as a prescribed set of steps that the analysis should follow.[2] A *method*, in the prescription model, serves as the guarantee of its final production: a guarantee that findings will both turn up on schedule and meet collegial standards for publication, that publication being the accreditation of the work as worth taking seriously, if still open to controversy. There has always been another tradition in which method is more ad hoc. Method in this tradition has precedents, guidelines, and especially exemplars, but it is not prescriptive.

This understanding of method as heuristic guide rather than procedural guidelines was given one of its clearest articulations by C. Wright Mills, who wrote his classic, *The Sociological Imagination*, in the late 1950s when courses specifically on methods were first being created in social science curricula.[3] Until then, consideration of method had been part of studying any research; the method was little more, but no less, than how that researcher had conducted that study. Mills writes as these ad-hoc procedures were being separated from the specific conditions of the research for which they were designed and represented as generally applicable templates for future research.[4] He advocates no specific method but rather what he calls "intellectual craftsmanship." Doing research requires discovering the method appropriate to that investigation, although happily this discovery is secondhand, based on a collective experience. Methods are not guarantees of anything. "Social research of any kind is advanced by ideas,"

Mills writes; "it is only disciplined by fact" (71). The priority of what counts is clear.[5]

Fast forward almost a half century from Mills to Paul Rabinow and Nikolas Rose, introducing the methodology of Michel Foucault, or what they call Foucault's "practice of criticism" as an antimethodology:

> Thus, the practice of criticism which we might learn from Foucault would not be a methodology. It would be a movement of thought that invents, makes use of, and modifies conceptual tools as they are set into a relation with specific practices and problems that they themselves help to form in new ways. When they have done this work, without regret, they can be recycled or even discarded.[6]

Much exegesis could be done on this dense statement; I note four points.

First, calling dialogical narrative analysis a "practice of criticism" rather than a method is useful, because the word *criticism* bridges social science, as in *critical theory*, with literary criticism. What makes thought *critical* is a refusal to accept immediate, commonsense understanding, while at the same time having the most profound respect for and curiosity about commonsense understandings.[7] The balance can be a fine one. Many of the intellectual successes of the nineteenth century were based on postulating limits-in-principle to people's self-awareness: Marx, Freud, and in sociology Durkheim developed theories that instilled suspicion of appearances; each emphasized how people's ordinary understanding of their world and their situation is somehow blind. They were not wrong, but suspicion has its limits. Many twentieth-century theories emphasized the knowledgeable, purposive actor.[8] The twenty-first century need not choose, however. Critical thought can appreciate how expert people are about their own lives while examining ways in which any person's or group's self-awareness is limited.

Second, instead of *methodology*, I prefer Rabinow and Rose's phrase "movement of thought." Too many methods seem to prevent thought from *moving*. Analytic or interpretive thought that is moving is more likely to allow and recognize movement in the thought being interpreted. Thought moves in dialogue, as those participating in research are given scope to upset the presuppositions of the researchers. This book's title trope of *breath* implies movement, reciprocity, and constant flux.

Third, as I read Rabinow and Rose, the "conceptual tools" are those of the analyst, while the "practices and problems" are those of people engaged in living their lives without having the leisure to suspend acting and think about how life is led and the extensive effects of living that way. But these two, conceptual tools and practices/problems, do not exist separately across a divide; they interact. Conceptual tools "help to form in new ways" how people understand their problems, and they can inform the practices people employ to deal with those problems. Any analysis is always already interactive with what is being analyzed; that interaction is part of what is *dialogical*.

Finally, Rabinow and Rose's lovely last sentence: "When they have done this work, without regret, they can be recycled or even discarded" (xv, quoted earlier). Just as a story is recycled when it has done its work—its fragments then taken up in the telling of new stories—so any method does its work within the time and space of some writing, and then the method fragments, without regret but with hope that some of its parts will be recycled elsewhere, as part of a larger movement of thought.

In summary, dialogical narrative analysis refuses to say, as too many methods do effectively say: *these are the rules; here are the steps to implement these rules; follow my direction or suffer rejection.* Such methods may allow adjudication committees to account for their judgments—they support what Mills called the "bureaucratic ethos"—but they do little to encourage thought to move. I prefer a message that plays on Thomas King's refrain, quoted in chapter 1.

Take this set of questions about stories. Do what you want with them. Use some in your work; forget others. Modify those you use to fit your scene of inquiry, the better to understand the people you listen to, to make sense to people you hope will listen to you, and to be responsible to the people who fund and employ you. Use dialogical narrative analysis to take care of yourself, which sometimes might mean not using it. But don't say no one ever told you that there is this way of doing narrative analysis. Don't say you never heard that dialogical analysis is an option.[9]

QUESTIONS OF STORYTELLING PRACTICE

The questions that follow initiate narrative analyses by calling attention to particular work that stories have the capacity to do. These questions are in no particular order, nor will they be equally useful in any given narrative analysis. If dialogical narrative analysis is a practice of criticism that seeks movements of thought, its work is to pose questions and then let those who do analyses decide which of these questions are the most useful to emphasize.

The issue that informs all these questions is: *what is at stake* for whom, including storyteller and protagonist in the story, listeners who are present at the storytelling, and others who may not be present but are implicated in the story? How does the story, and the particular way it is told, define or redefine those stakes, raising or lowering them? How does the story change people's sense of what is possible, what is permitted, and what is responsible or irresponsible?

What does the story make narratable? I take this question from Michael Bérubé's *Life as We Know It*, a book that is part memoir, part disability advocacy, and part treatise on moral and civic responsibility to the vulnerable.[10] Bérubé has two sons, Nick and Jamie. Nick is developmentally normal; Jamie has Down syndrome. As Nick grows up, stories are told of each of his milestones: taking his first steps, saying his first word, and so on. Jamie's milestones come so slowly that it was too easy not to tell stories about him, and therein lies a material danger to Jamie and a moral danger to society. Bérubé's argument is that if people whose children are developmentally normal do not hear stories about children like Jamie, then they will feel only the most minimal responsibility for the bare lives of these children. A life that is not fully narratable is vulnerable to devaluation. Certainly stories told about categories of persons can injure those persons.[11] But silences can be equally injurious, implying that there is no story to tell about lives such as these. Resistance to these silences begins by making lives narratable: telling the stories can make lives vivid and morally recognizable.

Michael Bérubé realizes all too well that having a material body is not much of a claim in a competitive world. A person becomes claimsworthy by virtue of being narratable. A real person like Jamie Bérubé is no less dependent on being made narratable than a fictional character like Mademoiselle Bourienne—that is the force of the narratability argument. Stories make people narratable because they are inherently performative, which involves more than recognizing that telling stories is always something of a performance. Stories *enact* realities: they *bring into being* what was not there before. Here, then, is another curious reversal of common sense: first, each person has a story; and then, in consequence of that story, she or he has a life that is enacted by that story.

To put this idea another way, for several years I wished that my own book could have had the title of Paul John Eakin's, *How Our Lives Become Stories*.[12] Gradually I realized that Eakin's title can be reversed to make an equally valid and more usefully provocative proposition: *How Our Stories Become Lives*. Stories by themselves may not determine whether people have fuller or diminished lives, but by setting the terms in which lives are or are not narratable, stories create conditions for enrichment or diminishment. When Michael Bérubé fashions a story of Jamie's life, what is at stake is whether that story can enrich Jamie's life. The core idea is that Jamie's life is effectively invisible until a story makes that life narratable.

Sometimes making narratable involves telling openly what had been secret, as in Maxine Hong Kingston's story. Related but one step removed is telling witness stories of events so terrible that most people have good reason for wanting them not to be narratable. These include stories of genocides, of state-sponsored terror and torture, of systematic neglect and mistreatment. People prefer to keep nonnarratable what they want to believe did not or does not happen. The pejorative phrase "victim art" might be reclaimed as empowering: stories are the preferred art form in which victims can make narratable their victimization.[13] Stories can cry out: *these things happen; I embody what happened.* Frederick Douglass's abolitionist sponsors hope his stories will do that, and today Douglass's stories still do. Or, stories can witness more quietly.

A different way to understand Mademoiselle Bourienne's story is that Tolstoy makes narratable the claustrophobic dependency of a minor class of comparatively privileged servants. *War and Peace* includes a number of characters who share something like Mademoiselle Bourienne's situation: tutors, architects, relations of questionable family connection, and others of the salaried entourage who get to eat at the family dinner table but whose presence depends on sustaining the favor of those whose place at the table is assured. The entourage is constantly reminded that their position is not assured. The conditions of favor require them to take what is offered, ask no more, and have no real options for life elsewhere. These lives do not scream for justice—they are comparatively privileged—but they deserve their moment of being narratable.

However effectively stories can make narratable, making narratable is not necessarily good work for stories to do. Allen Feldman's paramilitary indoctrination stories make narratable the fundamental wrongness of the existence of certain people, whom the story assembles into a group called interlopers. These people are evaluated as wrong not only for specific actions they take, but more fundamentally for being who they are, where they are. Stories are entirely too effective at demonizing, which is why the answer to the question posed in the title of Philip Smith's book, *Why War?* is stories.[14] Political leaders who would take their countries to war need the right story, and Smith explores how stories mobilize national spirit for the legitimacy of war. Put another way, war must be narratable before it can be fought. These mobilizations give the most compelling immediate relevance to what Hillis Miller, in the first epigraph to this chapter, calls the awful danger of storytelling.[15]

Stories make narratable, but often they do that not wisely but too well. Contests over whether entry into a war is good or bad proceed in narrations that generally are not stories, but stories work best for getting people marching. Stories are not very useful for getting troops into marching formation, but they are rich in capacity for making people willing to march—for making marching seem like a sensible thing to do. An inescapable duality is at work here. The same capacities of stories that are useful to the father of a disabled child to make visible and compelling the claims of his son's life are also useful for tyrants and terrorists. Chapter 6 will return to this crucial question—what are good stories and bad stories?

Who is *holding their own* in the story, but also, is the story making it more difficult for other people to hold their own? In all the stories with which this book began, the characters can be described as "holding their own." This idiomatic phrase describes situations that begin with a person who has a degree of self-regard; someone with sufficient self-consciousness of what is valuable and worthy of respect about him- or herself. This self-regard involves, at the high end, what a person is entitled to aspire to—for Mademoiselle, marriage to a Russian prince—and at the low end, what the person seeks to avoid—for Kingston's mother, the aunt's fate. Holding one's own can work up or down: either aspiring to a perceived opportunity, as Mademoiselle does, or avoiding a threat to the value of the self.

The problem is that one person's work of holding his or her own often becomes the threat against which someone else must hold his or her own. Princess Marya must hold her own against the threat of her suitor flirting with her friend, whose flirting is how she holds her own. Kingston must hold her own against the story that her mother tells her. Both mother and daughter are holding their own in their respective tellings of the story. Kingston then imagines how her aunt also was holding her own. Her pregnancy was most likely the result of rape or sexual victimization of which she could not speak.

Many narrative scholars have noted the utility of stories as enactments of resistance. In folklore, clever-fool stories and trickster stories are vehicles by which people experiencing various kinds of disadvantage or oppression—from being a younger son to being enslaved—can imaginatively enact getting the better of those who appear more powerful. The trickster perpetually confronts those who are more powerful and outwits them. But to return to the previous chapter's epigraph by Lewis Hyde, the story itself can be the trickster, as it enacts resistances that, for the present, lack other forms of enactment.

As exemplary as stories are for speaking truth to power, there is always the complementary, dangerous side: power can use stories to justify its entitlements. Stories can make it more difficult for some others—those who are the objects of righteous violence in the story—to hold their own. The story of Samson works to sustain the ability of the disempowered to believe in the possibility of their capacity to resist. But as David Grossman observes, the story turns dangerous when it becomes emblematic—literally, as the name of military units—of a dominant, if perpetually threatened, national power.[16] Plus, and tragic in its consequences, the story is out of control, as stories are always out of control. Samson's death sets a model for suicide killings that will be turned against Israel.

Who uses a story to hold their own, and how the story does that, are crucial questions. But it must always be complemented by the question of whom the story renders vulnerable; who now has an increased problem of holding their own, once the story has been told?

What is the effect of people being caught up in their own stories while living with people caught up in other stories? Julie Cruikshank addresses this question in a tale of two stories, or more exactly, two modes of story-telling that frame a murder case in the Yukon in the late 1800s.[17] The stories of that case continue to divide people in the region. Cruikshank begins with a question: "What consequences follow when different narrative models intersect on a 'frontier' where they are accorded unequal social weight?" (73). One of these models is Native oral storytelling. The other model is storytelling by the white prospectors, the basis of whose stories Cruikshank finds expressed in "Robert Service's poems about 'a land where the mountains are nameless' or Jack London's drama of individual men in stark confrontation with nature" (ibid.). "The paradox," Cruikshank observes, "is that the mountains were *not* nameless but were home to people rooted to place by narratives of connection" (ibid.). Here, then, is the basis of a conflict that will have violent and tragic consequences:

> To indigenous people, North Atlantic myths of individual autonomy set in opposition to a hostile land were probably incomprehensible, so little did the frames of reference overlap. If the problem facing individual prospectors in the late 1890s was how to escape economic constraints and forge autonomous identities, the problem for indigenous families was how to hold communities together and maintain networks of connection in the face of overwhelming pressures brought by the influx of thirty thousand to forty thousand men traveling through their territories. (Ibid.)

Both groups, prospectors and indigenous, were trying to hold their own. But each was caught up in different stories, rendering the others' stories mostly incomprehensible.

In Cruikshank's historical story, the conflict between various human antagonists follows from the disconnect between two stories that set these antagonists' respective HORIZONS of selection and evaluation. The facts seem simple enough and are not in dispute. Three Tagish men visit the camp of two prospectors, acting friendly. Later, when the prospectors are traveling down a river, the Tagish men shoot at them, killing one and wounding the other. A headline in the Dawson City newspaper of June 16, 1898, reads: "Indians Shoot White Men to Rob Them of Their Supplies" (83–84).

The trial judge is not an unsympathetic character, only a person limited by what stories he is able to hear and which stories are impossible for him to understand.[18] Cruikshank describes him "as a man of reason, [but] also a man of categories" that are based on "the cultural logic of the court" (87). Thus, one of the accused men was encouraged to "tell his story" (85). The problem was that the story made so little sense to the court that "it was recorded but went unheard" (ibid.), which is an eloquent statement of the generalizable problem: to those who are caught up in one story, a story that does not fit the same narrative parameters may be "recorded" but will remain unheard.

The Tagish men's recorded but unheard story is difficult to recover, and even Cruikshank's indigenous mentor, Mrs. Kitty Smith, was uncertain about the details. An indigenous woman "either found or was given a can containing some white powder which she mistakenly assumed was baking powder," Cruikshank writes. "The powder may actually have been arsenic, used in the refining of gold" (89). Several men died after eating bread made with the powder. By custom, the responsibility for avenging the deaths fell to clan members of the deceased, but generally the issue was resolved by negotiation leading to restitution: "Either the death of a social equivalent of the victim or a negotiated repayment in goods would be satisfactory compensation" (90). Custom also prescribed that the clan of the attackers should open the negotiations.

In this frame, a different story of the same events emerges. The Tagish men visit the prospectors' camp expecting negotiations to be initiated, because the prospectors are "seen as representing the 'clan' of white people responsible for the incident" (90). Tellers of the Native version of the story acknowledge "that the two men were chosen randomly as social equivalents of the deceased" (91). Cruikshank's dialogical analysis does not seek to assert the truth of either story. "More interesting than the question of which versions more accurately account for 'what really happened' is what differing versions tell us about the values they commemorate," she writes (92). At the time, each group found the other's values incomprehensible.

The prospectors' story dominates because the dominant institutions, newspapers and more significantly courts, require this version of events. Cruikshank's conclusion describes how stories work symbiotically with formal institutions like courts, which need stories but also select which stories they use:

> In effect, facts get established by enacting silences. Despite the judge's frequent admonition to the accused to "state your narrative," that is not what he really means. An institution differs from a dialogue in that it sets constraints on what stories can be told and when they are admissible. There are things to be said, and there are ways of saying them. (95)

In order to understand the shooting, it becomes necessary to ask the prior question of who these people were. Were the indigenous men autonomous individuals pursuing their own gain, which was the model of identity assumed by the prospectors and court? Or, according to the Native model of identity, were they clan members acting on behalf of one clan in response to another clan—the white newcomers—of which the men they shot were representatives? "One critical difference in the narratives is the way they construct categories of individual and society," Cruikshank writes, "and especially how boundaries between those categories are established" (92). Those categories, however, become real, because people are caught up in stories, whether these are indigenous clan stories or Jack London's stories. Stories construct what counts as individuals as well as the boundaries and categories relevant to those individuals' responsibilities and liabilities.

The historical narrative underlying Cruikshank's stories of the Yukon shootings is the displacement of oral culture by a bureaucratic culture based on written records; it is a narrative of imperialism in the broadest sense. In Wittgenstein's terms, two forms of life conflict, and the trial demonstrates the impossibility of translation between these forms of life. Cruikshank concludes: "Arguably any narrative representation of reality presenting itself to us as history invokes a social system" (97). I would prefer to reverse the order of predication: what is known as a social system is assembled and reassembled from the dominance of some narrative representations of reality over others, and history—as Cruikshank writes it so well—is the story of that contest for narrative dominance. What complicates this contest is that neither side can acknowledge it is contesting, because that would require recognizing an alternative narrative that is incomprehensible. Thus, the contest is played out in venues like courts that allow some stories and their form of narration and relegate other stories to silence.

Dialogical narrative analysis looks for how "facts get established by enacting silences," as Cruikshank puts it. Analysis asks what stories different actors are caught up in, what actions those stories authorize and even require, and how some stories silence other stories. The crucial and dense word for me in Cruikshank's history is *incomprehensible*. The power of stories, the hypnotic spell they cast over people caught up in them, produces an embodied assent that requires the incomprehension of other stories that fail to fit the underlying narrative of one's own stories.

Neither group in Cruikshank's story, neither prospectors and courts nor indigenous people, could exist without its stories. To paraphrase Foucault, stories are not *bad*, but they are inevitably *dangerous*.[19] Cruikshank's history, far from being a one-off incident in a distant time, is a disturbingly contemporary allegory for situations in which one group, living caught up in its stories, is brought into proximity with another group living with very different stories.

What is the force of fear in the story, and what animates desire? Stories make some things fearsome and other things desirable, yet stories do not invent people's hopes and fears. Stories shape fears and desires. They make fears more vivid, and they suggest appropriate and inappropriate objects of desire. But stories compel because they express in narrative form what begins in bodies.

The primal story of fear in the Western canon is *Beowulf*.[20] The monster, Grendel, comes out of the depths and darkness; he is darkness embodied. The Beowulf poet felt no need to explain Grendel's origins, nor did the listeners need an origin story. The human hero, Beowulf, has origins that the poet tells; he has a country and a genealogy. The monster has only a mother—which is to say, one monster usually leads to another—but he is otherwise originless, which may be part of what constitutes his monstrosity. The world includes such forces of darkness, and the work of men—heroes—is to keep these forces at bay; therein lies a narrative. The story is that Grendel breaks into a hall where people should be able to sleep safely and dismembers his victims. He is fear itself, and with his equally fearsome mother becomes a figure that expresses any number of fears that take different shapes in different ages: fears of war, death, and enslavement; fears of plague; fears of chronic disease, dependence, and impoverishment. Stories express these fears but they also contain them, in the sense of holding them within visible form. People may not master their fears through stories, but through them they do come to grips with their fears; or, put another way, they hold their own against their fears.

What, then, is a story in which desire weighs as heavily as fear does in *Beowulf*? Stories of the Holy Grail are told several centuries after *Beowulf*, and the figure of the Grail can be understood as a complement to Grendel, leading me to think of them as the G Twins.[21] If Grendel comes out of darkness and brings destruction, the Grail comes out of light, heavenly light, and brings healing. If Grendel breaks into apparent safety and brings death, the Grail stops suffering and brings healing. *Parzival* is the great Grail epic.[22] As a young hero, Parzival does not know who he is; he fights invincibly, but he lacks discernment about when and whom to fight. His epic is a journey toward self-understanding, culminating in his return to the Grail castle, which he has previously found by apparent chance. The mature Parzival can control chance. His development is described exactly by what Lewis Hyde says about tricksters: his *good* luck is no longer dumb luck.[23]

Fear and desire are, I believe, complementary aspects of a single whole, because each mirrors the other, albeit at a distance. A film version of *Beowulf* develops the clever conceit that Grendel's mother is a shape-shifting demon who appears as a beautiful woman to whichever hero comes to fight her. From their mating the next Grendel is born, who will eventually come back to haunt, fight, and finally kill the hero who is his father but denies it.[24] This plot twist loses something important in the original narrative, which is the otherness of monstrosity. The film gives Grendel not only a human paternity but, more significantly, human motives; Grendel's rage is now Oedipal, which significantly distorts the original story. But this revisionist version does bring fear and desire into their necessary complementarity. Desire is literally mis-taken: the mother demon assumes her enticing shape only for a moment of seduction, and the embrace is as much about fear as about lust—the hero's alternative to being seduced is to fight the demon and probably be killed. From this seduction there is no redemption. By contrast, Parzival's desire is purified in the course of his journey, eventually allowing him to be in the full presence of the Grail.

Any narrative analysis must, at some point, recognize the interplay of fear and desire that animates anything worth calling a story. Harvey Sacks's simplest story, "The baby cried. The mommy picked it up," expresses a child's fears of crying and no mommy being there, as well the desire for comfort and security. Stories are always about what makes people cry and what can pick them up. Among the Yukon prospectors whom Cruikshank describes, their desire for gold had its complement in their fears of the unnamed mountains and of the nameless people who already inhabited those spaces. The questions for narrative analysis are how stories not only express fears and desires—which makes these emotions seem to precede the stories—but also enact fears and desires. Stories are not mimetic with respect to fear and desire. They are performative.

How does a story help people, individually and collectively, to remember who they are? How does a story do the work of memory? "Stories connect," Cruikshank observes, "as by centripetal force, those areas of life that seem to be disintegrating" (94). She refers to Yukon indigenous stories that worked to sustain traditional connections of family and clan when the massive in-migration of white prospectors threatened those connections, and how they continue to do that work. But her statement has broader significance: stories are good at reconnecting that which is always drifting apart. Cruikshank's descriptive word *disintegrating* might at first seem extreme to apply to individual lives and groups most of the time, but just as bodies are constantly if imperceptibly disintegrating, so are lives and groups.

Lives and groups require constant *reassembling*, which is Bruno Latour's general descriptor, and stories reassemble, both individually and collectively.[25] But reassembly is as much about change as continuity; the act of reassembling does not mean keeping things, including memories, as they are. Reassembly enacts what Norbert Elias called *process*: what is reassembled is never exactly what was, but always a slightly changed version.[26] Most of the time these changes are imperceptible, and the process proceeds unnoticed. Mundane stories—kitchen table stories—imperceptibly reassemble. But sometimes—and the Yukon gold rush is a good example—the changes are all too apparent. Memorable stories are told at moments of visible, palpable change. To return to the former question, these stories help people deal with their fears of what change brings, and they express hopes for what change might bring.

Both individual and collective memory exist in a process of constant reassembly. A text from 1927, credited to V. N. Volosinov but probably by Bakhtin, states: "We see in the past only what is important for the present, important for the instant in which we remember our past."[27] Brian Boyd summarizes recent research on memory: "We recall only selectively, according to what we attend to and its recency, salience, and emotional impact."[28] Dialogical narrative analysis treats stories not as expressions of an archival memory that already has form and content somewhere outside stories. Rather, stories are the ongoing work of enacting or performing memory. Stories give memories recency, salience, and emotional impact. The sociobiologist Edward O. Wilson states the issue most forcefully and poetically: "The mind lives in half-remembered experiences of uncertain valence, where self-deception twists memory further from truth with every passing year."[29]

Stories enact *how* memory reconfigures; they are the process of memory-in-action as much as they are repositories where memories are kept. Legal courts need to understand memory as fundamentally accurate, if open to contingent distortion, and they require stories to serve as simplistic recording devices that can be switched on and set to particular times past. That perspective makes possible legal proceedings that cannot appear open to multiple interpretations, much less be out of control, but it is not the best way to think about memory in people's lives. People remember by telling stories of times past, but they tell in response to the needs of reassembly at the time when the story is told—what Boyd calls salience—and memory then takes that form. Memories are less accurate or forgetful than they are good or bad reassemblies, hardly distinguishable from the stories in which their reassembly work is performed.

Memoir is the genre of storytelling that self-consciously recollects memories. In suspenseful memoirs, this recollection proceeds out of necessity, because the memoirist is vulnerable to memories that endanger her or him. Memory must be outwitted and reassembled. Sharon O'Brien outwits memory by seeking family documents and other historical materials. She also brings her mature interpretive sensibilities as a literary critic to bear on family stories, thus opening these stories to interpretive possibilities that her younger self could scarcely recognize and not articulate. But O'Brien stays well within what could be called the boundaries of the real. In contrast, Maxine Hong Kingston outwits memory by playing with the real.

In *The Warrior Woman*, Kingston begins with what a reader understands as genre-appropriate memoir stories, that is, stories that recollect as accurately as possible scenes that actually took place in the author's life. Then the memoir genre seems to break down, as Kingston tells the story of the warrior woman Fa Mu Lan, who becomes an apprentice to demigods from whom she learns magical fighting powers that she uses to defend her village. Kingston does not set the story of Fa Mu Lan apart as a folktale. She effects a seamless transition into the folktale, telling it in the first person by assuming the persona of Fa Mu Lan. As the memoir is read, no clear boundary separates the first-person voice telling what "really happened" to her from that same voice inserting herself into the first person of a received story, shaping it (more or less) to fit herself.

Kingston may have to play with the real in order to be true to her memories of her family; in her own way, she preserves the family's rules of storytelling. In the first pages of *The Warrior Woman* when Kingston's mother, whom the memoir has not yet named, tells the story of the pregnant aunt, I as a reader understand that as family history. Later in the memoir, the same woman, now named as Brave Orchid, tells a story of how before she left China she defeated a ghost that terrorized her fellow medical students. In this story, the veil between accurate recollection and adapted folklore is thin indeed. Brave Orchid insists on the truth of her ghost story. The more accustomed I became to Brave Orchid's storytelling, the more I wondered: maybe there was no pregnant aunt, no attack of the villagers, no suicide.

If we readers continue to believe that these things actually happened, do we also have to believe that Brave Orchid defeated a ghost while she was a medical student?

Rather than seek to draw boundaries between the real and the fictive, it is far simpler to understand all these stories as doing their respective work of reassembling lives. It is more productive to ask: how is the way the story is told the best way that the storyteller can imagine—using an imagination for which stories set the parameters—to represent his or her life? And complementary to that: how do the stories and narrative resources available to the storyteller shape the process of reassembling his or her memory?

* * *

The five questions posed in this chapter are anything but exhaustive of how dialogical narrative analysis can start, and for any collection of stories, some of these questions will be more useful than others. These questions initiate practices of criticism, in the sense of helping thought to move. Each question revolves around some work that stories have the capacity to do and sometimes to do too well, to questionable ends. Stories are always on both sides of any fence at the same time, and very often so are storytellers. Kingston's mother tells her the story of the pregnant aunt, thus implicating her in a history of shame. Brave Orchid tells her daughter the story of the girl warrior Fa Mu Lan, which Kingston tells in the first-person voice, claiming its power as her own.

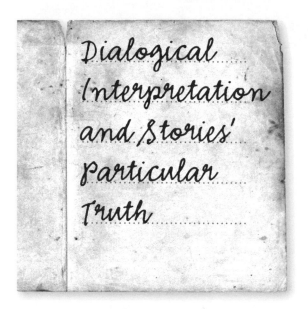

Dialogical Interpretation and Stories' Particular Truth

4

If you're ready, you'll get it. If not, then it will be just a story.
—Indigenous storyteller Robert Matthew, quoted by Jo-ann Archibald

This is where the specific reliability of oral sources arises: even when they do not tell the events as they occurred, the discrepancies and the errors are themselves events, clues for the work of desire and pain over time, for the painful search for meaning. —Alessandro Portelli

Stories call for interpretation even as they resist it. No matter how pure the pleasure that humans take in being caught up in a story, storytelling raises questions about both the characters in the story and who is telling the story. Brian Boyd writes that storytelling "arises out of our intense interest in monitoring one another . . . through *theory of mind*."[1] Boyd means the human capacity "to make inferences from other minds," and his point is that one evolutionary value of storytelling is to enhance both this capacity and people's ability to function in "situations fraught with difficult or subtle choices or to run complex scenarios" (49).[2] "Theory of mind" thus is a condition for entering into relations of storytelling—Boyd describes psychological studies seeking to determine the age when children develop a theory of mind—and is enhanced by participation in storytelling. To say humans depend on a theory of mind is to say that we interpret.

Interpretation is thus inherent in storytelling; both tellers and listeners constantly interpret each other. In a functional sense, storytelling prepares people for encountering difficult situations, but often the story itself *is* the difficult situation. Interpretation is necessary for deciding how to respond to a story: whether to pay attention at all; if attention is paid, how to react (laughter or tears, indignation or affirmation); and if the story is told in conversation, what story to tell next. Most of all: interpretation is the attempt to understand what the characters in the story and the storyteller are up to.

A good interpretation is a response that seems to fit the story, complementing it. Yet the trickster quality of stories—the slipperiness of meaning at play among multiple perspectives—defies their being pinned down. No single interpretive response is ever quite adequate; interpretation is always a work in progress. This interpretive work is often troubled, because as much as interpretation and story exist in mutual dependence—each allowing the other to be—there is also a tension between them. The need for interpretation implies something concealed or left unsaid in the story, that interpretation must clarify or fill in. But then stories mock interpretations for inevitably saying less than the story conveys in the sum of its effects.

Dialogical narrative analysis has considerable ambivalence toward interpretation. Some interpretations seek to finalize stories, cutting off dialogue by claiming to speak the last word. A different ambivalence is expressed in this chapter's epigraph from Robert Matthew. Interpretation is a claim to "get it" and to articulate what it is. Matthew raises the unmethodological contention that no one can "get it" until they are ready to get it.[3] I call this claim unmethodological because it implies that getting it cannot be brought about through any systematic, replicable analysis. Being ready, as I understand Matthew, is a state of embodied being, as much emotional and spiritual as it is intellectual; as much about who the analyst has become through contact with these stories as it is about the cognitive reorganization of the stories. "Being ready" is the objective expressed by the subtitle of Jo-ann Archibald's book: Educating the Heart, Mind, Body, and Spirit. Interpretation requires all four, together.

There is, however, nothing mystical about how to "get it." Nor does the dialogical narrative analyst wait passively for inspiration. Just as chance favors the prepared mind, interpretation is achieved by working on a set of questions, deciding which are most relevant to the materials at hand, and iteratively revising both the questions and the understanding of the materials. I believe what Robert Matthew says is true, but his statement as quoted omits the process of getting to getting it. My preferred understanding of method is what can be done to hasten getting it, so that delay is not frustration but progressive understanding; and the arrival of it does not seem to be any great epiphany, but only finding the words to say what has been realized for some time.

Interpretations generally seek to express some truth that the story says or at least points toward, so this chapter's first section begins by clarifying what kind of truth stories can offer. On the heels of truth comes the suspicion that interpretation reduces stories rather than letting them breathe. As an antidote to that suspicion, the second section presents a version of HERMENEUTICS. The objective of hermeneutic interpretation is not to display mastery over the story, but rather to expand the listener's openness to how much the story is saying. Dialogical interpretation seeks not to pronounce on the story or the storytelling scene, but rather to engage the story in ongoing dialogue. This chapter's third section asks what is *dialogical* about the narrative analysis proposed in this book: what interpretive commitments are involved in analysis seeking to be dialogical? Finally, after much of what interpretation is not, the chapter follows several storytellers whose suggestions for interpretative practice support dialogical commitments.

Robert Matthew is right. Any interpretation requires a moment that can be called intuitive. The intuition in dialogical narrative analysis, however, does not come out of the blue. There may be no rules to follow, but there are exemplars to learn from. There may be no system of interpretation, but interpretive competence can be worked on systematically.

THE PARTICULAR TRUTH OF STORIES

Stories tell the truth, but stories tell the truth by twisting it. The word *trope*, denoting those usages of language that include metaphors and similes, literally means a twisting of language. The twisting is not mere aesthetic display but is necessary to express what is genuinely complex about the kind of truth that is best told in stories. Recall the quotation from Boyd, at the beginning of this chapter, about stories preparing people for "situations fraught with difficult or subtle choices." Stories do their best work in such situations, when the truth being told often is twisted.

Those scholars of narrative analysis whom I most respect all reject what can be called a *mimetic* understanding of stories: the idea that stories merely imitate a reality independent of stories, that they are surrogate versions of what the story listener would have seen and experienced, had she or he been where the storyteller was, proximate to the events being described.[4] The most concise critique of mimetic understandings may remain the metaphor offered by the Russian formalist Viktor Shklovsky in the 1920s. Mimetic theories imagine stories to be clear windows through which those who receive the story can see the world that it describes. Shklovsky offers the alternative metaphor that if stories are compared to windows, a story is like a sketched window.[5] The viewer does not attempt to look through it to something beyond, much less assume that the sketch perfectly represents what lies beyond. Instead, the sketch itself is well worth looking at.

Stories' layering of imagination and realism is teased out in René Magritte's painting *La condition humaine* (1933).[6] A painted canvas sits in front of an open window, partially blocking the view through the window. The realistic image on the canvas is perfectly mimetically continuous with the view through the window. Yet even this mimesis cannot be seamless: the edge of the canvas interrupts the continuity of views. Moreover, even when mimesis is perfect, it is still something else: a painted canvas, not the world outside. And then the viewer remembers that the whole picture is painted. The view through the window that has been accepted as reality is part of the painting—Magritte's whole painting is *painting*. If the human condition is to experience the real through its representations, those representations are not necessarily distorting. But neither are they the real itself.[7]

Once narrative analysis rejects mimetic projects, it can study the storyteller's intended or unintended creativity in sketching windows on reality, and the contexts that make particular kinds of creativity seem necessary. Chapter 1 emphasized the capacity of stories to be *performative*, meaning not only that storytelling is a performance, but also that stories enact whatever truth they claim. Any claim to be reporting reality directly is a rhetorical device; reports fabricate reality. *Fabricating* here does not mean making something up out of thin air; it emphasizes the act of *making* as a weaving together of elements. The issue for narrative analysis is how to understand stories as *authentic fabrications* rather than second-rate reports, which they are.[8] Here we approach a more profound sense of stories being performative.

Once in the course of my studies I misread a crucial sentence in the writing of oral historian Alessandro Portelli, whose understanding of the truth of stories so clearly and beautifully expresses my own views that I risk quoting him to excess. The sentence occurs after Portelli has presented a transcription of a long story he recorded that recounts peasants rising up against a cruel baron who once ruled their village. The story is exciting, including details of the baron's greed and sexual exploitations, the courage of the surprisingly successful uprising that is instigated by a man who refused to surrender his bride for the baron's *jus primae noctis*, and the baron's eventual escape from the liberated village. What I misread Portelli to be writing at the end of this story was: it may not be a true story, *but at least it was told.* What he actually writes is: "It may not be a true story, at least as it was told; it contains too many folk motifs and stylemes to be factually credible. Also, I find no documentary confirmation."[9] My misreading, however, is not that far from Portelli's understanding of what stories do, both for the people who tell these stories and for the world that needs to hear them.

Stories often reflect more desire for what might have happened than commitment to an accurate description of what did happen. Stories give that desire a material reality, especially when told to oral historians who will record, transcribe, and eventually publish them. If life did not happen as a story tells it, *at least it could be told* that way. As Portelli succinctly summarizes the epistemology of oral history: "We learn the truth of the telling as well as the telling of the truth" (48). Dialogical narrative analysis has more interest in the former than the latter. But as Portelli's work exemplifies, one interest hardly excludes the other: to get to the truth of the telling, it is often necessary to sort out the telling of the truth—or to consider the extent to which external validation of the story could be provided, which in many cases is not very far at all.

Stories are not the best medium for telling what might be called definitive truth or singular truth. First, storytelling depends on memory that is most notable for its lapses, or as the previous chapter argued, for its constantly accommodating reconstructions. For the person who remembers, these reconstructions are not necessarily failures, but rather the useful reshaping of memory as the present situation requires. "We never thought of memory as an archive," Portelli writes, "as a freezer that preserves data and meanings, but rather as a processor that transforms and elaborates them in osmotic fashion and yields ever new data and meanings that include the old ones—if only to deny or get rid of them" (44–45).[10] What programs this processor to function as it does are previous stories.

Stories are cobbled together from a creative mix, beginning with memory of what happened and then adding what Portelli calls "folk motifs and stylemes," whether the relevant folk are agents at MidWest Insurance or those who wrote the story of Samson into what was compiled as the Hebrew Bible. Stories reassemble bits and pieces—character types and motivations, forms of action, symbols, tropes—recycle them in the present storytelling, and then turn them loose for future use, which now has added resonance. In storytelling, perception and memory are always filtered through narrative resources, shifting and expanding those resources.

When this cobbled-together story is actually told, that telling is what conversation analysts call "recipient designed." Any storytelling is tailored to fit the expected response of the listener(s), including the listener's apparent needs and purposes, sense of humor, likes and dislikes, and readiness to approve or disdain. Portelli states categorically that participants tell what they tell, as they tell it, within a relationship to a specific interviewer: "The myth of noninterference" of the interviewer in the participant's storytelling is central to "the attempt to create the fiction that the informant is speaking directly to the reader [of the eventual report], and—just like a book—would have spoken in the same way to anyone" (12–13).[11]

A final limitation on what truth stories can tell includes most of the capacities of stories described in chapter 1. If stories are suspenseful, if they are open to multiple interpretations, if they express an inherent morality, if they shape-shift, then the utilization of these capacities rarely sits easily with the needs of truth telling. What makes a *good story* is how the artfulness of the telling elaborates some truth, as Portelli's source elaborated his peasant-rebellion story. What makes a truthful story is its refusal of elaboration. That refusal is ritualized in the storytelling conventions required by newspapers and courtrooms. But this stripped-down, facts-only telling remains a style; its adoption is more a rhetorical display than an actual guarantee of truth. This book's opening story from Frederick Douglass exemplifies a storyteller's recognition of the gap between telling-as-facts and the truth. Douglass has no doubt there are truths about slavery and these need to be told, yet he feels the twisting inherent in any telling.

Portelli values historical accuracy. Neither the ideal nor the real possibility of that accuracy is in dispute, either in Portelli's oral history or in dialogical narrative analysis.[12] What dialogical narrative analysis can learn from Portelli is how complicated people's struggles to tell the truth often are, with their stories mixing memories, narrative conventions, expectations of listeners' needs, and what Portelli calls the "process of authorization" of the telling (9). What he means by this is, for example, how a research interview authorizes storytelling, as opposed to the different authorization of a published memoir. No story is told, whether in print or in person, outside some process of authorization, just as no memory is free of distortions—*distortion* being a deceptive word to pair with *memory*, suggesting that transparent recall is normal and distortion is the exception. The reconstitution of memory is so normal that calling it a distortion misses what memory is and what the truth of stories is.

These recognitions about the particular truth of stories—the truth of expressing the storyteller's "painful search for meaning," in the words of this chapter's epigraph[13]—lead Portelli to express his preference for "hybrid genres" (45), a good example of which is the story that this book begins with, Galeano's "Christmas Eve."[14] The story is told as one of a series of short pieces, some of which refer to events that would admit what Portelli calls documentary verification; others are clearly folkloric and fantastic; and many present a mix that defies disentangling. Yet as Galeano's stories accumulate, none are so *clearly* folkloric or fantastic, as opposed to some that are *clearly* realistic. The effect that is generically called magical realism is to render the reader uncertain as to which is documentary and which is fantastic.[15]

In "Christmas Eve," the third-person narrator is almost certainly not present in the hospital witnessing the scene between the dying child and Fernando Silva; the narration is a rhetorical device. But is the story a literal report of what was told by a real person, Fernando Silva, and thus the work of literary journalism, similar to the social scientific reporting of stories told in interviews? Or, if the story is a work of Galeano's imagination, on what is that imagination based; what reports and observations provided the materials for the storyteller's imagination? How are the story's twistings necessary to tell what Galeano holds to be the truth of those reports and observations?

One effect of the genre hybridity (eliding boundaries between fiction and nonfiction, fable and report) of "Christmas Eve" is to leave any response suspended between the telling of the truth—events that happened—and the truth of the telling—a truth materialized *in* any telling. This oscillation emphasizes and complicates the question of *what the story requires* of those who receive it. And what the story requires is the central concern of a dialogical interest in stories. Here we reach one of the densest words that is unavoidable in the study of narrative: *meaning.*

Meaning means many things.[16] For purposes of dialogical narrative analysis, I find it most useful to think of meaning in terms of these questions: who continues to tell the story, when and to whom, with what effects? Understanding meaning as a chaining of narrative enactments might be called a pragmatic understanding of meaning. What counts is not fixing meaning in some propositional content, but rather to understand meaning as an ongoing process of retelling, with attendant effects on different occasions of telling.

To return to my artful misreading of Portelli: "Christmas Eve" may or may not be a true story, but at least it was told. Or to return to the first of the questions posed in chapter 3, a truth is made *narratable* by that story being told. The story performs the truth of *making a situation real because it is now narratable*. An opening is created. Something has been spoken that previously was not fully acknowledged, and no one can say they have not heard it. Lest this argument go too far, however, it seems important that no claims are made about the truth of "Christmas Eve." The value of genre hybridity depends on not making false claims, for example claiming the nonfictional status of what blurs the boundary between fiction and nonfiction.

Whatever limitations stories have for telling the truth, their genius is in creating openings by making narratable. As Portelli writes about a story that he takes to be wholly imaginary: "What counts is less the event than the telling of the event. It may not be a true tale, but it was really told by a real person."[17] And then he adds, suggesting "Christmas Eve": "As long as the story is told, [it] will not end there" (43). The work of narrative analysis, like oral history, is to be part of making it not end there.

DIALOGICAL INTERPRETATION: FROM DECODING TO HERMENEUTICS

For several years I worked hard to avoid accepting that narrative analysis involves interpretation. That avoidance now seems silly, because it is impossible: even to transcribe a story is to engage in some level of interpretation.[18] But my reasons for being suspicious of interpretation are worth rehearsing, as they lead to a less suspect form of dialogical interpretation.

One major paradigm of interpretation begins with Karl Marx and continues through Emile Durkheim and Sigmund Freud to Claude Levi-Strauss. For these thinkers, individual consciousness (Freud), myth (Levi-Strauss), and society (Marx and Durkheim, with different emphases) all have commonsense appearances that are more or less mystifying, and interpretive analysis is the work of decoding, to comprehend the underlying reality of these phenomena. The object of interpretation differs—for Freud, the unconscious; for Levi-Strauss, a structure, ultimately of the mind; for Marx, class conflict and capitalism; for Durkheim, forms of solidarity—but interpretations promise to reveal truths not readily accessible to those who see only appearances. The attraction of these thinkers is also their danger: to those who master their schema, they offer the ability to claim privileged access to realities that the uninitiated are necessarily unaware of.

Interpretation becomes a decoding scheme: the capacity to sort what makes a difference from what is secondary or contingent, to trace the cause of what matters, and to *name* that cause. These interpretive schemes do yield genuine insights. Marx's concept of false consciousness and Freud's psychic mechanism of repression seem to me to have considerable validity as observations of the human condition. But these concepts make people's inability to know their own truth a principle of the human condition. Marxist and Freudian systems of thought institute dependence on the analyst privileged to speak whatever truth can be spoken. As a student, the more I gained access to these decoding schemes, the more I grew suspicious of interpretation. The problem was not the validity of Marxist, or Freudian, or structuralist interpretations. The problem was their politics of interpretive privilege.

Perhaps my suspicions about interpretation crystallized in the 1960s when I acquired the first paperback edition of Susan Sontag's *Against Interpretation*. Exactly why Sontag opposed interpretation might not have been clear to me, but like many readers I was stirred by the prophetic call that ends her title essay: "In place of a hermeneutics we need an erotics of art."[19] What particular hermeneutics Sontag had in mind when she wrote is not specified; she seems to refer to nineteenth-century attempts at interpretive certainty, especially certainty in the interpretation of biblical texts. In the early twentieth century, hermeneutics shifted radically to emphasize the *limits* of uncertainty. Josef Bleicher summarizes this shift: "The real power of hermeneutical consciousness is our ability to see what is questionable."[20] I propose that the hermeneutics available today, based on the work of Wilhelm Dilthey, Martin Heidegger, Hans-Georg Gadamer, and Paul Ricoeur, can offer an alternative to interpretation as mastery. Which brings me to the following brief, slanted, but I hope not misleading summary of hermeneutics as a dialogical form of interpretation.

Hermeneutics begins with the premise that any understanding of a text, which I will now restrict to stories, is enabled and also limited by understandings that have already been set in place by knowing previous stories—a stance reflected in Pierre Bayard's ideas, discussed in chapter 2. The possibility of an interpreter's understanding depends on his or her *horizons*, formed by what Gadamer called prejudices: what is already known and believed.[21] Prejudices provide the necessary basis for any understanding. Brian Boyd states the general principle in psychological terms: "A mind equally open to all possible links would have no way of deciding what information would prove useful."[22] Hermeneutic analysis is founded in this tension between the practical necessity of not being "equally open" to all interpretive possibilities, and the countervailing need to be sufficiently open, lest some valid interpretation be foreclosed.

That tension underlies interpersonal relationships. Understanding either a text or another person hangs between two principles: no two people's horizons ever overlap entirely, but neither do these horizons completely diverge. Dialogue requires difference, or else people would have nothing to say to each other. Dialogue also requires similarity, or else people would have no basis for understanding what others say.[23] Hermeneutic interpretation is a process in which *initial understandings shift in response* to the story and the storyteller. An example is required.

Alberto Manguel, discussing the Inuit film *Atanarjuat: The Fast Runner*,[24] describes how the film's storytelling effects a shift in the audience's horizons: "Something new, something that demanded a different receptive method for a different voice, was being shown, and, in the process, the audience was taught another way of seeing, a viewpoint from within the other culture itself."[25] The audience to such a film cannot passively depend on their prejudices about what good storytelling—in this case, filmmaking—is. They have to make themselves available to this different way of seeing, and that can be considered an ethical task, because making oneself available to others is ethical. Horizons, like Bourdieu's habitus discussed in chapter 2, are durable but never fixed. Hermeneutic interpretation requires and observes the shifting of horizons, based on an ethical will to understand what is not immediately accessible to the self but matters crucially to the other. In the case of memoir, an older self seeks to understand what was not accessible to his or her younger self—the younger self is the other.

To return to one of the stories that began this book, when Sharon O'Brien, as a small child, first becomes aware of the family silver as the symbiosis between the material objects and the stories told about her family (her grandfather having the silver shipped from Paris, and so on), that symbiosis and its explicit prejudices form her horizon.[26] The family-silver stories become her prejudgment of herself within her family, her family in its community, and the community within the world that includes an exotic place called Paris from which her grandfather could summon silver place settings, monogrammed. The child grows up, hears a lot of other stories, lives in different places, and becomes able to see her family from the perspective of those places. She ends up at a kitchen table, listening to her mother tell familiar stories about the family silver, including the story about O'Brien's grandmother crying when the silver arrived. Her mother tells the story of the silver's arrival without irony, sensing no contradiction between the tears and the gloriousness of the silver and, by extension, the family. For O'Brien as memoirist, whose horizons are now considerably different from her mother's, the family-silver story is filled with ironic contradiction.

Memoirs practice applied hermeneutics when they contrast different understandings of the same story as it is heard within the different horizons of the memoirist's younger and older selves. O'Brien is gentle with her mother and with the family story. Her memoir asks the story of the family silver to do a different kind of work in her present life: to be a different kind of story that will allow her to be the person who is able to write her memoir without bitterness, even though it is a tale of self-deception, acrimony, and considerable collateral damage.

O'Brien interprets her mother's story, but she does not impose any decoding on the story. She interprets by hooking the story up with other another take on 2 stories as "non violence", offny anothr story as a way of analysis.

stories and understanding it from different perspectives, including that of her grandmother. She invokes considerable historical material about Irish immigrants of her grandfather's generation, attempting to understand their horizons. She also accepts the family-silver story as having formed her own horizons, even as she shifts these horizons to realign herself in a new relation to the story and the storyteller, her mother. A problem of memoir writing is to conclude the book without implying that the process of realigning horizons is finished. O'Brien never speaks as one who has ceased to be a member of a family affiliated by stories that she now has serious problems with. She is both inside and outside those horizons, remaining in relationship to her family, both living and dead. Her memoir is a dialogue between horizons, including those of O'Brien's younger and older selves, those of recent immigrants and the securely established, and those who question their horizons and those who accept family stories without question.

In perhaps the book's most significant metaphor, O'Brien describes how the family silver finally ends up belonging to her. She uses it daily, but its pieces are now mixed among other utensils in her kitchen drawer. That metaphor expresses beautifully Gadamer's hermeneutic fusion of horizons.[27] The original pieces of silver are still distinct and recognizable, but they work with and among other knives, forks, and spoons. O'Brien's silver drawer represents the play of sameness (all forks are forks) and difference (this fork was part of the family silver) that dialogical thinking is always concerned with.

Hermeneutic interpretation does not stand outside the story and decode it in terms of a master schema, the access to which privileges the interpreter. Dialogical interpretation begins with the interpreter's recognition of being caught up in his or her own stories, which may overlap with the narrative habitus of the storyteller or may require a substantial shift in horizons, in order for the other's story to be recognizable. Hermeneutic interpretation is a commitment to work with one's prejudgments, recognizing the need for these but also their inherent danger. The hermeneutic commitment is to ask not only what the story means within my horizons, but also how far I can understand what it means within the horizons of the storyteller and other listeners. Perhaps most important: how does the story call on me to shift my horizons? A hermeneutic interpretation presupposes the interpreter's personal transformation but then redefines the personal within the dialogical. Hermeneutics is clear that the issue is *someone else's* story, but knowledge of that story always proceeds within the horizons of an interpreter as knowing subject.

Presenting hermeneutics within the horizons of this book, I foreground the complementarity of Gadamer and Bakhtin and assimilate hermeneutics to dialogical philosophy. I turn now to what constitutes the specific force of *dialogical* narrative analysis.

DIALOGICAL INTERPRETIVE PRACTICE

Dialogue refuses what monologue aspires to, which Mikhail Bakhtin calls FINALIZATION. Here is Bakhtin telling a story within a story within a dialogical analysis. He analyzes how Makar Devushkin, a character in one of Dostoevsky's early novels, objects to Gogol's short story, "The Overcoat," and how that objection expresses Dostoevsky's commitment to writing dialogical novels.

> Devushkin had glimpsed himself in the image of the hero of "The Overcoat," which is to say, as something totally quantified, measured, and defined to the last detail: all of you is here, there is nothing more in you, and nothing more to be said about you. He felt himself to be hopelessly predetermined and finished off, as if he were already quite dead, yet at the same time he sensed the falseness of such an approach.[28]

Devushkin deserves to be the central character of this chapter. He is the hero of dialogical interpretation, because he recognizes the falseness of the approach that attempts to finalize him — "there is nothing more in you, and nothing more to be said about you."

Reading about Devushkin, I imagine a governess or lady's companion of the early twentieth century, while such occupations still existed in much the same form that Tolstoy describes. She reads *War and Peace* and there, in the character of Mademoiselle Bourienne, is her own fantasy of being carried off in rich marriage. But the novel presents this as a spectacle for public derision. The reader feels humiliated, no less so for possibly having learned something about her own situation. The problem is not that Tolstoy is wrong about Mademoiselle; the problem is exactly how right he may be. Tolstoy not only exposes Mademoiselle's inner life of storytelling, he grants her no further room to learn from her aborted seduction by Anatole. His finalization of Mademoiselle Bourienne contrasts with his treatment of Natasha, who also enters into a near-seduction by Anatole but then matures to become a great deal else. Tolstoy's fable of Mademoiselle remains, as I have presented it throughout this book, an insightful story about the power of stories to create experiences. But his narration also exemplifies the monological style: he knows all there is of Mademoiselle, and he makes all of her knowable to the reader. Her secret fantasies are stripped bare for the reader's judgmental gaze, and she is *used* by the plot, used both to prefigure Natasha's moral lapse and to provide a display of Princess Marya's generosity in forgiving Mademoiselle.

Social scientific research practice too often *Devushkinizes* the participants: it silences people with its enumeration of *all* that is significant about them. Dialogical analysis understands that approach as not only ethically wrong but false, because it creates a pretension of knowing what cannot be known. As one example, over the last twenty years I have talked to many medical patients who felt, in Bakhtin's phrase, "finished off" by diagnoses of chronic and critical illnesses. Like Devushkin, they felt the falseness of an approach that scanned, measured, and analyzed every detail of their being and then claimed to pronounce the truth of that being. Many sought other narratives. Some turned to uncredentialed health practices, some to forms of spirituality, some to psychological journeying, and some to altruistic engagement in helping others. Too much social science actively aspires to the level of Devushkinization, for which medicine's more unfortunate practices provide a model. This aspiration is entirely rational in that it recognizes what is most readily funded and rewarded. It may be a good career choice. But it is not the only choice.

The dialogical shift in research practice begins with the important semantic difference between the research *subject* and what increasingly becomes the preferred term, the research *participant*. The research subject, like the medical patient, is the object of another's investigation, allowed to act only in ways that the other prescribes and subjected to the investigator's interpretive authority. Dialogical research seeks to take participation seriously, rather than using the term *participants* as a politically correct euphemism with no effect on research practice, either in data collection or in analysis. Participants *do things*. Specifically, they are not data for investigators; instead, they co-construct with investigators what count as data. Alessandro Portelli describes oral history as "what the source and the historian do together,"[29] and that emphasis on *doing together* speaks to all dialogical research, whether the participants are physical presences or textual presences.

Participants retain the right to change. Portelli, cited again because his practice is as exemplary as his capacity to articulate what he does, writes of oral history "putting back together, in some kind of temporary unity" (47). Avoidance of finalization does not mean giving up the unity of an account. Portelli's key word seems to be *temporary*. A unity is proposed, but this unity is not claimed as some transhistorical absolute. Any generalization is limited, both in scope of who this generalization might apply to, and in the openness of this unity to revision—not only by future interpretive reanalysis, but more significantly by the participants changing who they are. The dialogue is not only between participants and investigators as contemporaries. Dialogue is also between participants as they are and who they might become in the open future that investigators watch with respectful curiosity.

Participants are experts, at least in their own lives, and the dialogical interviewer is there to learn from the participant. Bruno Latour expresses this well when he describes his research as "studying up," as opposed to the conventional social scientific practice of "studying down."[30] Latour studies science, and scientists command respect; their research grants are much larger than those of the ethnographers who study their work. Scientists can make their own decisions about who will get into their labs and who will not. Their participation has to be elicited, as it can rarely be coerced or purchased. The dialogical ideal is to enter any research encounter as an occasion of "studying up," beginning with the premise that the *participant is the expert* from whom the researcher hopes to learn. In time, the researcher might offer back his or her own expertise, and that mutuality of offerings extends the dialogue. But it remains mutual.

Perhaps most important, *participants* make their lives meaningful, and research is one occasion for enacting meaning. And, like all humans, research participants co-construct meaning with other people. Research is no one-way transmission of information about lives; rather, it is an ongoing dialogue between participants' meanings; the meanings that researchers attribute to their words, their actions, their lives, and their stories; and how participants change in response to researchers' responses. No one's meaning is final, and no one meaning is final. What counts is two's meaning, which is enacted through a process of those two creating meanings as expressions of their relationship. In a dialogical framing, no one can ever take him- or herself out of relationships with others.

The dialogical attitude toward participants and interpretation of their stories can be summarized in three working principles. The first is *non-finalizability*, as summarized by Bakhtin, who is describing Dostoevsky's writing but could be advising social scientists on how to represent interview materials:

> This is no stenographer's report of a *finished* dialogue, from which the author has withdrawn and *over* which he is now located as if in some higher decision-making position: that would have turned an authentic and unfinished dialogue into an objectivized and finalized *image of a dialogue*, of the sort usual for every monological novel. The great dialogue in Dostoevsky is organized as an *unclosed whole* of life itself, life poised *on the threshold*.[31]

②

⤳The second principle is that of *second-person address*. Again, what Bakhtin recommends for novelists applies equally to how dialogical social scientists should write about those who participate in their research: "By the very construction of the novel, the author speaks not *about* a character, but *with* him" (63). And: "One cannot talk about him: one can only address oneself to him" (251).

Lest speaking not *about* but *with* seem nothing more than a literary-philosophical ideal, Mitchell Duneier's ethnography of New York street vendors, *Sidewalk,* offers a practical example.[32] Duneier includes—and this inclusion is itself a critical dialogical gesture—an afterword written by Hakim Hasan, his key informant during the research. Hasan exemplifies the difference between being a research *participant* and being a *subject*. He is well aware of the risks of turning over his life to a social scientist who then withdraws to what my previous quotation from Bakhtin calls "a higher decision-making position." Hasan's description of his initial reluctance to participate recalls Bakhtin's description of Devushkin: "How could I prevent him from appropriating me as mere data, from not giving me a voice in how the material in his book would be selected and depicted?" (321)

One of the most demonstrably practical ways that Duneier kept his project dialogical involved bringing a draft of his book back to New York. As Hasan describes, Duneier "rented a room at the Washington Square Hotel, and brought each and every man and woman involved with his project there. He read chapters of the book to them and solicited their opinions. This was not easy" (327).[33] Hasan is clear that in the final writing, Duneier "made his own judgments," and he has no quarrel with that, because he made these judgments "after listening to everyone first" (ibid.). Hasan concludes:

> My determination to participate in this project forced me to discover that a dialogue with Mitch, in his capacity *as a social scientist*, was possible. This was no small achievement. This was a departure from the "scholar knows best" paradigm. The romanticized idea of "the subject's voice" that I often hear about from graduate students studying at New York University and the New School for Social Research who come to my table is one thing. The radical willingness of the social scientist to listen is quite another. (Ibid.)

③

The third principle of dialogical research relationships takes up the question: what does the dialogical researcher say, speaking to participants? The principle is best phrased in the negative: say any number of things, depending on the project, but claim no privilege of interpretive authority. Bakhtin's most important pronouncement on dialogue and the limits of interpretation may be this:

> In Dostoevsky's works there is literally not a single word about a charac-
> ter that the character could not have said about himself (from the stand-
> point of content, not of tone). (278)

Reading this as advice for researchers, the conditional verb *could* seems crucial, for reasons that raise a fundamental question for any narrative analysis: Why not stop at collecting and publishing people's stories as they are
told? What is added by any interpretive analysis? The risks of interpretive
commentary are now clear: Devushkinizing the participant, finalizing him
or her, claiming that the unity created in the research report is more than
temporary. What, then, gives analysts or interpreters resources to say anything, once they accept the dialogical strictures on speech? Quite a bit can
be said, at least plenty to justify interpretation beyond transcription.

The investigator might add external verification of the participant's
story. In oral history, documentary verification of the story's truth is an
important task, and Portelli shows how that verification need not lapse
into monological judgment on the story. Whether or not a story can be
verified matters to historians, but verification is not any last word, because
absence of verification (either impossibility of verifying or discovery that
the story is wrong in some respect) still leaves the "truth of the telling."

For many if not most stories, however, external verification is not feasi-
ble. One good reason is that verification is often unethical. It would require
access to confidential records or involve third parties who have not agreed
to participate in the research and whose involvement the participant has
not agreed to. Sharon O'Brien offers readers her book, but that does not
authorize seeking out her relatives still living in Elmira.

The more complex problem with verification is whether those aspects
of the story that could, in principle, be verified are what make the story
important. If I had permission to locate and interview O'Brien's relatives,
could they verify what she writes? In some superficial respects they could,
but not with respect to what makes O'Brien's story memorable, which is
how her family affected her. Among the four nonfiction stories with which
this book began, verification seems to make any difference only with respect to Allen Feldman's paramilitary stories, which is one reason those
stories are best told within the genre of anthropological report, in which
verification should be possible, at least in principle.

Placing too much emphasis on verification relegates the storyteller
to being a mere source and holds the story hostage to its mimetic value.
When verification arbitrates reception, the story cannot act but can only
report actions that have already taken place; the interest is in those actions.
But beyond verification—important as it may remain for some narrative

analysts—the dialogical narrative analyst can add to the story in ways that do not violate Bakhtin's injunction against saying something that participants could not say.

First, the analyst's work and practice lead to hearing multiple stories about similar events or experiences. Analysis can connect these stories. Portelli writes: "Each person is a crossroads of many *potential* stories, of possibilities imagined and not taken, of dangers skirted and barely avoided."[34] Most people, I believe, realize this about themselves. But most people hear only a limited number of other people's stories. They have a limited understanding of what lies beyond the particular crossroads at which they live, even as they feel affected by what lies beyond. The analyst hears those other stories that remain as possibilities for the person who has not yet ventured down those roads. Situating any one story within those multiple stories does not finalize participants either singly or as a collective. It is not more than any participant *could* say but is more than any participant is currently *located* to say.

Second, the dialogical narrative analyst knows more about stories and socio-narratology. Anyone could acquire this knowledge—no false consciousness or repression blocks that acquisition. But few people have the time to tolerate the distraction of employing this knowledge on an ongoing basis; it gets in the way of practical pursuits. What is known about stories only articulates what participants, who are storytellers, already know tacitly. That articulation is, however, no small thing, and can offer participants new perspectives on their stories and their lives. A participant might be surprised, for example, to hear his or her story discussed as a shape-shifted variant of another story, but describing the story in that way need not finalize the story or the participant. Such interpretive talk does not claim what Bakhtin criticized as a "higher decision-making position."[35] On the contrary, recognition of the linkage between stories expands the dialogue by opening another connection that is a potential resource for participants. Rather than carrying the monological message, *this is all you are*, dialogical research can offer the possibility, *this is what else you are connected to*. A participant's story is no less his or her own for that connection; it is more.

Third, dialogical narrative analysis can help people, both individually and collectively, to reassemble stories that are remembered only in fragments, when the loss of the whole story is experienced as an individual or community loss. Jo-ann Archibald describes her work with Indigenous researchers to help Elders to recover a story that, in their marvelous phrase, had been "put to sleep in people's memories."[36] The description of this narrative reassembly work exemplifies one form of dialogical narrative analysis:

No one had the whole story. Eventually, they got the whole story pieced together, but it went through a . . . transition of convincing each other that their particular part of the memory was valid. It didn't matter if they didn't know all of it. Once they put it all together it became a whole story . . . It was incredible listening to the arguments and [talk about] how long it had been handed down. (Shirley Leon, quoted by Archibald, 80–81, ellipses and brackets in original)

The dialogical principle here is that no one—especially the researcher— ever has "the whole story," whether that story is told around a campfire, or in an interview, or in a published book. Dialogical narrative analysis participates in the ongoing work of reassembling what never will be a whole story, because claiming wholeness would finalize the story. What Shirley Leon describes as the Elders' arguments are dialogue. A dialogue can be reported on, as Archibald reports on one here, without the report ending that dialogue. On the contrary, the analysis becomes another voice in the polyphony, connecting the story in other ways, as my quotation of Shirley Leon does here.

As a necessarily provisional summary: what is *dialogical* in dialogical narrative analysis is a refusal of making the subject/participant/other known in his or her finalized and too-often naked being. The positive commitment that dialogical researchers offer participants is *mutual recognition* that begins when the story is first heard and is carried forward through whatever reports are written as the analysis of that storytelling. But a phrase like "mutual recognition" means little until it is animated by a story. Portelli tells a story of such recognition. He interviews a labor organizer, and in the course of the interview the man asks Portelli if he knows anyone who might be a useful contact to help secure the man's daughter's admission in a selective secondary school. Portelli writes how he could have experienced this request as a break in the agreed-on research relationship. But he decides, upon reflection, that it was a moment when he and his "source," which is oral history's preferred term, truly recognized each other as people whose lives extend beyond the research and their respective work. Each has needs and can call on the other for assistance. "Our gazes crossed and we *viewed* each other," Portelli writes, offering as good an evocation of dialogical recognition as I can imagine.[37] He refuses to Devushkinize the man as only a source; he allows him also to be a father whose concern for his daughter results in a request that seems incongruous to the research relationship and to the man's politics—because the school would be considered elitist—only if Portelli finalizes the man as a source for research and a type of political actor.

Dialogue always begins in difference and aspires to freedom. Devushkin's freedom feels reduced when he reads himself as measured and quantified. The measures render him subordinate to the knowing interpretive gaze that specifies him—a gaze to which there is no speaking back (the mixed metaphor seeming unavoidable). Thus subjected, Devushkin cannot be free. I give Portelli the last word here, although I hear him channeling Bakhtin. Portelli expresses what can be enhanced through multiple dialogues between researcher and participants, between multiple participants, between participants and the multiple addressees of an eventual research report: "To be truly different we need to be truly equal, and we cannot be truly equal unless we are truly different" (60). I return to this complex idea later in this chapter.

ACTS OF INTERPRETATION: FOLLOWING THE STORYTELLERS

Interpretation, in its hermeneutic and dialogical tradition, is less a matter of decoding stories than of seeing all the variations and possibilities inherent in the story. The narrative analyst opens him- or herself to these possibilities, in order to invite others to open themselves. Interpretation seeks *not* to say: all the story is here, analyzed and stated in clear, explicit terms. Interpretation seeks not to stand over the story, speaking about it. Interpretation aspires to be an ongoing dialogue with the story.

How to interpret has been the topic throughout this book. Figuring out how any particular story realizes the capacities discussed in chapter 1 generates interpretation: what counts as the trouble that sets the story in motion; how the story allows its characters to respond to this trouble, and so on through each of those capacities. Describing how a story does the forms of work described in chapter 2 is interpretation: how does the story teach people who they are, and what sort of people are likely to be instructed by this particular story? Each of the questions in chapter 3—What does the story make narratable? Who is holding their own in the story?—opens a line of interpretation. What can be added?

In Barry Unsworth's novel *Morality Play*, a medieval troupe of players arrives in a town to put on a series of passion plays.[38] The town is agitated: a twelve-year-old boy has recently been murdered, and everyone is convinced that a young woman is guilty. Perhaps because of that excitement, the plays draw poorly. In an effort to increase attendance, the leader of the players hits on a new idea: they will write their own play, depicting the crime that has just occurred, according to the story that everyone believes about what took place. Not all the players are comfortable with that—for them, plays should depict only stories from the Bible, nothing more—but they agree and begin to plan the production. As they retell the accepted, public story of the murder, adapting it into a play, a strange thing happens. The story proves to be a weak narrative: one thing does not happen in consequence of another; holes in the plot become evident. To fix up the story, the players turn detective, and we need follow them no further in those adventures. Unsworth's players exemplify a form of dialogical narrative analysis.

The players' ad-hoc method of analysis is to tell the story in a different and more disciplined way. By translating the tavern tale into a staged play, they raise questions that never occurred so long as the tale remained told in the tavern. Their translated story opens a dialogue with the earlier story, and in the course of this dialogue, the players' horizons shift. Like the viewers of the film *Atanarjuat*, as described by Alberto Manguel, "They [had] to make themselves available to this different way of seeing."[39] In other words, the players-as-researchers find that the privileged route to telling the truth of the boy's murder is found by refining and expanding the truth of their theatrical telling. Dialogical narrative analysis may differ most from the strategy that the players in *Morality Play* stumble onto, because they are characters in a detective story, and that genre requires finding *the* singular truth. In dialogical narrative analysis, the truth of the telling is being sought, but that truth is never finalized.

I once read how musicians enjoy an advantage among students of different art forms in that they actually perform, note by note, the texts they study, having to make all the decisions that performance requires. Painters approximate this when they copy great works. Narrative analysts can use performance (most often to oneself only, but also within research teams) as a mode of analysis. The question of interpretation thus becomes how to enter into dialogue with a story, translating it and discovering unnoticed aspects, whether these are linkages or discontinuities. Interpretation is less a matter of commenting on a story than of retelling it in a varied form to create new connections. In the initial moves of this dialogical translation-as-interpretation, the storytelling scene is bracketed, and attention focuses on the content of the story. Later, the focus expands to bring the storytelling scene back into the analysis. Throughout, I follow the advice of storytellers themselves, respecting them as experts.

First, translate the story into images. David Grossman, a novelist whose interpretations of the story of Samson were prominent in chapter 2, offers the advice "to fix in our mind's eye" scenes from a story.[40] Social scientists who most often work with stories in the form of transcriptions and other written texts think of stories as collections of words, but stories are also collections of images that the words create. Once, a performance storyteller surprised me by describing storytelling as primarily a *visual* art. Not a verbal art, but a visual art. He meant both that he remembers stories as a succession of images, and that he aspires to create images in the imaginations of his listeners. Interpretation begins with seeing the story, off the page. The storytellers whom Archibald interviewed make the same point when they talk about the need for inexperienced storytellers to let go of a line-by-line grasping of the story and instead to "go into the story."[41]

If these master storytellers were asked what "go into the story" means in practice, their reply might have been something like this chapter's first epigraph: when you're ready, you'll get it. A first step in interpretation as a work of going into the story is to stop reading or listening and *see*, then asking how the story positions you to see. The point is not to connect these images. The point is to let them connect. Translating the story into images is only a beginning.

Second, translate the story to tell it from the point of view of a previously marginal character. If a story positions its listener to see what happens from one position, interpretation requires seeing from other positions and imagining their possibility. Grossman recommends you choose a character other than the central protagonist and "see the story through her eyes."[42] He begins his interpretation of Samson by seeing the story through the eyes of Samson's mother, noticing that the biblical text calls her simply "the woman," although it repeatedly names Samson's father, Manoah. Yet the woman is the far more active, kinetic character—something that could be learned by repeated reading but would be realized more quickly by telling the story and having to work with the woman as a character. Grossman points out that Manoah always seems one step behind her, in thought, deed, and step. One anomaly of the biblical text is its description of the husband going "after his wife" (Judges 13:11), an ordering of gendered bodies so unheard of that it is notable. Grossman sheds new light on the Samson story by asking what the events would look like through the eyes of this unnamed, formally peripheral but very significant character.[43]

Each of the multiple perspectives that are immanent within a story begins a potential translation of that story. Yet opening the story to those alternative perspectives is remarkably difficult. A workshop exercise that I sometimes encourage is for one person to tell a story and then another to tell it back, but the retelling must shift the point of view, elevating a peripheral character to the protagonist through whose perspective the story is told. Workshop participants' unexpected difficulty with that task teaches me how deeply invested listeners become in the point of view from which they first hear the story told. Yet stories incorporate multiple points of view—that is their polyphony. Interpretation begins with letting each point of view have its moment of being the perspective that directs the consciousness of storyteller and listener.

By translating the story into different points of view, any unity that the story displays as a narrative becomes understandable as a provisional achievement: not a reflection of reality as it is and must be, but a creative act of story and storyteller working together. Dialogical interpretation requires *making the achievement of the story questionable*, in order to ask what that achievement achieves.

Third, notice which details might have been expected but are omitted. Grossman's example is that when Samson's mother tells her husband the news of the miraculous birth-to-be, she repeats most of the very specific instructions that the divine visitor told her, but she omits a couple of other instructions.[44] His point is not to attribute any specific significance to those omissions; again, interpretation is not decoding, and there is no presumption of a hidden text to be uncovered. Samson's mother may have reasons for holding back what she omits, or she might simply be in a hurry, or the storyteller might want to speed up the narrative. But giving attention to the mother's omission makes it more interesting how Samson, throughout the story, omits details about himself in what he tells people, specifically women. One aspect of his trickster quality, shared most notably with Odysseus, is holding back part of the story, so far as he knows that story himself.

Attention to omissions reminds us that stories, more than other forms of narrative, make silences significant. What happens is not the only thing to attend to; what does not happen can be equally worthy of interpretation. To notice what is omitted, the easiest way is to tell the story as if in performance, asking what every performance storyteller needs to ask: Am I offering the audience all they need to make sense of the story? Do the parts fit? What is better left imagined than specified, and thus is well omitted? How does an omission engage and direct listeners' imaginations?

These three interpretive suggestions are not yet socio-narratology; the *socio* is bracketed. Those brackets can now be removed and attention shifted to the storytelling occasion, restoring the *socio* to narratology.

Fourth, attend to differences between the storyteller and the analyst. Portelli's oral history practice suggests the advice to specify the differences between the storyteller and various recipients of the story, ending with the narrative analyst. Portelli describes doing fieldwork in Kentucky studying political activists. An African-American woman who agrees to an interview nevertheless tells him:

"There's gonna always be a line" between us . . . "I don't trust you"—and that's why, she implied, I am talking to you—because the world I'm working for is one in which a black proletarian woman and a middle-class white man might be allowed to trust each other at last, abolishing their hierarchies and keeping their differences.[45]

Here hermeneutics transpires in the moment when two people seek to communicate between different horizons. What this woman taught Portelli is that to interpret a story, foreground the differences between yourself as interpreter and the other person as storyteller; pay attention first to all that separates you, taking it very seriously. In Portelli's fieldwork story, oral historian and participant share a goal of equality, but abolishing hierarchies depends on sustaining recognition of differences. Bakhtin returns repeatedly to the point that without difference, there can be no dialogue. Well-meaning narrative analysts are often inclined to emphasize what they share with participants. Interpretation finds a better beginning in difference.

Fifth, slow down. Jo-ann Archibald offers what might be the most difficult advice for academic narrative analysts to follow: interpretation can only proceed *slowly*. "Learning how a story fits within a people's belief system requires that one live and interact with the people for a long time," Archibald writes.[46] She writes later about research as "a process that involves going away to think about [stories'] meanings in relation to one's life" (90) and the importance of "creating time to listen and having patience to learn" (108). Archibald offers this advice as a researcher who turned herself into a storyteller. On my interpretation, she is exquisitely aware that stories are anything but secondary effects of belief systems. Belief systems are the performative effects of stories; in stories, beliefs are enacted into being. A back and forth movement between story and context is required, and that takes time. A view of both stories and belief systems as ongoing is also required. Both are dynamic, changing in response to each other. As *research* becomes another actor in the dialogue, it will—if it is a good actor—create changes of its own.

"We should listen and wait," says Portelli.[47] He is talking about interview technique, not rushing the participant to tell the story that the researcher thinks he or she wants to hear. But the advice is equally important for interpretation: listen and wait. When my interpretive work is stuck, my advice to myself is to go off—preferably off for a walk—and tell the story again, as if I were practicing for a performance. Listen and wait. You won't get it before you are ready, but readiness is an active achievement, including the achievement of patience.

Sixth, *appreciate* the story and the storyteller. Any dialogical relationship is based on some kind of appreciation of the other: perhaps appreciation for the other's forbidding and unfinished struggles, but still appreciation. A final interpretive technique can be adapted from narrative therapy.[48] Compose at least two letters, preferably written (but *not* sent and probably not included in eventual published analyses) to both the protagonist of the story and to the storyteller, if they can be separated, and also to the story itself—though this may take some practice. In these letters, offer thanks for what you learned from the story or how it benefitted you. As ways to open up interpretation, these letters are only as valuable as they are specific about exactly what is appreciated about the story; avoid adjectives. The letters should emphasize how the story enlarges your perspective; be specific about what can now be seen and understood differently. In this translation of the story, responses should be personal, but again, the point is to express appreciation in specifics, not generalizations about how the story made you feel. Part of any story's work is to produce feelings, but noting feelings advances interpretation only when reasons for such reactions are offered that expand appreciation for how the story is told—the storyteller's art.

These letters need be no longer than the story itself. For example, to the child who tells "The baby cried. The mommy picked it up," I might write: *Thank you for reminding me what it is like to be very small in a world that is large and to depend on adults so very much.* That would be an easy letter.

Allen Feldman might have difficulty writing appreciative letters to the Irish paramilitary indoctrinators who tell the origins stories discussed in this book's introduction. Writing those letters would require spending time dwelling on how these storytellers are trying to hold their own and what they are trying to make narratable or keep narratable. Feldman, I think, could have written such letters, because he does what Archibald recommends: he learns how a story fits into a people's belief system. Feldman spent enough time to free himself from being overcome by what I, at least, initially experience as an overwhelming sense that the storytellers' beliefs are horribly wrong. He does not lose his moral compass—the issue is not relativism—but he does make himself available for useful responses to the stories he heard. That is why interpretation, proceeding with dialogical commitments, always begins best with appreciation in the broadest sense: appreciation for the story that is told, and appreciation for what makes that story not only tellable but necessary to tell.

* * *

These interpretive techniques, or ways of translating a story, are acts of *preparation* for dialogical narrative analysis. Actual forms of that analysis are described in the next chapter. The issue is approaching those forms of analysis and choosing the most appropriate among them from a position of dialogue with the story. And in this dialogue, what counts is opening up as many of the story's multiple possibilities as possible.

FROM VALIDATION TO RESPONSIBILITY

Nondialogical social science methodology seeks validation for analyses: interpretations must have some guarantee that excludes other possibilities. Dialogical analysis has little interest in excluding—it welcomes a proliferation of possibilities, which confirms that the story or stories can never be finalized. From a dialogical perspective, *validation* risks imposing what Mabel McKay, in this book's prologue, calls "somebody else's rules." The dialogical position is that interpretations are valid when they are responsible. But what is responsible is complex: people represent their lives and truths in stories because they recognize that others' responses, and their terms of responsibility, are complicated in multiple ways. The capacity of stories is to explore complications, rarely to resolve them.

As I wrote earlier in this chapter while discussing genre hybridity, the dialogical interest is always in what a story requires of those who receive it. Interpretation in scholarly narrative analysis, like interpretation in everyday life, comes down to deciding what a story requires and whether or how to act on that. The question of responsible interpretation is well summarized by Archibald: "Jeannette Armstrong, of the Okanagan Nation, speaks about a way of listening as preparation for taking responsibility for the effect on others of one's words/thoughts when shared publicly."[49] Armstrong makes the necessary link between responsibility in listening and responsibility in telling, the one preparing for the other. I hold Armstrong's statement alongside what German novelist Alfred Doblin said, speaking in Berlin in 1948: "You have to sit in the ruins for a long time and let them affect you, and you feel the pain and the judgment."[50]

Both statements point toward what chapter 1 called the material-semiotic nature of stories. Armstrong talks about real, material effects of stories. Sometimes people hear a story and take a new pride in who they are. Sometimes they despair. Doblin calls for responsibility in interpreting the signification of rubble, as that interpretation prepares Germans to rebuild their lives and their country. The people he speaks to need to take time to be with that signifying rubble. They need to feel their own participation in the story ending in that rubble, and they need to imagine the stories that others would tell. Only when all those stories are heard can those people rebuild responsibly.

A responsible relation to stories is a moral imperative, one aspect of which is never to aspire to control stories through their interpretations. The inescapable loop is that stories teach how to be responsible in response to stories. In Armstrong's Indigenous community, people tell stories about imagined pasts and possible futures as a means of learning and contesting which effects of these stories are responsible. There need be no agreement, only enough mutual understanding. Among Doblin's ruins, different people will feel different judgment. They will tell stories about what happened and dispute the truth of others' stories. Narrative analysis seeks not to resolve these contests, but rather to enhance the dialogue. Narrative analysis aspires to have some affect on whether and how long people listen to each other's stories and how open they are to those stories.

Interpretation is responsible when it *opens*, not closes; when it creates links to more stories, anticipates effects, and asks why some stories affect judgments rather than others. I return to these issues in chapter 6. Chapter 5 turns to specific forms of dialogical narrative analysis, bringing more voices into the conversation. The chapter describes analyses that exemplify some of the many different ways to be responsible.

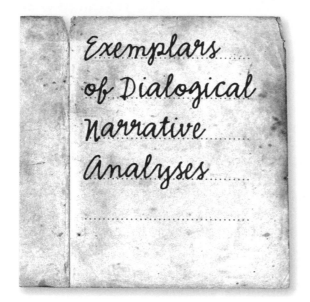

Exemplars of Dialogical Narrative Analyses

5

A scientific activity is acknowledged or rejected as good science by how close it is to one or more exemplars, that is, practical prototypes of good scientific work. —Bent Flyvbjerg

Oral history does not cultivate the average, but often perceives the exceptional and unique to be more representative. —Alessandro Portelli

Every narrative analysis needs to discover its own singular way to proceed, but no one does narrative analysis for the first time. As Bent Flyvbjerg writes in the first of this chapter's epigraphs, analysis claims to be science by following exemplars that are recognized as science.[1] That is another level of dialogue: between the present analysis and previous ones. Because this dialogue, like any other, depends crucially on difference, following exemplars does not mean mimicking them. The distinctive originality of each previous analysis is its creative discovery of how to represent stories in a manner most appropriate to the research interests but also true to the stories themselves. These exemplars are resources for future work, but they are not templates.

This chapter presents six forms of narrative analysis. I discuss them not to synthesize some unified method from their practices, but rather to suggest what makes each exemplary. Specifically, what makes each a *narrative* analysis and also a *dialogical* analysis? If the *socio* aspect of socio-narratology was sometimes bracketed in the last chapter, here it returns full force. Each of these exemplars is committed to understanding how stories make life social, or in some cases, how stories reveal the loss of what makes life social.

In all these exemplars, either stories are working, or the analysis is about what prevents them from working and the problems that causes. The work the stories do is not all good, but that is the topic of the final chapter.

One presupposition these exemplars share is expressed by this chapter's second epigraph, from Alessandro Portelli. That statement begins a passage in which Portelli discusses the truth of stories and the different objectives of narrative truth versus factual truth. As an example, he cites historical research about slavery in the American South. The research concluded that "slaves were likely to be whipped an average of 0.7 times per year."[2] But what does this statistic—representing what Portelli notes is a physical impossibility—mean to those who were slaves, and thus what does it say about the system of slavery? Portelli observes:

> The slave who was whipped one hundred times may illuminate the institution of slavery more than those who were whipped 0.7 times per year; the tiny number of drug victims in an industrial town may give us precious clues to youth experience as a whole. And one creative storyteller, a brilliant verbal artist, is as rich a source of knowledge as any set of statistics. (58)

Flyvbjerg, who does not cite Portelli, makes the same point:

> When the objective is to achieve the greatest possible amount of information on a given problem or phenomenon, a representative or a random sample may not be the most appropriate strategy. This is because the typical or average case is often not the richest in information. Atypical or extreme cases often reveal more information because they activate more actors and more basic mechanisms in the situation studied. In addition, from both an understanding-oriented and an action-oriented perspective, it is often more important to clarify the deeper causes behind a given problem than to describe the symptoms of the problem and how frequently they occur.[3]

Social scientific methods differ as to where the significant action takes place. The studies discussed in this chapter do not emphasize sampling or coding, nor do they make strong claims about generalizable cases. Frequencies, either of a type of story or of incidents within stories, are not counted. *Analysis* often seems to emerge from recollection. As analysts think about and also with the stories they have heard, the significance of those stories crystallizes, and how to tell the metastory of the stories becomes sufficiently apparent to begin writing and revising. Most consistently in all these exemplars, what counts is which stories occur in what settings, and how different types of stories work in the setting where they do work.

What Portelli and Flyvbjerg say about the value of atypical but information-rich cases within research also applies to my choices of studies discussed in this chapter. Some of the studies taken up here are acclaimed (by awards, reprinting, and/or frequent citation), and others are newer and less known. My claim about their value as exemplars is not that they would all receive high scores in a survey of scholars (although I believe all would). Instead, I present each study as being what Portelli imagines his ideal research participant to be: "one creative storyteller, a brilliant verbal artist."[4] Not a "source," but a teacher that is also a partner in dialogue.

BEGINNING WITH AN ANALYTIC INTEREST

Some narrative analyses, like many stories, begin in the middle of things. Gareth Williams's often reprinted article, "The Genesis of Chronic Illness: Narrative Re-construction," begins with a moment during a research interview.[5] The participant, Bill, leans forward and asks Williams: "How the *hell* have I come to be like this?" (175). Bill then answers his own question by telling a story about how he came to suffer from rheumatoid arthritis, which he was diagnosed as having at age fifty.

Williams's opening is as artful as it is true to his stories. The artfulness is that he makes his analytic interest in the *genesis* of chronic illness seem to arise spontaneously from his interviews: Bill's question points backward toward some genesis—whatever started the process of becoming as he is. Bill is not the only one engaged in what Williams calls narrative reconstruction; Williams himself is doing his own reconstructive work. He reconstructs Bill's story and those of the other two storytellers in the article, Gill and Betty, to focus on their understanding of the genesis of their illness, or, how they have come to be as they are. Bill, Gill, and Betty are clearly concerned with how their disease began, but Williams's representation of their stories makes genesis the foreground.

Williams's article exemplifies narrative analysis that begins with an analytic interest. That interest becomes a device to organize the multiple stories that participants tell according to how the device selects from and among stories; Williams's device is genesis.[6] The focus on genesis works especially well for narrative analysis, because genesis is as much a storyteller's problem as it is an ill person's problem.

The genesis of illness, as Williams uses that term, refers specifically to lay versions of what medicine would call the etiology of the disease. Genesis in personal storytelling is less about alignment with medical explanations— Bill has some concern with this alignment, but it seems of marginal interest to either Gill or Betty—and more about a need for the disease to fit the narrative trajectory of a life. Bill's "how the hell" outcry is an impassioned and poignant expression of this need; his life story was not supposed to lead to disability. But Bill reconstructs his story so that it does lead there.

Williams's decision to focus on genesis seems to derive as much from previous ideas about narrative and illness experience as from what people with rheumatoid arthritis tell him. These ideas begin with the sociologist Mike Bury's argument that illness constitutes a "biographical disruption" in someone's life.[7] Williams reasons that a biographical disruption requires repair in the form of a narrative reconstruction. That reconstructive work hinges on telling a particular origin story about the illness. This origin story works to align life-during-illness with life-before-illness. What begins as disruption is thus reconstructed into continuity—perhaps a contingent continuity, but nevertheless a single narrative trajectory that holds different aspects of a life together as a whole. Life-as-a-whole, bound by causal connections, is the artful accomplishment of the self-story.

Williams complements this sociological interest in narrative reconstruction by asking a question about narrative based in literature. He quotes Ulrich, the protagonist of Robert Musil's novel, *The Man without Qualities*, who says that narrative order is "the simple order that consists in one's being able to say: 'When that had happened, then this happened.'"[8] From this, Williams extrapolates a research question about some people's stories:

> In confronting the experience of chronic illness, then, like an unusual or disturbing experience, Musil's narrative thread—"when that had happened, then this happened"—becomes *questionable*. The individual's narrative has to be reconstructed both in order to understand the illness in terms of past social experience and to reaffirm the impression that life has a course and the self has a purpose or *telos*. (179, original emphasis)

People's work of narrative reconstruction is teleological, in Williams's use of that term, because illness is the telos to which people reimagine their life before illness leading. How they have lived has not necessarily caused that illness—although Bill believes it has—but illness *makes sense as a sequential next part* of their life story. Williams writes that Bill, Gill, and Betty each tell a story that "imaginatively reconstructs the past so that it has meaning or purpose for the present" (179), which is close to what I wrote in chapter 4 about memory reassembling a past to enact a present.

Williams builds Bill's story through details of how he first experienced disruption in his working life: "Every time I had a session like, my feet began to swell and my hands began to swell. I couldn't hold a pen. I had difficulty getting between machines and difficulty getting hold of small things" (180–81). The story moves backward in time to Bill's earlier career in the military, and it eventually focuses on his belief that workplace toxicity caused his disease. In Bill's reasoning, his good health while living the punishing life of a paratrooper is the comparison case that excludes alternative explanations of his disease, including inherited predisposition to rheumatoid arthritis, which is the etiology his doctors favor. Bill's storytelling is most vivid when describing the workplace as a cause of disease: "There was a special section, and that was quite hot up there. Your entry and exit was through the fire door, and there was no air intake, no fresh air from outside . . . It's totally enclosed, it's double thick glass, and they always had the damn things shut till we opened them" (186).

Gill's story presents the genesis of her illness as the cumulative effects of stress. If Bill situates himself among working men, Gill places her life story among women who experience the multiple demands of work and family: "Not simply the stress of events that happened but the stress perhaps of suppressing myself while I was a mother and wife; not 'women's libby' but there comes a time in your life when you think, you know, 'where have I got to? There's nothing left of me'" (188). Stress may not have caused Gill's condition, but her condition makes sense as being where a stressful life leads.

Betty's story revolves around her strong Christian faith. Her account of the genesis of rheumatoid arthritis requires a self-fashioned theodicy in which the illness is an aspect of God's will. However, as Williams interprets Betty's account: "'God's will' does not imply self-blame where the individual is bad and illness is retribution; at least, there is no direct relationship" (195). He then quotes Betty saying: "You see, there's a beauty about everything and you can sort of go through it in this way, you know, talking to the Lord and entering into it. He knows all about it. So people say, 'why you?' Well, why not me? Better me who knows the Lord" (ibid.).

Williams makes no specific claims for how typical these stories of Bill, Gill, and Betty are among the thirty people whom he interviewed, nor does that issue seem to require discussion. These three stories are valuable for understanding the experience of chronic illness not because they are typical, but rather because they are *vivid*. This vividness allows the three stories to fulfill the role that Portelli holds for oral history: "to connect life to times, uniqueness to representativeness."[9] The dialogical achievement of Williams's writing is to make Bill's, Gill's, and Betty's stories seem representative of the generalized problem of telling a life story that includes a debilitating chronic disease, but to do this without conscripting these participants as typical, which would be a form of what chapter 4 critiqued as Devushkinization. Each person's story can remain unique while being representative in that uniqueness.

Williams's stories are vivid because readers feel like they are in the presence of Bill, Gill, and Betty. Williams is as good a storyteller as his participants are, maybe better. As clear and systematic as the analytic framing of the article is, what remains most memorable are the three stories and the *characters* who tell them. Williams writes what truly is a *narrative analysis*— not simply an analysis of narratives—because his research report allows these characters and their stories to breathe.

The analysis is dialogical not only because Williams's telling respects the narrative arc of the whole story, but also because he does not finalize Bill, Gill, or Betty by imposing a psychosocial evaluation of their storytell- ing. For example, when storytelling is relegated to being a form of *coping*, dialogue suffocates, because the analyst takes the position of an external evaluator of another person's success or failure. Although Bill's, Gill's, and Betty's accounts of the genesis of illness each represent a subtype of the general form of reconstruction narrative—the environmental/political exploitation narrative, the stress narrative, and the religious narrative— Williams does not present them as a typology. Again, the stories are not typical instances of three frequently occurring categories of stories. Rather, they are representative because of the creativity that Bill, Gill, and Betty demonstrate in finding their respectively different solutions to the typical problem of "Why me?" More specifically: how is the younger, healthy me continuous with the chronically ill me?

If each individual story is not exactly suspenseful, readers are led to care about the characters. Among all three stories, a kind of suspense does emerge, as readers recognize that any account of the genesis of illness could be otherwise; any single account is *fragile*, in Cheryl Mattingly's sense.[10] Bill, Gill, and Betty are holding their own against the adversity of their bod- ies, and their stories of the genesis of their illness are companions that play a significant part in enabling them to hold their own. Reading Williams, I may know that he is reconstructing the stories he has heard, but his pres- ence is primarily that of a witness, putting these stories in dialogue with one another and then inviting his readers to enter this dialogue.

BUILDING A TYPOLOGY OF NARRATIVE FORMS

This form of narrative analysis describes my second book, *The Wounded Storyteller*.[11] To shape many stories of illness experience into a book, I had experimented first with a stage theory of illness. I foregrounded aspects of the stories that exemplified what sociologists would call the "career" of an ill person; stages might include, for example, presentiment of illness, diag- nosis, treatment, complications, remission, and reentry. I went so far as to write a complete draft manuscript on this basis.

Not the least problem with this organization was that it required cut- ting up individual stories of illness, pulling out what each had to say about that stage, and then seeking what seemed most typical in what different accounts said about that stage. Although I could not have articulated the problem at that time—about fifteen years before writing this book—what that approach produced was an analysis based on narratives, but not a *narrative* analysis. The storytelling got lost as sound bites were extracted from different stories. The results were not false in the sense of being untrue; people had said those things about their illness. But how this rejected draft represented these stories was unfaithful—not necessarily to the content of the stories, but to the art of the storytellers.

People have their art—how they work with the stories around them to tell a story they can call their own. What we refer to, often vaguely, as people's *dignity* is not simply expressed in this art; dignity is enacted in the space of being artful and being recognized as artful. Imposing a stage theory denied people's art by treating their stories as material for me to cut up and arrange. Any retelling of a story involves editing and selection, but the editing required by a stage theory went beyond telling a shorter version of the story in a different context (as I do throughout this book). In constructing a stage or career theory of illness, I risked making the uniqueness of individual voices disappear entirely. I *finalized* their material in my rearrangement. Or I could have, if I had written that way.[12]

The Wounded Storyteller proposes that any unique story is fabricated through a weave of at least three core narratives, which I call the restitution narrative, the chaos narrative, and the quest narrative. *Restitution* narratives have a plot of someone getting sick, being treated, and having some version of health restored. The protagonists who do all the acting are medical workers who enact the restitution; the sick person is cast as an almost exclusively passive character, appropriately called *the patient* because she or he waits for someone else to do something. The plot of *chaos* narratives is not much of a plot, because the protagonist is stuck within an immovable complex of obstacles, including untreatable medical problems, financial problems, family problems, and more—always more problems. The chaos narrative is an anti-narrative, because one thing does not lead to another. Everything gets in the face of the ill person, blocking movement toward any kind of meaningful response. In the *quest* narrative there is movement. The ill person is an active character who does find some kind of meaning in illness, and that may take different forms. Illness is not a good thing by any means, but protagonists of quest narratives find ways to work with illness, keeping their lives moving in a direction they experience as forward.

Why should narrative analysis proceed by typology construction? What advantage does a typology provide, and for whom? Typologies risk putting stories in boxes, thus allowing and even encouraging the monological stance that the boxes are more real than the stories, and the types are all that need to be known about the stories. In a world where simplification is a pretext for knowing, and knowing is a pretext for controlling, typologies are risky. But if hermeneutic openness is sustained, typologies can also enhance appreciation, both mutual appreciation and self-appreciation.

Elaboration of types of narratives allows recognizing the uniqueness of each individual *story*, while at the same time understanding how individuals do not make up stories by themselves. Each story is singular; none is a mere *instance*. Yet, stories depend on other stories: on recognizable plots, character types, conventional tropes, genre-specific cues that build suspense, and all the other narrative resources that storytellers utilize. A typology of *narratives* recognizes that experience follows from the availability of narrative resources, and people's immense creativity is in using these resources to fabricate their stories. The types in a typology are of *narratives*, not people. No individual storyteller is reduced to any narrative type, but all storytellers work with these types as resources for telling and expectations for hearing. Experience is understood as residing as much outside persons as inside them; it is borrowed even as it is felt.

Years of responses to *The Wounded Storyteller* have taught me that people use typologies as guides to listening and to storytelling. With a typology as a reference, those who listen to people telling stories can more readily hear how these stories are woven together and what changes in storytelling occur over time.[13] The typology in *The Wounded Storyteller* enables listeners, who are mostly clinicians and family members, to hear different threads in the fabric of an ill person's story, because each story will draw on aspects of all three narrative types. The listener can attend to which thread—restitution, chaos, or quest—seems to dominate the story that day, and how that gestalt of foreground narrative to background narratives changes over time. The typology's complementary value for people working to tell their own stories is to assist in *naming* differences between narrative representations of experiences. Naming types of narratives can help people think about what story they are telling and what story they want to tell. Naming narrative types can authorize the telling of particular stories, and it also can liberate people from stories they no longer want to tell.

How to develop the specific types in a typology is not easy to specify, and the process takes time. In my own work, approaching illness stories as one who had already told my own story[14] led me to read or hear other stories not only for their content, but also for how storytellers dealt with the problems of narration that I had worked through myself, including but hardly limited to what to tell and what to omit, how to present intensely personal material without embarrassing listeners or readers, and perhaps most of all, how to keep the story personal but open it up to listeners who have no reason to be interested in me, the storyteller. I understood tellers of restitution stories as fitting themselves into a narrative that institutional professionals prefer; chaos storytellers as unable to tell a fully developed story; and tellers of quest stories as fully engaged in storytelling, albeit dependent on narrative resources going back to the earliest myths and folktales that shaped their sense of what a quest is and how to value it as a form of life. The point with respect to typology building is to think not only about content but also about storytelling itself.

Typology building can also begin with an analytic interest or, more often, plural interests. The types can, for example, name clusters of typical solutions to a common problem that research participants have. Types can be arrayed along one continuum, such as compliance to resistance, or two continua can generate a matrix, at which point the typology becomes more formalized. Matrices look authoritative, but they risk imposing closure on what can be heard in people's stories, because the number of boxes is limited. At worst, formal typologies lead to fetishism: actual stories can end up serving as exemplars of types, rather than the types helping to understand what work the stories are doing for the different people who tell and receive them. These risks, however, are only cautions of what to watch out for. Research can begin with an analytic interest—biographical discontinuity, group formation, or the causes of war—and still remain narrative in how stories are represented.

Stories also cluster into types according to all the distinctions advanced in chapters 1 through 3. A typology can divide stories according to which capacities are paramount, or how some stories realize certain capacities in similar ways. Or, a typology can reflect types of work that stories do and how they do it. Or, a typology can reflect such issues as who is holding their own and how. Much of this book has presented ways that stories can be shown to cluster into types. But the best way to develop a typology is to tell the stories oneself, as recommended in chapter 4. Musicians impress me by their ability to hear compositional similarities between pieces that I would never have associated with each other. But I only listen to the music, while they actually play it. To hear these similarities, playing it at all matters more than playing it well—playing well has other values. The struggle to tell a compelling story requires attention to what that story's distinctive capacities are, what work the story is doing, and what issues it raises. Typology building depends on these foci of attention.

Types become identifiable as they are named, and a typology compels or collapses depending on the descriptive force of its names. Names can describe the stories (for example, "diagnosis stories"), or they can borrow some phrase that reoccurs in that type of story, or names can be descriptively evocative, like my types of restitution, chaos, or quest. Some names are immediate and obvious fits; some clusters of types seem resistant to naming. The process of naming a type proceeds iteratively with changing understandings of which stories fit that type. Stories that do not fit within proposed types require decisions whether to expand a type that has already taken shape and may have a name, or to create a new type. As in putting clothes into a new closet or arranging a new desk, things have to be taken out and put back again multiple times before the proper fit is found. The passive voice in that last sentence is intended. Good typologies emerge, because like stories, typologies have their own vitality. But the analyst does not wait passively for that emergence; resorting and renaming bring the typology into being. No rule says when to stop; eventually, the analyst and enough others recognize the types as expressing something significant about the stories they describe.

Typologies should never be considered final. I did not intend my typology in *The Wounded Storyteller* to be closed; on the contrary, I expected others to add other types. The closest to a fourth type that I have heard might best be called the illness-as-normality narrative. The plot involves minimizing the effects of illness. Life is lived around the illness, accommodating it as necessary, but ignoring it as much as possible. Claims are often made to be living a "normal" life, despite the illness.[15] The heroism of this narrative is its will to live as fully as possible in spite of the illness. Meaning is sought not in the illness itself, as in quest stories, but in life around the illness. Diseases involving long-term deterioration seem to lend themselves to illness-as-normality narratives. The methodological point is that a dialogical typology builder is always listening for another type.

* * *

A different exemplar presents a narrative typology that does not involve life-story narratives and is especially clear in its distinction between *narrative* and *story*. The medical historian Anne Harrington organizes her history of mind-body medicine around five narratives.[16] Harrington understands stories, as I do, as "living, local, and specific" (24). Narratives, in contrast to stories, are templates that people use as resources to construct and understand stories. Harrington compares narratives to rules of grammar that are learned by constant exposure until reliance on them becomes second nature, even as a speaker continues to refine use of those resources (24–25). Again, people's abilities both to tell stories and to understand stories depend on their narrative resources. Stories depend on their respective narratives; a story outside any narrative is a fish out of water: it can't breathe and usually will have a quick end, although, to press the metaphor, the occasional fish out of water becomes a new species on land. This occasional story persists and becomes the basis of a new narrative.

Based on this narrative/story distinction, Harrington proposes six narrative templates into which most stories of mind-body medicine fit. The stories might be clinical, promotional, experiential, or pop cultural; Harrington's argument is that each gains traction by its appeal to a narrative template. She calls these narrative templates "The Power of Suggestion," "The Body That Speaks," "The Power of Positive Thinking," "Broken by Modern Life," "Healing Ties," and "Eastward Journeys" (25), names that are as evocative as they are descriptive. As one example, the power-of-suggestion narrative "begins by introducing at least two characters: a vulnerable, naïve, or needy person (often a patient, quite often a woman) and an authority figure (typically a doctor, healer, hypnotist, or priest, and invariably a man)" (33). The narrative then moves to "a series of exchanges" between these characters, in which "the patient is helpless to resist." The patient believes, does, and actually experiences whatever the authority figure says. The resolution of the narrative occurs when "the authority figure's words and acts seem to open up channels of communication between the patient's mind and body that are normally impassable" (ibid.). That opening results in some form of healing, which is where the story ought to end. But as Harrington notes, usually "recovery is only temporary" (ibid.).

Not all of Harrington's narrative types are chronologically sequential, but the power-of-suggestion narrative is older than the broken-by-modern-life narrative. This latter template corrects flaws in earlier narratives by casting humans as a new kind of character, as Harrington summarizes:

> When we tell stories based on this narrative template, we are no longer the passive creatures who are healed in response to the suggestions of powerful authority figures ("the power of suggestion"); nor are we people who find ourselves physically healed when we have the courage to face and confess our secret sins and traumas ("the body that speaks"); nor, again, are we the fortunate possessors of wells of energy we can tap to heal ourselves ("the power of positive thinking"). Instead, we are complex, self-regulating machines who must husband our energies properly if we are not to risk permanently damaging ourselves. (140)

In the final narrative type, Eastward Journeys, the body-as-machine metaphor is repudiated in favor of "appreciation of the sufferings of the whole person" (206). In this narrative someone takes a journey: either physicians or scientists go east, or spiritual leaders come west. An ancient wisdom is imparted, and at the end "we can have the best of the East without abandoning all that we value from our own traditions" (207).

Harrington's goal is neither to debunk these narratives nor to find the one true narrative, any more than my goal in *The Wounded Storyteller* was to recommend a single narrative according to which people ought to tell their illness stories. Harrington writes that in the course of her research on how bodies behave badly—that is, not according to the prediction of Western biomedicine—she "learned the stock narratives of this community—heard them told and enacted over and over by my colleagues" (252). She found herself "struck by what a 'storied' world I had entered. I wondered where the stories had all come from, and what roles they were serving" (ibid.).

Here again a narrative analyst speaks about stories as if they had lives of their own, which I contend they do, in a symbiotic way. The same language is used in Harrington's initial rules for what stories are: "a story selects . . . ," "a story identifies . . . ," and a story "affirms the importance of certain values" (21). To call the field of mind-body medicine "a storied world" is to recognize that in this field, *stories are actors*, but these actors are constrained by a finite number of narrative templates. Stories in any field can and often do draw on more than one template, but the templates are the fundamental narrative resources that set the terms of thinking, acting, and even imagining in this field. Nor are stories all that is acting. In the field[17] that both *The Wounded Storyteller* and *The Cure Within* describe, bodies get well or die, often regardless of the stories being told about them. Bodies also resist narratives, giving rise to stories about that resistance, and these stories will gain traction or not depending on whether they show sufficient affinity to existing narratives. Sometimes a new story can create what appears to be a new template, but in the world of narrative, very little is ever new.

Harrington does not use Donna Haraway's and John Law's term *material semiotic*, but if I understand her correctly, she could have. Harrington's narrative configuration of the mind-body field understands both stories and bodies as equally fleshy and symbolic, thinglike and signifying. Her goal seems to be that of any typology building: naming the fundamental types of stories to enable a better reflective grasp of practices, their motivations and their ideals. Her types focus on specific characters who engage in prescribed courses of action toward ends that become taken for granted within that narrative frame.

To return again to the fundamental question of the value of such a typology, there may be nothing outside stories, but naming the types of narratives enables people to understand what stories they are telling and how their own responses and plans—their sense of possibility—are conducted by those stories. Harrington's analogy to rules of grammar is useful. People can tell stories without conscious awareness of narrative types, just as they can speak without a self-conscious knowledge of grammar. But without that knowledge they cannot speak reflectively. Aligning stories within narratives is ultimately aligning decisions about how to live. Narratives make some possibilities available and foreclose others. In Harrington's work, people face choices whether to engage in mind-body medicine, either as a practitioner, a patient, or a spectator. They need to know what kind of stories they are getting themselves into. And that is the ultimate value of any typology of narratives. Humans live their lives getting themselves into stories. We need help reflecting on what these stories are, and what the choices among them are.

Harrington does not present her typology as closed; she works hard not to finalize mind-body medicine or claim to know its possibilities or limits. She does offer a kind of mapping, so that those within the storied world can better know themselves, and those outside can perceive forms and regularities, where before there seemed to be only oddities and eccentricities. The dialogical trick with typologies is keeping them open.

STORIES AND STORYTELLING AS DOCUMENTS OF AN EFFECT

In 1973 the sociologist Kai Erikson was asked to travel to Buffalo Creek, West Virginia, to document the effects of a flood that occurred on February 26, 1972. A dam burst, releasing 132 million gallons of black water, a by-product of mining, onto the villages on the hillside below.

> It was already more than water, full of coal dust and other solids, and as it broke through the dam and landed on the banks of refuse below, it scraped up thousands of tons of other materials, the whole being fused into a liquid substance that one engineer simply called a "mud wave" and one witness described as "rolling lava." The wave set off a series of explosions as it drove a channel through the smoldering trough of slag, raising mushroom-shaped clouds high into the air and throwing great spatters of mud three hundred feet up to the haul road where a few men were returning from the mines. The rock and debris dislodged by those explosions were absorbed into the mass too. By now, there were something like a million tons of solid waste caught up in the flow.[18]

The wasteland caused by this wave is difficult to comprehend. "And scattered somewhere in all this litter were 125 bodies," Erikson writes, "hanging from tree limbs, buried under piles of silt, or washed up limp on the banks of the creek" (40). At the time he wrote, seven bodies had still not been recovered. Others were too damaged to be identified and had to be buried in a common grave.

Erikson was retained by the law firm representing the survivors of Buffalo Creek in a class-action suit against the mining company. His narrative analysis is thus uniquely focused in origin and purpose. He was to write a report and then testify in court to show the extent of the suffering caused by the mining company's negligence in the dam's construction. The core of his testimony is his description of what he calls the "loss of communality," using that word rather than the more familiar *community* "to underscore the point that people are not referring to particular village territories when they lament the loss of community but to the network of relationships that make up their general human surround" (187). The interest of his work as a form of narrative analysis, however, centers not on what survivors of the flood told him about their lives since the disaster, but rather on how they told their stories.

Erikson notes "the extraordinary repetitiveness of the comments people make" in stories about their current lives. His analysis of this repetitiveness exemplifies how to study stories as documents of an effect—in this instance, the flood—on those who experience it. Erikson focuses more on the mode of storytelling than on the content of the stories. The stories are documents of the continuing effects of the flood; those effects are made visible in the material form of the storytelling:

> This study is based on thousands of pages of transcript material, whole packing boxes full of it, yet a researcher is very apt to conclude after rummaging through these data that there is really not very much to say after all. This is not because the material is contradictory or difficult to interpret but because it is so bleakly alike. I noted earlier that the psychiatric evaluations seem to indicate that virtually everybody who managed to survive the flood has suffered at one time or another from anxiety, depression, apathy, insomnia, phobic reactions, and a pervasive feeling of depletion and loneliness. What makes these data so frustrating is that one reads and hears the same remarks again and again, almost as if a script had been passed around the creek. (198)

Erikson does not put his research team to work coding the data; instead, he listens, and he thinks about what he is hearing, which is repetition. He then asks how every story could sound "as if a script had been passed around," which is not likely because "the survivors are scattered all over the area and do not keep in close touch with one another." And, "those who do keep in touch generally make a point of talking about something else" (ibid.).

Erikson presents survivor stories in long transcribed segments, often following the same participant for several pages. The quotation length is closer to common practice in oral history, which Erikson's work is often close to. These segments are organized within chapter sections with titles that might be expected: "Morale and Morality," "Disorientation," "Loss of Connection," "Illness and Identity," and "The Illusion of Safety." These titles do not designate themes of individual survivor experience. They are segments of what emerges as a collective or community story. Again, the content of what survivors report matters less than their tone of reporting, and Erikson's sensitivity to that tone does as much to make his work a narrative analysis as the quotation length of participants' testimony.

The measure of the effect of the disaster—how it can be heard in survivors' stories—is not exactly silence but more precisely absence. With the loss of communality, survivors "lost their navigational equipment, as it were, both their inner compass and their outer maps" (200). Survivors "found that they could no longer mobilize whatever resources are required for caring and nurturing" (227). Among these resources are their stories. What was lost in the flood was the crucial connection of stories to place and of stories to relationships with others who share the same narrative habitus: people who not only knew the same stories but who shared an unspoken but compelling understanding of what any story required of them, be that laughter, or a knowing nod, or action. The flood so thoroughly disassembled people's lives that they had no resources left with which to reassemble. Reactions that could be described in individual, psychiatric terms are better understood as the loss of affiliations that make subjectivity possible. Erikson writes: "A good part of their personal strength turned out to be the reflected strength of the collectivity—on loan from the communal store—and they discovered that they were not very good at making decisions" (215). Not very good, that is, once the "communal store" was no longer there.

Stories should work to affiliate people, as discussed in chapter 2. But stories' ability to do this work is symbiotic, especially with places and their familiar junctures for encounters, their typical issues of weather, and the memories that they hold. When other bases of affiliation are lost, when there is nothing with which to be symbiotic, the stories go flat. They no longer work for people or with people. They become, in Erikson's phrase, "so bleakly alike" (198, quoted above). Stories become alike when they no longer bring together people who are different and contain those differences. Without interpersonal difference, bleak sameness replaces dialogical affiliation. People need communality to enable their differences by holding these within communal boundaries.

Erikson documents the traumatic effects of the Buffalo Creek flood first by listening to the stories as a whole corpus, and understanding what they tell by attending to how they do the telling. Second, he hears individual sto-

ries as expressions of a collective story, that collectivity being what
individuality possible, or not so possible after the disaster. His a'
dialogical, because Erikson does not finalize the survivors in some
diagnostic theoretical schema. The book ends like a story, describing a.
evening in August 1974 when all those who had been involved in the liti-
gation met to celebrate the award of $13.5 million and to distribute that
money. "A stranger might very well have mistaken it for a graduation exercise," Erikson writes (248):

> It was a graduation in the sense that it ended a period of uncertainty,
> vindicated a decision to enter litigation, and furnished people with suffi-
> cient funds to realize whatever plans they were ready to make. But it was
> also a graduation in the sense that it propelled people into the future at
> the very moment it was placing a final seal on a portion of the past. The
> time had come to seek new housing, to make overdue decisions, to put
> the many pieces of a shattered life back together. (248–49)

This is not a happy ending, because Erikson also recognizes "the fact that
many of the people in the school auditorium did not really know what
they would do next and had not really decided how to use their new resources" (249). That is what *unfinalized* often means: moving into a future
with little sense of how to use the resources available or even what these
resources are.

* * *

Paul Draus's study of inner city tuberculosis control in New York and
Chicago in the 1990s is a more recent exemplar of dialogical narrative analysis that balances stories' reports of what affects people in the research
field with consideration of how the storytelling performatively exemplifies
those effects.[19] Draus's fieldwork involved literally working in the field. He
was employed by city health departments to locate patients, primarily men,
who had left hospitals' infectious-disease units before their treatment was
completed. The objective was not to take them back to the hospital but to
enroll them in a program in which Draus would bring medication to them
and watch them take it. Because most of these people were homeless, finding them for each dose of medication was a considerable part of the job.
Draus had a talent for getting the men to like him. Most were not intentionally uncooperative, but keeping scheduled appointments was not part of
their repertoire, nor was it something that fit their means of survival.

Draus's stories take two basic forms. Some are stories that people tell
him in the course of longer conversations, in which these people describe
aspects of their lives: being in hospitals, suffering assault and other injuries,

meeting friends, and doing things. Other stories describe how these conversations took place. The core narrative of these stories is Draus searching
for patients, finally finding them with the assistance of contacts who may
also be patients of his, convincing them to accept treatment, and keeping
them in the treatment program despite other aspects of their lives that pull
them away.

Draus frames his study in dialogical terms. He sees the risk of perpe-
trating the "stigmatization of subjectivity itself," in which his work might
"contribute to the continued subjection of the poor and the sick" (8). He
thus commits himself to having "the actual words of subjects share space
with those of the author" (ibid.). Method here follows ethics, which produces good method, because it responds to the reality of the situation being
studied rather than tacitly colluding in perpetuating the power relations
that permeate that situation. Incremental relations of power are always reflected in the stories: most limited is Draus's power that includes no coercive authority at all and can offer only minimal rewards; then the somewhat
more coercive power of hospitals that can commit people to treatment but
cannot effectively keep them there; and finally the fully coercive power of
police who never actually appear but remain in the background.

Draus's method can be called hermeneutic insofar as he refuses ever to
take himself out of the dialogue and present his participants' stories as doc-
umenting a space that they occupy but he is not part of. Stories do describe,
certainly. "Narrative," Draus writes, "allows us to see homeless persons as
part of a larger whole, both socially and historically" (152), which in itself
is a conventional methodological statement. But then he adds: "These are
not 'illness narratives,' in the sense that they chronicle a person's subjective health experience; rather they are stories about particular individuals
as they interacted with me, and the medical institution I worked for, over
a period of time" (ibid.). In Bakhtin's terms, stories are always *addressed*.[20]
Draus understands himself not as collecting data but as being the addressee
whose presence enables people to tell their stories. "Just by being there
and listening I may have provided a form of care that she had never before
had" (211), he writes about one of his clinical relationships that is also a
research relationship.

Draus's responsibility as addressee is as much an ethical demand as a
methodological problem. His response is to allow his participants' words to
carry their own message—not to analyze their stories but to witness them
and to connect them. These connections are between multiple participants'
stories, between participants and medical institutions, and between lived
realities and social policies. But in demonstrating these connections, the
ethnographer never usurps the participant's perspective. How Draus writes

of his participants exemplifies what Bakhtin claims for Dostoevsky's dialogical practice: "The character . . . I perceived as the author of a fully weighted ideological conception of his own, not as the object of Dostoevsky's finalizing artistic vision."[21]

As in most fieldwork, the researcher forms a particular relationship with one participant who becomes the center of the report. For Draus, this character is Isaiah. Much of what Isaiah says and does is interpretable within categories of disease and psychopathology. Draus refuses those interpretations. Here is a brief segment—some interview transcriptions go on for several pages—of Isaiah telling a story about how health-care workers who know he has TB respond to him:

> You'll be sittin' at the desk talkin' to someone and they'll get up and walk away from you like they got to do something very urgent, and they, when they come back, they keep their distance about two or three feet from you. And you wondering what's wrong. You wondering what's wrong, and then, when you're into the hospital, or something, you got doctors that tells you the good things that you can deal with about this, and some of the bad things too. You get confused, and you constantly want to know, what gonna happen to me, how will it hurt me, what is this gonna do, is it gonna be swift, fast, or, you know, slow: bit by bit. (162)

The continuous present tense of this story omits details of time and place, but one thing clearly leads to another, characters are established, and Trouble (with Kenneth Burke's capital *T*) generates suspense. I have heard Isaiah's story of stigmatized invisibility told with only slight variation in support-group meetings by any number of middle-class cancer or heart patients. They spoke differently but were no more articulate in their indignation. As Draus writes: "Beneath Isaiah's demographics and diagnosis lived an intelligent, independent, and somewhat troubled man, existing within a dense set of enduring social networks which he loved but also deeply distrusted" (163). If Isaiah's thoughts often are disconnected, even to himself, Draus tells readers enough about the shelters where Isaiah sleeps, the street corners and vacant lots where he hangs out, and the hospitals where he is treated for us to understand Isaiah's troubled nature to be what those conditions seem most likely to produce and what they certainly would sustain.

Draus's dialogical balance is in showing his participants' lives as inextricable from the places where they live, the endemic problems like violence and substance abuse that define those places, and the personal, communal, and institutional networks that they both love and distrust. Yet the participants are never reduced to a set of conditions that produce them. To finalize them as nothing more than the inevitable product of their living conditions would be another form of oppression. Draus respects Isaiah too much not to allow him to make choices, even when these choices are blatantly self-destructive, which is a word that is difficult to use in a purely descriptive sense without doing what Draus worries about: stigmatizing a person's subjectivity.

Draus appoints himself a task very close to that for which a law firm hired Erikson: to speak of how conditions have affected people. Like Erikson, he hears their stories not as descriptions but as performative evocations. Unlike the people of Buffalo Creek, Isaiah is not a victim, yet *flood* as metaphor seems appropriate to describe his life: it is flooded, and he is swept along. The real commonality between Erikson's work and Draus's is, for me, their use of narrative analysis to express indignation. Draus describes the reemergence of tuberculosis in American cities:

> The threat that TB posed to the American population as a whole was not great, even at the peak of the resurgence. Because of those very same factors of inequality and segregation, its spread was largely limited to the urban cavities inhabited by the poor. Therefore, the lesson that tuberculosis should have taught—that inequality and poverty have a price— was not learned. Or rather, that *price was seen as acceptable*, compared to the much larger cost of pursuing equality and social justice, both essential elements of community health. (252, emphases added)

Erikson goes to court to prevent the price of the Buffalo Creek flood from being seen as acceptable. That disaster also occurred in one of those "cavities inhabited by the poor," but a rural one. Dialogical narrative analysis is one way to represent people whose afflictions are regarded, or disregarded, by others as an acceptable price.

STORIES AND GROUP ASSEMBLING

Within academic sociology, scholars of social movements focus most consistently on how stories bring people together into groups and hold those groups together.[22] Yet the best description of what stories do for groups may be Bruno Latour's term from science studies, FABRICATION MECHANISM.[23] Latour's presupposition is that groups do not exist as fixed entities like buildings (although how fixed buildings actually are depends on how closely one looks at materials, their flux and decay). Groups are processes of people coming and going, pushing and pulling, weakening ties and strengthening them. Thus Latour's maxim: there are no groups, only group assembling. The work of assembly is done by fabrication mechanisms. One example is the spokesperson who by speaking for the group assembles it as having a voice and unity of purpose. Spokespersons make groups recognizable not only to outsiders but to the members. I propose stories as another fabrication mechanism.

The research question is how particular stories fabricate particular groups. Francesca Polletta studies stories in a variety of social movements, and her research on the American civil rights movement in the 1960s exemplifies narrative analysis as a way of understanding how groups come together and hold together.[24] Polletta argues that premovement stories— stories of atrocities and indignations that showed the need for a civil rights movement—did less work than stories about the movement itself. A social movement generates stories that fabricate the growth and future direction of the movement. Premovement stories are left behind as less useful fabrication mechanisms.

Polletta, like an oral historian, is interested in the correspondence between stories-as-fabrications and how events actually unfolded. Here is a historical account that Polletta offers of how action turns into a story that fabricates collective action:

> On February 1, 1960 four black students from North Carolina Agricultural and Technical College in Greensborough purchased a few items in the downtown Woolworth's and then sat down at its whites-only lunch counter. Told that they would not be served, they remained seated until the store closed. "Four guys met, planned, and went into action. It's just that simple," Franklin McCain explained later to those who wondered who had planned the demonstrations. The Greensborough Four came back the next day, and the next, now joined by students from surrounding colleges. Students in other cities began to sit in. Within a month, the sit-ins had spread to thirty cities in seven states. Within two months, they had spread to fifty-four cities in nine states. By mid-April, fifty thousand people had taken part in the protests. (32)

One version of the sit-in story is the student account that becomes the title of Polletta's book: "It was like a fever" (320). But using this phrase as her title is ironic, because Polletta shows that the spread of the sit-in movement was not like a fever. For the spokesperson whom Polletta quotes to call the movement's origin "that simple" is more useful as a fabrication mechanism for the movement—spinning a story that will continue to collect people and move them—than as a historical description. It was not that simple. Polletta offers a different descriptive account:

> The Greensborough Four were members of an NAACP Youth Council and were in touch with activists who had led sit-ins in Durham in the late 1950s. When the protest began, a network of ministers, NAACP officials,

and other adult activists contacted colleagues to spread the news, trained students in sit-in techniques, and persuaded other adults to support the cause. This was far from the "grass fire" that protesters and observers described. (32–33)

Polletta describes the same narrative reconstruction process in what became the story of Rosa Parks's refusal to sit in the back of the bus, as segregation laws required. "They had considered a boycott after fifteen-year-old Claudette Colvin was arrested but abandoned the idea when the unmarried Colvin became pregnant. Parks, who was married, middle-aged, and a churchgoer, fit the bill as a test case . . . the ground work had been laid long before Parks boarded the bus" (33). Rosa Parks made a better story than Claudette Colvin, and one task of movements is to make good stories.[25]

Movement stories that fabricate the group are fabricated; actions are planned to generate an already imagined story of those actions.[26] Then a story is told that reconstructs what happened as spontaneous. "It was like a fever" is a great trope for spontaneity. What matters is not that it is also a poor trope for what actually happened, although on Polletta's account it is. The trope may be bad history, but it is a vital fabrication mechanism. The trope expresses what the group needed for its development.

Polletta's analytic question then becomes *why*: "Why do [activists] cast themselves not as strategic actors but as swept up by forces over which they have no control?" (33). Studying Polletta's work as an exemplar of narrative analysis, we need not follow how she answers this question. She seeks to avoid depicting activists as being overly rational in their strategizing. She understands that no one can control stories, because stories always lend themselves to multiple and thus unpredictable interpretations. This capacity for openness to interpretation is what makes stories good fabrication mechanisms.

Stories, Polletta observes, blend the predictable and the unpredictable. The story makes sense because, as she writes: "it is familiar. Indeed, we find a story coherent because it resonates with stories we have heard before" (10). Yet stories need a complementary element of unpredictability because "a story that was so familiar as to be entirely predictable would be no story at all" (ibid.). Listeners have to work to sort out the unpredictable aspects, and that work generates engagement. Polletta writes:

> Stories require our interpretive participation. They require that we work to resolve ambiguities as events unfold, to anticipate the normative conclusion to which the story is driving. Indeed, the closure stories promise may never be fully realized. A story's meaning may remain elusive. Stories are thus distinctive in their openness to interpretation. (Ibid.)

Polletta's narrative analyses return to this fundamental insight that stories do their work by requiring interpretive participation. Once again, the crucial point is that people get caught up in stories. Stories and social movements have a natural affinity because stories *move* people, in the sense of both generating emotions and in creating agitation that shifts people's position.

Stories are also good fabrication mechanisms because they offer a common focus of agreement for people who, in many respects, do not agree and would not act together. In a non-civil-rights example, Polletta describes the mobilizing effects of a 1962 news story about a woman who sought a therapeutic abortion because she had used Thalidomide. The story, she observes, "is actually open to various interpretations" (19), and in this case the interpretation that determines the story's principal use is not the intention of the storyteller.

> It could be read as the story of a mother of four and her husband who were subjected to the whim of a hospital board (and therefore as an argument for abortion on demand); or as about the clear need for therapeutic abortions (and therefore as an argument for clearer rules); or as about the dangers of Thalidomide (as the reporter actually intended the story). (Ibid.)

Here we reach the crux of why stories are good at assembling groups:

> Far from discouraging concerted action, the story's ambiguity may have enabled groups with very different agendas to come together in a common stance of indignation. The groups that rallied to support a legislative bill that would relax restrictive abortion rules included public health officials concerned about the incidence of criminal abortions, medical professionals who wanted legal protection for the therapeutic abortions they were already performing, activists who wanted the repeal of all abortion laws, liberal religious groups, and civic groups such as the Jaycees and chambers of commerce—the latter comprising mainly family men who disliked granting professionals the right to make family decisions. These groups did not form a natural coalition of interests. The story's openness to interpretation probably did not *create* interests in contention, but it may have allowed diverse groups to see their interests as alike enough to act collectively. (Ibid.)

The story held together the groups that it mobilized because it did not require any one group to state too explicitly what its interest was. Narrative ambiguity allowed disagreements between cooperating groups to remain latent.

Stories often express values, but as Polletta observes, "a narrator rarely announces the moral explicitly" (88). Stories make good fabrication mechanisms, and people tell stories rather than present arguments in other forms, because stories keep their principles implied. The scope for individuals and groups with differing values to have some stake in the story is thus left open. Polletta recognizes that "all discursive forms are, at some level, allusive." "But," she continues, "audiences *expect* good stories to be interpretable more than they do good arguments or good reports" (89).

Polletta had a unique opportunity to study exactly how people engage one another's stories. She followed an online site in which people with diverse memories of and emotional investments in the terrorist attacks of New York City on September 11, 2001, exchanged views about how the site of the Twin Towers should be reconstructed. The stories never actually fabricate a group, but the sheer number of stories and the capacity to follow message threads allow some provocative observations about how people respond to stories. Polletta was especially interested in whether and how stories facilitate dialogue. She offers two possibly contradictory observations. First, most stories are *responsive*, told in response to another story. "Far from being aimed at personal self-expression rather than mutual understanding," she writes (98), "personal storytelling in the online dialogues was both occasioned by other people's remarks and invited commentary, interpretation, and more storytelling."

This impetus to dialogue is noted with reservations, however. "Perhaps the most sobering finding was that, more often than not, people did not respond to their fellow participants' claims at all. Less than half of the claims people made, whether by way of stories or reasons, elicited at least one response" (98). Those like me who wish to remain optimistic about the human propensity for dialogue might reply that amid so many postings exchanged among people who are otherwise strangers, it is good news for dialogue that as many as half the messages were responded to. But that also shows how numerical data, like stories, are always open to interpretation.

INSTITUTIONAL EMPLOTMENT OF INDIVIDUALS' STORIES

At the risk of pressing the breath metaphor entirely too far: on some occasions, stories seem to suck the air out of those who are constrained to tell them; in such instances symbiosis can edge closer to being parasitism. Those situations occur at one end of the continuum of variation in how much creativity people can exercise while working with the narrative resources available to them in an institutionalized setting. Dialogical narrative analysis can study either end of this continuum; the following concerns research on stories imposed on people by groups and institutions.

James Holstein and Jaber Gubrium, reporting research on a support group for relatives of persons with Alzheimer's disease, describe how groups impose a particular narrative on their members, even when those members "felt [this narrative's] experiential stages didn't apply to them."[27] In other words, groups tell people what their stories ought to be. Holstein and Gubrium show an experienced member, Dora, not so subtly tutoring a new member, Dee, about how she should tell her story, which is also how Dee should live her life. Dee has told her story based on a narrative of continuing to care for her husband at home. Dora rejects this narrative:

> Well, then, dear, what's your problem? We're all in this together. You're no different, you just think you are. I was like you once. [Elaborates] I did everything. I had no time to think. It was get this, do that, and take care of Ben [her husband] 24 hours a day. Well, I learned the hard way and nearly put myself in the hospital. Ben's on the waiting list [for nursing home placement] at Pine Crest. God, help me, it won't come too soon. (277, brackets in original)

To assert the group's preferred narrative of caregiver experience, Dora tells a story beginning with an orientation ("Well, then, dear") that sets up a complicating action ("what's your problem?"). The complication is not Dee's husband's illness, but Dee's attitude toward that illness. Dora tells her own story as a proposed resolution to Dee's problem. Her story is that she first "did everything," which brought her to the verge of breakdown ("nearly put myself in the hospital"), until she arranged for her husband to be admitted to full-time care. How Dora resolved her problem is proposed as the resolution to Dee's problem, as she begins by saying, "You're no different." When Dee responds by persisting that her experience is different, another group member plays the trump: "You're denying it. We all try to deny it" (ibid.).

Dora's story has a broader purpose than proposing a narrative that Dee should adopt as the proper template in which to tell her story and according to which she should live her life. Dora enforces narrative conformity in the whole group, which she addresses indirectly. Details of the group's preferred stage theory of caregiving experience are less significant than the observation that most groups have templates of members' experience, expressed in a narrative. The Alzheimer's group did not make up this narrative; in its skeleton form, it reflects the recovery narrative preferred in Alcoholics Anonymous and other support groups. A person engages in behavior that is leading to destruction (for Dora, caring for Ben); she or he hits bottom (Dora's "nearly put myself in the hospital"), stops denying what the problem has been, and with external assistance, takes some action (Dora putting Ben on the nursing-home waiting list). Dora's equivalent to AA's "higher power" is the nursing home, in which she invests final authority.[28] Participation in the group hinges on new members realizing that their story is "no different" from what the recovery narrative describes but also prescribes. The price of admission for new members is telling their story as an instance of the template narrative that the group maintains as the only possible truth. A person telling any other version is in denial, an accusation that cannot be denied.

Leslie Irvine studies the same process of narrative conformity in meetings of Codependents Anonymous (CoDA). "At the meetings," she reports, members "learn to piece together events of their lives using an institutionalized formula. Each meeting brings a new installment to the story."[29] Irvine observes a distinction between narrative and story that is a crucial resource for the group to balance internal cohesion with sufficient flexibility to sustain an ideal of individual authenticity. There is a "narrative formula" that creates "a good story of codependency" (51); however:

> This is not to say that everyone in CoDA tells exactly the same story. To the contrary, they tell quite *different* stories—using the same formula. Much of the discourse's appeal no doubt stems from its ability to do both, to work at the somewhat universal level of a legitimate account of uncoupling and at the idiosyncratic level of a unique, personal history. (50)

In a footnote, Irvine distinguishes between "lite" and "greedy" groups, the difference being how much groups expect members to "forsake competing claims to time and identity" (190). In narrative terms, how much variation does a group allow in individual stories, and how closely do members have to follow the narrative formula in which the group instructs them?[30]

To call CoDA groups' recovery narrative a fabrication mechanism is to understate the extent to which the group *is* its narrative. The civil rights movement can be imagined without the Rosa Parks story or the sit-in story. Those stories were supporting actors, albeit hardworking actors. In contrast, recovery groups cannot be imagined without the recovery narrative—life spiraling downward, hitting bottom, ceasing denial and giving up control, finding some higher power that enables changed behavior. The narrative more than breathes and more than fabricates; the narrative is the group's claim for existing. Groups that exist as their narrative still vary between lite and greedy, to use Irvine's terms. Members tell stories with greater or lesser variation from the core narrative, and they maintain more or fewer ties outside the group.

A jargonistic term for what groups do when they enforce a preferred narrative is *emplotment*. That term's usefulness is most evident in Cheryl Mattingly's research with occupational therapists. To emplot is to propose a plot that transforms what are still incoherent things-that-are-happening into experience that has meaning. Mattingly writes: "A plot gives unity to an otherwise meaningless succession of one thing after another."[31] She takes the word *emplotment* from the philosopher Paul Ricoeur, for whom it is the act of making a coherent sequence out of what was simply a succession. She quotes Ricoeur's phrase, "action is in quest of a narrative" (46). Emplotment in its most basic sense is what everyone does every moment: make sense of the ongoing flow of life by endowing what happens with direction, boundaries, and general rules about what leads to what else. "To have a story at all is to have made a whole out of a succession of actions," Mattingly writes (ibid.). She understands *meaninglessness* as "when lived experience seems to be driven by no form other than brute sequence" (47). Brute sequence is a good description of how patients often feel when they arrive in the spinal-cord injury unit where Mattingly studied the work of occupational therapists.

In the spinal-cord units, debilitating injury is in quest of a narrative. In the work of occupational therapists, emplotment denotes helping young men—men being the typical victims of spinal-cord accidents—to experience their postaccident lives as not necessarily driven by brute sequence. "Although therapists do not always start out to do so," Mattingly writes, "they very often end up negotiating with patients about what dysfunctional problems therapy will address in terms of the very deepest issues of how a patient's life story will be remade to accommodate a new body" (52). Emplotment in Mattingly's sense is close to what Gareth Williams calls narrative reconstruction, discussed earlier in this chapter. But if Bill, Gill, and Betty look back to discover continuities between the present and lives already lived, occupational therapists emplot potentially livable futures. Their emplotment is positive, as opposed to the negative emplotment of cautionary tales, as when Maxine Hong Kingston's mother tells the pregnant-aunt story as a future her daughter must avoid.

Mattingly observes that occupational therapists propose emplotments such as "disability not as horrifying shame, not as existential drama, but as inconvenience—something that calls for clever practical sense rather than deep anguish" (60). That emplotment is not yet a narrative, much less a story, but it can become the basis of a narrative and of multiple stories about working out solutions to disability as a practical problem. Therapists do not assert these emplotments but propose them, and that proposal opens a negotiation as the patient adopts the emplotment or resists it. Emplotment takes definite shape as stories are co-constructed about ongoing activity. In the talk between Dee and Dora that Holstein and Gubrium report, there is no invitation to co-construct a story as caregiving progresses. Dee will either adopt the narrative that Dora emplots, or, if she remains

[handwritten at top: situations where alt stories are brought into the mix, through neg'n & enforcement.]

a group member, she will be the one who has a problem and denies it. As a group practice, that process could be called strict narrative adherence. In contrast, occupational therapists propose emplotments loosely; they change their initial proposal according to how the patient responds. They lead by seeming to follow.

The occupational therapists whom Mattingly depicts are as good at manipulating storylines as they are at working with bodies. During therapy sessions, stories emerge in conversation as co-constructions. One person does not hold the floor for the duration of the story; instead, the story emerges through conversational turn taking.[32] This storytelling-in-process fits the therapeutic task of occupational therapists, to transform patients' meaninglessness into the sense of an unfinalized future in which good things might happen. This emplotment of an open, possible future serves the practical needs of therapists who work with patients whose sense of a limited future would make them uncooperative, especially those patients with high-level paralyses for whom little improvement is possible. But Mattingly also recognizes the therapists as moral actors who are engaged for more than instrumental purposes, just as she recognizes stories as doing more than mimetic representation. Stories emplot future actions; they breathe.

Recently injured spinal-cord patients are uncomfortable with a narrative absence that equals meaninglessness. Members of CoDA groups may be too comfortable with a narrative that explains everything for them. To claim that dialogical narrative analysis helps people find the balance between narrative resources and narrative imposition that is *right for them* risks skipping over the crucial point that whoever people are is already the result of multiple emplotments. People have no "right for them" narrative outside emplotment, and most emplotments have some institutional basis or linkage. Yet Dee's resistance to Dora's asserted emplotment shows that people are not narrative dopes, ready to fashion themselves within any emplotment. What people need is the broadest range of narrative resources to work with.

HOW STORIES EFFECT ACTION

Francesca Polletta recommends the potential for narrative analysis to "zero in on the conditions in which stories gain and lose influence."[33] Such research requires observing both "how stories operate rhetorically" and "tracing variations in the story told across groups, institutional settings, and time periods" (20). The most fully realized example of this research program may be Philip Smith's *Why War?*[34] Smith's basic answer to the question posed by his book's title is that countries go to war or not because stories gain traction or not. Stories effect the "ramping up or talking down of threats" (29) that incitement to war depends on.

Smith's research is a comparative case study examining the participation or nonparticipation of four countries—Britain, France, Spain, and the United States—in three wars: the Suez crisis of 1956, the Gulf War of 1991, and the war in Iraq in 2003. His interest is in how the stories told in countries that engaged in these wars differed from those told in countries that stayed out, and so his narrative analysis is at the opposite end of the continuum from personal stories. The stories are told mostly in mass media, often quoting or paraphrasing a story told by a political leader. "This is a discourse of persons speaking not so much to each other in the concrete," Smith writes, "but rather to a generalized, overhearing Other who accumulates and assesses not only 'good reasons' but also . . . 'good interpretations'" (12). The issues, however, still follow from the fundamental questions of narrative habitus: who gets caught up in which stories, with what effect, and to the exclusion of what other possible stories?

Smith argues that stories are built in a process of "symbolic bricolage" (15) that involves characterizing people, events, and relationships—generally among nations—according to three sets of binary oppositions. "We make sense of the world, including world events, using astoundingly simple cultural resources," he writes (14). One set of oppositions involves "the civil discourse of motives," including active/passive, rational/irrational, and sane/mad as characterizations of different characters in a story (15). A second set is "the civil discourse of social relationships," including trusting/suspicious, truthful/deceitful, and straightforward/calculating (16). Third is "the civil discourse of social institutions," including rule regulated/arbitrary, law/power, and equality/hierarchy. In practice, Smith writes, "these three codes are zippered together to build up a unified discourse" (17).

This unified discourse does not, however, determine what is said or believed. Smith writes: "Binaries help us make sense of the world but do not offer an instruction manual for what to do next" (17). Stories instigate war by positioning themselves on the side of a "Discourse of Liberty" while characterizing the enemy's stories within a "Discourse of Repression" (ibid.). They establish characters who are identified with liberty or repression in specific situations. The storytelling work of such characterization is as artful for a politician as for a novelist. Storytellers can count on listeners knowing the code for hearing discourses and identifying characters within those discourses. This code is a potent resource, but as Smith puts it so well, a code is not an instruction manual. Using it requires being artful.

Smith presents what I understand as socio-narratology, because he recognizes that the same process of producing multiple stories out of few cultural resources "hold[s] true not only for myth, folktales, and fictions but also for the stories that are told about real world events" (23). Smith is doing narrative analysis because he looks to stories not as descriptions of how the world is, but as vital actors affecting how the world comes to be. His analysis is dialogical because he gives people space to interpret the stories they are told. Interpretation also has a code that is not an instruction manual. Smith understands people's key interpretive resource to be *genre*: the expectations listeners have for the kind of story being told, which in turn affects their assumptions about the kind of person telling the story. "We might look to a politician with respect, empathy, or contempt," Smith observes, "depending on the genre through which we perceive them" (20). Genre possibilities precede any particular story, but each story must *claim* its genre, and genre claims are contested.

Smith distinguishes only three genres.[35] Again, narrative resources are limited; people work with "a relatively fixed repertoire of genres and tropes" forming limited "narrative templates" (19). In the "low mimetic" genre, stories are mundane reports of mundane lives. "Characters are not strongly polarized in terms of their moral worth and nothing much is at stake . . . there is no clear trajectory to events . . . Life as represented in this genre is drab and routinized and characters are reliable and stoic," or, characters are "just like us" (24).

The tragedy/romance genre has two sides, which for Smith are complementary; unlike low-mimetic telling, both amplify what they narrate. On the tragic side are themes of descent, struggle, and fatalism. "There is an amplified awareness of suffering, an atmosphere of pathos, and a belief that human motivations are misguided and can lead only to poor outcomes" (25). On the romance side of this genre, stories follow "an upward movement of the hero, and the environment of struggle, and sometimes the conversion for the better of the forces of evil, too" (26). *Transformation* is a key theme of romances.

The third genre, the apocalyptic, depends on complete polarization between characters. The amplification of the narration now requires an all-encompassing conflict. Apocalyptic genre stories depict "events as a struggle between radical evil and the forces of fundamental good in a supernatural setting" (27), although secular versions can be told. Smith concludes: "Apocalyptic narratives are the most effective at generating and legitimating massive society-wide sacrifice and are today the only narrative form that can sustain war as culturally acceptable" (ibid.).

Smith presents these genres not as static categories into which stories can be placed, but as dynamic because each genre is subject to characteristic inflationary and deflationary pressures. Narrative inflation occurs "as the powers and freedom of the actor increase" and motivations "become more ideal and abstract and less material and base" (21). Low-mimetic genres, already base and material, can only inflate. Both tragic/romantic and apocalyptic genres are open to deflationary attacks. Because telling stories as apocalyptic ramps up threats—such stories get people marching to war—deflating that genre by retelling the story as low mimetic dampens the sense of threat. Smith describes this deflation: "If the gap starts to close between the good and the evil or events start to look less apocalyptic we can negotiate. If the object of struggle turns out to be simply some local issue then the future of the world is no longer at stake and we need not send troops to die for it" (27). Public narratives for and against wars are a contest between inflationary and deflationary pressures on genre. To decide between contesting versions, people simply have to guess. Going to war depends on genre guesses.

A brief return to Mattingly's ethnography of occupational therapists can show how flexible and useful Smith's genre scheme is. When therapists emplot disability as a series of practical problems requiring inventive solutions, they deflate the tragic genre of disability as "deep anguish" in favor of a low-mimetic genre.[36] If they emplot a future in which unanticipated good things can still happen to the patient, they inflate a low-mimetic story that is unbearably base and material into a romance. Therapists' work of emplotment conducts genre revising.

Maxine Hong Kingston's mother tells the pregnant-aunt story in the apocalyptic genre. As Kingston retells the story within her memoir, it becomes part of a romance, with the plot of how the little girl who was told that story grew up to become the memoirist. Frederick Douglass has a more complex genre problem, because the last thing he wants is for the stories about slavery in the early part of his memoir to become absorbed within a romance about how he became the confidant of presidents. Douglass needs to keep the apocalyptic story vital so that it can have political effects, but the story of his own development has aspects of romance.

Smith thus sets up a meta-interpretive schema, that is, a theory of how stories generate contests between different interpretive claims. To repeat my refrain: he is doing narrative analysis not because he takes stories as his data, but because he studies how stories act, taking people to war or keeping them at peace. Of course, stories act symbiotically with people. "Aware in a practical way of the power of narratives, actors struggle in sometimes self-interested and sometimes disinterested ways to align genres with events," Smith writes, describing this symbiosis of stories and actors.[37] Contests are often not over facts but rather are "over interpretive frames, the encompassing systems that enable us to make sense of all those details" (28). Here Smith reaches the core of his understanding of how stories work with and for people. The issue is "just why and how actors are able to act at all" (210). People are able to act, and vulnerable to be mistaken in their action, because stories require and circumscribe *genre guesses*. A genre guess asks: What outcomes follow in this kind of story? If I am in this genre of story, what therefore should I do?[38]

Before wars are fought on battlefields, they are *genre wars* "in which interested parties try to impose their version of reality."[39] That imposition is done by aligning facts into stories that make sense because they are recognizable as certain genres: "The narrative genre that is applied might work to amplify or diminish the apparent threat to which a nation is exposed, select some facts as relevant and not others, adjust the valence and spin of particular items of information" (29). Political leaders and editorialists stake their claims by telling stories in different genres, and ultimately citizens have to decide which story to believe. Smith follows the literary critic E. D. Hirsch, whom he quotes: "Every disagreement about an interpretation is usually a disagreement about genre" (29).

Genre guesses are not made all at once but are ongoing, collective efforts. "Citizens, journalists, commentators, and politicians take prior knowledge and the bits and pieces of information at hand and then, to put them together into a meaningful whole, each makes a genre guess" (31–32). As stories are spun, events "that may or may not be discrete" are brought together into a story that must establish its own boundaries. In interpretation, part of the genre guess is what these boundaries are (32). At some point the guessing has to stop and troops march or stay home. Rarely are the material and the semiotic fused with such consequence.

Smith leaves no doubt that stories play a significant part in starting wars. What he says about the inextricability of interpretation and action is so important to the rationale for socio-narratology that I quote him at length:

> In his Eleventh Thesis on Feuerbach, Karl Marx famously wrote the aphorism that although philosophers had only interpreted the world in various ways, the point was to change it. It is regrettable that such an intuitively appealing and crisp dictum should be predicated on a false distinction between interpretation and action. The genre politics of civil society can be thought of as a practical philosophical activity not as disinterested speculation, a form of engagement in which efforts are made to change history by means of interpretation and dialogue over interpretation. Readings of events and actors are thrown out into the public

sphere as speech acts with the hope that there will be some illocutionary force or performative impact. There is anticipation that these will confer legitimacy or withdraw it, change opinion, lead to political pressure. Hence this book [*Why War?*] is more than a formalist study of genres of political discourse, it is a demonstration of genre wars as a mode of human praxis. (33)

The best definition I know of Smith's last word, *praxis*, is provided by the philosopher Simon Critchley: "our historically and culturally embedded life as finite selves in a world that is of our own making."[40]

Human praxis consists in making our world, and stories are both what is made and a means of making. Socio-narratology insists that stories have, if not their own praxis, at least a symbiotic capacity to *make*. Stories make by requiring interpretation, which institutes contests; and the results of those contests have as real material effects as anyone could want or shudder to imagine. Whether the venue of activity is politics, or business, or clinical work, or family life, the performative impact of storytelling and the genre guesses made about stories are the human praxis of making the world. War is hardly the only human activity in which either threat or promise (or fear or desire) is ramped up or damped down. People tell stories to themselves and to others about their marriages and partnerships, their jobs and careers, the dependability of institutions they depend on, how their children are doing, whether the neighborhood or city is a good place to live, what the future holds. Each of these stories is told in some genre that implies a guess as to the future: is this story a romance promising transformation, or a tragedy spiraling downward; or, is it low mimetic, promising less but also risking less; or, is what looks to be low mimetic really the first act in an apocalypse?

Guesses that inflate or deflate threats do not by themselves make the stories come true. The German Jews in the 1930s who guessed that Nazism fit the low-mimetic genre were tragically wrong. Too many other Germans were acting in a different genre—the low-mimetic guess scarcely had a chance. History is not anybody's preferred story, but it is a contest between genre choices, including which groups are capable of what violence to assert their preferred story.

* * *

Smith refrains from asking whether countries were right or wrong to fight or abstain as they did. That would require another book, about how contemporary standards of right and wrong depend on the genre contests over stories of past wars: was the war a tragedy or a triumph, was it avoidable (low mimetic) or necessary (apocalyptic)? There is no outside of genre choices. As stories work with and on us humans, they create the terms of what we consider good or bad, just or unjust. Within different genres, the same danger would be considered well risked or foolish. "From the fairy tales, I've learned exactly who the enemy are," writes Maxine Hong Kingston.[41] From stories we humans learn whom to trust and distrust, what to hope for and what to fear. We are always guessing, and we learn to guess by hearing stories. How well or badly stories teach what to do is the topic of the last chapter.

How Stories
Can Be Good
Companions

6

"I bring nuisance and I bring news," said the Sly One, the corners
of his crooked mouth curling.—Loki, *The Lay of Thrym*[1]

*They are all modeled on an ineffable ideal: the dream of a perfect
social machine that will unerringly select what is good from what is
bad, and eliminate the noxious while preserving only what is
wholesome.*—Alberto Manguel, *The City of Words*

*Lives are built, so we had best become good craftspersons with the
other worldly actants in the story.*—Donna Haraway, "The Promises
of Monsters"

A *good story*—a story that people become caught up in because
it holds them in suspense, engages their imagination, and calls for interpretation—is not necessarily a *good* story, in the sense of encouraging goodness among those who tell and retell it. Stories can be the most engaging
companions but still make life dangerous precisely because they engage so
thoroughly. Many *good stories* make one point of view paramount; other
subjectivities are disregarded. People caught up in these stories forget what
the story means to those who are the objects of actions taken from the perspective that the story encourages. As one story leads to another, that next
story will probably take up the same or a complementary point of view, and
understandings of others become entrenched as a form of truth.

In the social sciences, narrative analysis generally limits itself to what
makes for *good stories* either as competent sociolinguistic accomplishments

or as narratives serving different professional, institutional, or cultural needs, thus perpetuating these groups. Socio-narratology needs to extend its concerns to the normative questions of what makes life not just performatively competent but actually good—this question is what people's lives truly depend on. This chapter opens a dialogue on living well with stories. Living well is as much about avoiding stories' dangers as about learning from their wisdom. Stories receive plenty of endorsement these days, including my own writing during the last two decades. The value of stories is no more in doubt than their inevitability. The dangers of stories are explored less often.

My basic argument is that a good life requires telling any story from as many alternative perspectives as possible and recognizing how *all* the characters are trying to hold their own. Frederick Douglass chafes at what his abolitionist sponsors ask of him, but he has the generosity of spirit and the political acumen to realize that they are trying to hold their own and do some good in a world that is hostile to their goals and dangerous to their persons as well as to his. Memoirists who work hard to get out of their family's stories realize that even when family members told hurtful and damaging stories, they did so to sustain the family as they knew it. In *War and Peace*, Princess Marya forgives Mademoiselle Bourienne's betrayal because she realizes that Mademoiselle is only trying to hold her own.

STORIES AS DIGNITY AND CALAMITY

Dialogical narrative analysis is not exclusively about people holding their own, but the stakes on what stories *do* are highest when storytellers are working hardest to sustain their dignity and sense of life's coherence against forces to which they are vulnerable. The epigraph in my book *The Wounded Storyteller* quotes Jean Améry writing about his experience of the Holocaust: "My body . . . was my calamity. My body . . . was my physical and metaphysical dignity."[2] My trope of letting stories breathe is a claim that stories are as much physical as metaphysical. As stories tell people who they are, those people are embodied as much by stories as by their flesh.[3] Stories, like bodies and in symbiosis with bodies, are people's dignity and their calamity. All the characters in the opening stories of this book's introduction are at risk of some calamity, and except in "Christmas Eve," a story supports the forces of imminent calamity. These storytellers also depend on their own stories to salvage their lives from calamity wrought by others' stories.

To distinguish stories that enhance dignity from those that precipitate calamity, the wrong approach would be to assert criteria that sort stories into the good, the bad, and the ugly, or some such categories. Unlike censorship, dialogical narrative analysis has no illusion of prescribing criteria that would proscribe certain stories. The dream of specifying criteria is another example of what Alberto Manguel gently satirizes in his epigraph to this chapter:[4] the ideal of a machine that could unerringly sort out good from bad, whether this sorting is of our stories, our beliefs, or our forms of organization and affiliation, including government. The issue of good and bad stories requires a loopier, more dialogical formulation, reflecting the recognition that stories are rarely if ever bad in themselves. What go badly are story-person-situation companionships. Things go badly most often when people who are caught up in their stories run up against other people living in companionship with different stories, and neither can hear the other.

Stories can be troublemakers but not on their own; as always, they are symbiotic with people who tell them and with situations in which telling happens. The Norse myths are wonderful stories that were notorious troublemakers when many Germans became caught up in them in the historical context of the 1930s. Not that the stories were innocent, even as isolated narratives. The Greek myths have never, to my knowledge, been appropriated for political purposes to anything like the destructive effect that the Nazis appropriated the Norse myths. In part, that reflects a difference between the moral luck of Greeks' and Germans' respective histories. But the stories themselves differ, and the differences may have played some part in shaping those histories. When the Greek gods fight, as they do in Homer's *Iliad*, they do so in loose coalitions, acting in ways that are ultimately arbitrated by Zeus; and however intense the mayhem, the conflict remains local and limited. The Norse stories are all told under the shadow of an eventual, inevitable apocalyptic battle: *Ragnarok*, the final, deciding contest between order and chaos. People who grow up on different stories develop different ideas about the aims and conduct of war.

Stories act and enact, but the responsibility falls on people to recognize which stories cause trouble in which situations and to avoid that trouble. This chapter's epigraph from Donna Haraway poses what must be the payoff of dialogical narrative analysis.[5] To paraphrase Haraway: *how can people become better craftspersons as we craft the stories that are "other worldly ACT-ANTS" in our lives?*

Responding to that question—which does not admit answering but does set before us an ideal—begins by recognizing how complex the weave of multiple stories is in any situation, how many different stories are doing different things for people and to people. Here is a story about storytelling. The journalist Jacqui Banaszynski describes her experiences in what she calls "a famine camp in Sudan on the Ethiopian border":[6]

You watch the little girls walk to the river and dig in the mud, soaking their rags with moisture that they wring, drop by drop, into their plastic jugs. You sit in the clinic where the waiting line is hundreds long. Desperate fathers thrust their babies at you, thinking that because you are a *khawaja*, a foreigner, you must be a doctor. You must be able to help. But all you have to offer is a poised notebook and some questions—suddenly too little to accommodate this reality. (3)

At night Banaszynski hears "coughing and vomiting and whimpering and keening . . . shouts, angry bursts of life, and rasps that rattle to silence as seventy-five more people die" (4). But she hears something else as well: singing. "You hear the sweet chants and deep rhythms. Each night, over and over, at about the same time" (ibid.).

The singing intrigued me. It took me several days to find out what it was. I had to go through several translators before someone finally told me that it was *storytelling*. When the villages in Ethiopia and what is now Eritrea finally got too parched or too bombed for people to survive there, they got up, en masse, and walked to the famine camps. Then they settled, in whatever little huts they could find, as a village. They continued whatever rituals they could. One of their rituals was their nightly storytelling. The elders gathered the children around, and they sang their songs. (Ibid.)

The stories that refugees sing at night work hard to sustain connection among these people and to sustain their possibility of connection to whatever gods or ancestors represent the transcendent for them. As Banaszynski tells this story, I imagine little disagreement that the refugees' stories are good. Although she tells nothing of the stories' content, of which she seems to know little, she predisposes how her readers imagine that content by describing the singing as "sweet chants and deep rhythms." Stories are good in Banaszynski's storytelling because they help people to hold their own in circumstances of calamity where dignity and identity are as much at risk as physical existence.

But the dialogue between people and stories always includes more people and more stories. If the stories that Banaszynski hears sung at night are keeping the refugees alive in the famine camps, other stories played a part in putting those people into those camps, and stories are part of what keeps them there, slowly dying. Perhaps these other stories were about ancient feuds; whatever their content, the stories precipitate one group's sense of entitlement to dehumanize another group. Stories, for all that they can be open to multiple interpretations, also have the capacity to make one truth seem inevitable. People become caught up in that truth and act on it.

A complexity of acts of omission and commission occurred for these Ethiopian refugees to be pushed to the brink of existence. The stories that precipitated commissions of violence cast the refugees as characters existing outside boundaries of moral obligation. These stories authorize pitilessness. Other stories more subtly authorize omission of efforts at refugee relief. In these narratives of omission, the refugees are cast as representatives of a problem imagined to be so extensive that response to local instances of this problem can be legitimately deferred, on the grounds that such efforts will be fruitless until the problem as a whole is addressed. The stories that omit and commit are the refugees' calamity. The stories that their elders sing to the children at night are their dignity.

LIVING WELL WITH STORIES

How, in the midst of such a complexity of stories, can dialogical narrative analysis guide people to be good companions of stories, and through that companionship become good craftspersons of their individual and collective lives? To repeat again this chapter's epigraph from Manguel, there can be no "perfect social machine that will unerringly select what is good from what is bad," because what counts as good and bad emerges only from the symbiosis of stories, people, and situations. But there can be a process of living well with stories, and I sketch one such process in three stages.

Recognize That Stories Are out of Control

Chapter 1 described Thomas King's retelling of Leslie Marmon Silko's story of how evil came into the world. An evil story was told, and once told, it could not be taken back.[7] Stories take on lives of their own; tales of ancient feuds are tragic examples. Everyday stories can go imperceptibly out of control in their useful capacity to be what Philip Smith describes as "machines for the reduction of complexity."[8] Stories make dangerous companions when they reduce too much complexity and are too good at concealing what they reduce.

Recognizing that stories are out of control requires being careful about which stories are told, and also not trusting first reactions to stories as they are heard. The need to resist being compelled by the evaluation that a story apparently proposes is evoked in an extraordinary passage by the literary critic and social theorist Tzvetan Todorov, reviewing Susan Sontag's *Regarding the Pain of Others*, a meditation on photographic and artistic images of atrocities, especially war. Todorov seeks to distinguish between the different evocative powers of images and of words. My argument will be that most of the problems Todorov associates with images are equally problems of stories, despite the significant distinctions that he observes between the two forms of signification.

> One of the great platitudes of our epoch is that images, in particular photographic or filmed images, transmit messages that are much clearer and stronger than words, which disguise the truth more than they reveal it. But in truth nothing could be less certain: a photograph can stun us, but taken out of context it may not convey any significant meaning. You see a mutilated corpse, you are moved and overcome by shock or pity; but you do not yet know who this corpse is, nor why this person has been killed, nor by whom; nor whether this is a case that warrants an appeal to vengeance, or on the contrary an appeal for peace, or whether it is only an incitement to meditate on the fragility of human existence. Sentences have a subject and a predicate, a part that delimits what is being discussed and another part that says something about it. But images are subjects without predicates: they evoke the world intensely, but they do not tell us, of themselves, what we should think about it.[9]

Todorov thus distinguishes images from words, presumably including stories, and all he says is true. But stories, despite their use of words, share many of the dangers that Todorov so clearly attributes to images.

Stories, no less than images, *evoke the world intensely*, in Todorov's memorable phrase. Listeners, like viewers, find themselves caught up in a story that claims primacy of attention. Stories put listeners in the position of hearing one perspective on one slice of reality. This selection is already an evaluation, because it excludes from consideration other slices seen from other perspectives. "What is decisive," Todorov writes, "is the choice to photograph *this* and not *that*" (29). Or, to tell this and not that. Reconsider how Banaszynski tells the story of the Ethiopian camp, using sentences like photos, directing the reader's attention to an image, then to sounds. The hypnotic effect is to cause at least a temporary breakdown of the reader's capacity to think outside the story's direction of attention. Todorov quotes Sontag: "To photograph is to frame, and to frame is to exclude."[10] This exclusion is not exactly concealment, but because the story evokes so intensely, interest is suspended in what is excluded—*that* no longer counts, only *this*. The art of storytelling is to effect that suspension of listeners' attention to anything except what the story frames. Like all arts, that effect can be put to any use. Its danger lies in its power.

Experienced storytellers know they are using the story no more than the story is using them. Among many quotations recognizing this duality, recall Eric Ormsby from chapter 1: "We do little more than hitch a ride on some obliging syllable or accommodating phrase."[11] We humans like to imagine the rides we hitch on stories—obliging plots and accommodating characters that simplify reality—as being like driving our own cars: we can go where we want, and we take for granted having to stay on roads that are already there and obey speed limits and traffic signs. The fearful possibility is that some stories are like amusement park rides that take you where they want, at their speed, and once a decision has been made to get on, the possibilities for getting off are very limited.

Todorov attributes considerable importance to stories being told in words and thus having advantages he associates with syntax. "Sentences have a subject and a predicate," he writes, "a part that delimits what is being discussed and another part that says something about it."[12] Images are comparatively deficient, being only "subjects without predicates," which certainly is correct. If we recall from chapter 1 William Labov's schematic for storytelling, the complicating action, which is the story's *subject* in Todorov's terms, is eventually subjected to an evaluation. That evaluation is Todorov's *predicate* that "says something about" the subject and can include a caution about how to understand and apply what has been evoked intensely. But in storytelling practice, such cautions are too rarely offered. Evaluations too often work as reaffirmations, not qualifications. They put a monological seal on belief in the story's point rather than qualifying or complicating belief, opening dialogue.

Stories become troublesome when evaluations—in Labov's sense of a concluding phase of the story—do not limit the intensity of the story by calling to attention the questions that Todorov elaborates: What exactly has been shown in the telling, and what response is warranted? More often, evaluations assert one response to the story as self-evident. Stories are very good at evoking intensely. One story by itself is often not good at eliciting reflection on what that story has framed, and what it leaves out of that framing; what perspective it takes, and which perspectives it excludes. Few storytellers *interrupt* the plot to call attention to everything else that is also going on at the same time.[13]

Todorov argues that humans can complement being caught up in stories with *thinking* about stories. "But images," he writes, "do not tell us, of themselves, what we should think about it"[14]—that is, what we should think about the world those images evoke intensely. Todorov separates critical *thinking* about a story from being caught up in what the image or story evokes, and such thinking is clearly a moral responsibility. Here is a significant caveat to dialogical narrative analysis's recommendation to think *with* stories, learning stories and retelling them as a way to enhance interpretive

possibilities. Companionship with stories does begin by thinking with stories, but eventually that has to be balanced by the capacity to think *about*
stories. To skip over thinking with a story risks failing to understand how
that story does its work of engaging; allowing oneself to be engaged is a significant first step to interpretation. But once engaged, to refuse the inter-
ruption of thinking about the story risks missing what the story excludes:
the other perspectives it silences or marginalizes.

The distinction between being caught up in a story and thinking about
it is not a rigid dichotomy, as Todorov illustrates. Because there is no outside of stories, Todorov has to describe *thinking* by telling another story;
he thinks *about* one story *with* another story, which may be the only way.
Todorov retells Sontag's story of a documentary photography exhibition
in Sarajevo during the war there. The exhibition presented photographs
that "mixed the images of their sufferings with those of similar atrocities
in Somalia." The residents of Sarajevo found it "intolerable" to have their
suffering "twinned with anybody else's." To which Todorov concludes: "Intolerable, yes; but it's also indispensable to anyone who wishes to think,
rather than simply to be outraged" (28).[15]

As Todorov's necessary use of a story illustrates, no *thinking about* is ever
purified and abstracted from thinking with stories. The plural in that last
sentence makes all the ethical difference: *two* stories are the beginning of
thinking, as opposed to being caught up in one story. *Two* stories instigate
dialogue. Todorov offers a significant distinction between allowing oneself
to be caught up in whatever evokes, "simply to be outraged," as he puts it,
and achieving the critical distance to reflect on that outrage, its sources,
and the cost of alternative responses to the story, including the cost of being outraged: what that outrage prevents and possibly protects the listener
from hearing or the viewer from seeing.

Two stories are necessary for thinking because each opens a critical distance from the evocative intensity of the other. The second story is most
necessary when twinning it with the first story seems most intolerable,
and those who are living through such a story insist that their situation
is incomparable. That claim to incomparability carries privileges that are
the beginning of danger: one group saying "Because of our incomparability
we can . . ." precipitates trouble for whomever becomes the object of that
group's entitlement. Introducing a second story restores complexity; that is
not the least of what is intolerable about the second story, and not the least
of what is ethical about it. If it is impossible to think outside stories—to
banish the poets, as Plato wanted—it is possible to do what the Sarajevo
exhibition accomplishes: expand the scope of the stories that people think
with. The exhibition requires dialogue, and often the most ethically nec-

essary intrusions of dialogue are experienced as intolerable to those fully caught up in a cause.

Bring In More Stories

The Sarajevo exhibition exemplifies the beginning of what Haraway, in this chapter's third epigraph, calls becoming good craftspersons with the other worldly actants in our lives, those actants including images and stories. A good craftsperson expands the dialogue to include more stories. The best response to the recognition that stories represent the world from one particular and often restricted perspective is not to dream of a perspective outside stories; that would be a view from nowhere. The response should be to bring in more stories.

"We exist in a sea of powerful stories," Haraway writes. "They are the condition of finite rationality and personal and collective life histories."[16] She then adds the antidote to the dangers and limits of humans' irremediably storytelling existence:

> There is no way out of stories; but no matter what the One-Eyed Father says, there are many possible structures, not to mention contents, of narration. Changing the stories, in both material and semiotic senses, is a modest intervention worth making. (246)

How do we change the stories? Stories are always changing as they are retold, and they are resistant to change—they change inevitably, but slowly. What stories do readily is to attract other stories, and therein lies faster leverage for change. Part of letting stories breathe is letting them do what they do, which is lead to another story. If there can be any inherent, nonrelational quality that makes a story *bad*, it is that bad stories discourage moving to another story that presents the same content from a different perspective. There are greedy stories, just as Leslie Irvine, in chapter 5, described greedy groups that want to limit members' stories and ties.

On Donna Haraway's interpretation, the biblical story of the Garden of Eden (Genesis 2–3) is a greedy story. Her objections to the story are familiar: the story's interpellation of women as the daughters of Eve, who caused the Fall; the foundational injunction against knowing; and more complex, how the story institutes categories that God sets in place—the hierarchy and separation of living beings—as forceful principles for organizing reality after the Fall. But the Garden of Eden becomes a dangerous story only when it is told by people who assert this story as *the* one creation narrative and can back up this assertion with force. Fortunately, that assertion can never be totalizing. Because the Garden of Eden is a great story, it goes out of control. The nineteenth-century poet William Blake expressed this out-of-control quality in his famous observation that John Milton, retelling the Garden of Eden story in *Paradise Lost* with the intention of justifying "the ways of God to men" (1.26), was "of the Devil's party without knowing it."[17] Milton's greatness is his ability to write a story that escapes the trap of his intentions; he creates too vivid a character in Satan. But I think Haraway wants more than a reinterpretation. She wants to bring in more stories, imagining entirely different conditions of creation.

Thomas King offers such an alternative when he juxtaposes a Native creation story to the creation story in Genesis. The Earth Diver story, which made the briefest appearance in chapter 1, begins with a woman named Charm, whose main attribute is her curiosity.[18] Charm asks parts of her body, like her toes, why they are the number they are, and this being a story, they answer. She asks Moose why it is bigger than she is. Charm also happens to be pregnant, which expresses her openness to different experiences. Fish and Rabbit recommend that Charm eat some Red Fern Root to help her cravings. She digs a hole to find some, and to make a long story far too short, she falls through the hole, which opens into the sky. So the world is going to be created not by an omniscient God, but by an inquisitive pregnant woman who makes the mistake of falling through a hole she has dug.

The earth to which Charm falls is still covered with water. The animals see Charm falling, and knowing some applied physics (which seems to be King's interpolation), they realize that her hitting the water at terminal velocity "was going to create one very large tidal wave and ruin everyone's day" (15). The water birds fly up, form a net, and catch Charm, easing her into the water. There the sea creatures realize she is not one of them, so they put her on the back of the Turtle, which is a good solution until her baby is about to arrive and more room is needed. Otter, with the help of some magic, dives deep enough to bring some mud to the surface. Charm dances and sings and grows the mud until it becomes enough space for her to have what turn out to be twins: "A boy and a girl. One light, one dark. One right-handed, one left-handed" (18). The Twins drain water off the mud into what become rivers; they create forests with trees that have nuts and fruit so that the animals can move onto the land and have something to eat. They create seasons, and finally they create human beings, assuring the animals that they will get along fine with these creatures.

King's summation of the contrast between this creation story and the Garden of Eden is another way of expressing Haraway's observation that there are many possible structures of narration:

> In Genesis, all creative power is vested in a single deity who is omnipotent, omniscient, and omnipresent. The universe begins with his thought,

and it is through his actions and only his actions that it comes into being. In the Earth Diver story, and in many other Native creation stories
for that matter, deities are generally figures of limited power and persua-
sion, and the acts of creation and the decisions that affect the world are
shared with other characters in that drama. (24)

When creation is imagined as a cooperative act—a material-semiotic dialogue—accomplished by fallible beings engaged in making the best of their
own or others' mistakes, then the story is open to other stories. Other creation stories are not *competing* narrations but complementary, participating in the still uncompleted work of creating.

As I understand King's objection to the biblical Genesis story, the greediness lies less in the story itself and more in how it has been told in historical
collusions between church missionary work and state colonization:

> If we see the world through Adam's eyes, we are necessarily blind to the
> world that Charm and the Twins and the animals help to create. If we
> believe one story to be sacred, we must see the other as secular. (25)

But does seeing through Adam's eyes *necessarily* blind anyone to the Earth
Diver story, or can it be one in a shifting sequence of perspectives? Seeing
through Adam's eyes is blinding only in settings that enforce the exclusion
of other stories. And happily, the trickster in the narrative is the narrative;
the story itself eventually turns against monological enforcement, as Blake
observed in Milton's telling of Genesis. — *creates too vivid a character of Satan.*

The Garden of Eden story, like any story, exists not only as a text but also
as a telling or a history of multiple tellings. How stories are told reinforces
their openness or closure to other stories—their comparative greediness.
King tells Charm's story in a conversational way, full of colloquialisms and
side-comments. He interrupts himself, reminding himself and his listeners:
hey, enjoy it, it's a story. He reflects on his own narrative style as adapting a
typical Native way of telling. He tells the Genesis story by quoting verbatim
from the King James Version of the Bible, which he says is typical of how
that story is told—and it may be, but only for some people, some of the
time.[19] In the Midrash version of the Creation, God creates two women,
not only Eve but also Lilith, who opens up very different possibilities.[20] The
medieval passion plays adapted versions of the Garden to fit the habitus
and the humor of their audiences. Most stories eventually slip the trap of
institutionalized, canonical telling, and any story becomes how it is told
by the community in which that story acts as a fabrication mechanism,
holding the group together. King's and Haraway's important cautionary
argument is that communities define themselves by their creation story

re-telly Garden of Eden
→ remix
occupy stories great + small

or stories, setting boundaries by the level of greediness with which these stories are told.

Comparing two creation stories—the potentially monological Garden of Eden in which one voice has the first and last word and the necessarily dialogical story of Charm with its multiple voices, each contributing to a cooperative work—is a long but possibly entertaining and thus memorable way of making a simple but politically crucial point: some stories and their communities are more open than others to the proliferation of stories. Among those who tell Charm's story, no one would find it "intolerable," going back to the word Todorov uses to describe the reaction to the Sarajevo exhibition, if the Earth Diver story were followed by a creation story of Raven stealing the light that he brings to earth. That does not render the Earth Diver story "merely an instance" of creation stories; instead, it imagines creation as a far richer possibility than any one story can evoke by itself. In dialogical storytelling, there must always be at least two stories. At least two stories are necessary to begin *thinking*, that is, thinking with stories.

Haraway favors the biblical injunction to be fruitful and multiply, as long as that does not carry the secondary injunction to restrict fruitfulness within boundaries, with that injunction legitimated by institutions that make a single creation story seem greedy. Haraway and King, each in his or her own idiom, reject the mistrust that seeks to defend itself by fixing categories. But after all the stories have been fruitful and multiplied, what then? What Todorov recommends as *thinking* entails a refusal "simply to be outraged" in favor of a commitment to dialogue.[21] Yet at some moments in life, people do have to judge between two stories, or between two versions of one story. Conditions no longer allow sustaining the difference between those two. At such moments, people take individual responsibility while also participating in a collective. The resulting action may assert a principle even at the risk of arrest, as in Francesca Polletta's civil-rights protest stories, or it may be going to war or refusing a war that others go to, as in Philip Smith's stories.[22] When the proliferation of stories has to end, how can stories guide action?

Cultivate Trickster Luck

Acting on stories is highly fallible, which is why many philosophers seek to supplant reliance on stories, especially in ethical decision-making.[23] But acting on stories is also deeply, inherently, and probably inescapably human, which is one reason why this book follows the tradition that stays with stories while seeking to minimize fallibility. The other reason for sticking with stories is that claims based on some version of reason seem no less fallible. There is no machine that can unerringly sort good actions from bad, and if the world is a place where stories do breathe and where human freedom is a perpetual project, the lack of such a machine is just fine. But how do we humans live in such a world as best we can? My quite serious response is that we need to be lucky, but luck is not simply chance. Luck can be cultivated.

The issue is hardly new. Allan Janik and Stephen Toulmin's *Wittgenstein's Vienna* describes a major ethics debate of the late nineteenth century. On one side was the project informed by advances in the sciences that imagined grounding all ethical action in systematically accountable reasons akin to scientific propositions. The other side understood ethics as ultimately requiring some kind of leap, akin to faith in Kierkegaard. On this latter account, an ethical action is based on commitments that can never be fully accountable or reasoned.[24] A narrative theory of action sides with the neo-Kierkegaardians, holding that people act on the basis of stories they are caught up in. Reasons follow stories, because stories teach where and how principles apply.[25] Post-hoc reasons can hold a story accountable, which is what Todorov wants, but reasons acquire their sense of rightness because they fit the stories that people think with.

Here we reach another symbiosis: if people are asked why actions in stories are good or bad, they offer reasons or principles. And when those people are pressed to account for their reasons or principles, sooner or later they fall back on stories.[26] People's belief that an act is the right thing to do, at minimum acceptable and at most ethical, is embedded in stories they learned years before, as those stories have been adapted through the narrative trajectory of repeated telling. Few of these stories may be actively recalled; they are mostly a tacit resource. Oral histories, research interviews, and therapy sessions are among the rare occasions when life's narrative sedimentation is excavated and stories are articulated. These forgotten stories are not an instruction manual, to use Philip Smith's metaphor from chapter 5.[27] And even if these forgotten stories were a kind of instruction manual, people need not follow *those* instructions—they can and do seek other instructions from other stories.

To find the heroic exemplars of this paradoxical recognition that stories are highly fallible but also humans' best companions when life reaches an impasse, I turn to memoirists. While I wrote this book, I asked myself why I kept coming back to stories from memoirs; why are they my chosen genre? One answer is that memoirists live always on the cusp of some next circle of stories. They know there is nothing outside stories, but they also know that the story they have grown up on is either a ghost, as it is for Sharon O'Brien and Maxine Hong Kingston, or too limiting as a horizon of who they might become, which seems to be Frederick Douglass's recognition as he grows increasingly uncomfortable telling his slavery story, night after night, constrained to comment as little as possible. To slip out of this trap, memoirists create a new story in which the old story becomes one actor cast to play a supporting role. What could be called critical memoirs, or maybe trickster memoirs, originate with an existential break when the old story no longer sets the terms in which the memoirist will hear or disregard the call of new stories. The old story no longer selects and evaluates for the memoirist. Life after this break is best described by O'Brien's wonderful metaphor of the family silver, once such a potent force as it elevated her family and then divided them, now distributed among the other knives, forks, and spoons in O'Brien's utensil drawer. Old stories *take their place* in a past that is still resonant but no longer has the power to set parameters of the future.

Memoirists retell the stories they have grown up on to sort out which companions they want and need in the present moment of their lives. In doing this, memoirists share certain qualities with the trickster character in folktales: they slip out of traps, they shape-shift, they have a sense of humor, and most relevant here, they accept the moral ambiguity of their acts. "We may well hope our actions carry no moral ambiguity," writes Lewis Hyde on the need for trickster figures in human thought, "but pretending that is the case when it isn't does not lead to greater clarity about right and wrong; it more likely leads to unconscious cruelty masked by inflated righteousness."[28] True enough—but how do memoirists help the rest of us as we humans struggle to find clarity and avoid unconscious cruelty? They teach us how to cultivate being lucky.

"In classical Greece," Hyde writes, "the lucky find is a *hermaion*, which means a 'gift-of-Hermes' . . . Hermes is a generous thief" (129). Hermes' greatest gift may be offering himself as a model of how to be lucky. Hyde points out that in Latin mythology, separate figures existed for "smart luck" and "dumb luck" (139). He elaborates:

> That's "dumb luck," the luck of all gamblers whose winnings never enrich them, the luck of the hotel clerk who hits the lottery and quickly spends himself into bankruptcy. It's sterile luck, luck without change. "Smart luck," on the other hand, adds craft to accident—in both senses, technical skill and cunning. Hermes is a skillful maker of the lyre, and he is canny as well, leveraging the wealth his *hermaion* brings . . . Thus does Hermes show us how "smart luck" responds to hermetic windfalls. (Ibid.)

Narrative habitus—the stories we grow up on—is a trap only for those who rely on dumb luck. All of us humans are cast into stories according to our luck. The memoirist adds craft to accident, turning the stories she or he grew up on into a *hermaion* and leveraging that. To learn smart luck, listen to enough stories and retell the stories that are listened to, in order to hear different possibilities within them, especially the possibilities that at first seem most intolerable.

Listening to stories can be dumb—sterile and without change, in Hyde's characterization—or it can be smart, seeing opportunity for change. Smart listening does not simply react to a story according to its fit with previous stories. Smart listening hears the story as a potential *hermaion*, a lucky find, a gift that will require working with but can bring riches. Having heard a story, retelling it in the right place at the right time and especially to the right people also requires luck that can be smart or dumb; that right occasion of telling is another *hermaion*.[29]

THE ETHICS OF DIALOGICAL NARRATIVE ANALYSIS

Dialogical narrative analysis begins with how stories give people a sense of who they are. Then it addresses how stories connect: how affiliations, groups, and communities form because people know the same stories and make sense of these stories in the same way; these stories make people's actions and choices recognizable to one another. Dialogical narrative analysis considers how stories make human lives good by providing ideals, imagining hopes, providing models of resistance to injustices, and feeding imaginations of how life might be not only different but better. But dialogical narrative analysis also has to recognize the dark side of narrative imagination, which is its exclusivity. Stories make too evident and easy the separation between *us* who have names and faces and *them* who are known only by their unjustified opposition to us and who must therefore be opposed. Stories lend themselves to the binary logic most clearly exemplified by stories that precipitate war: *our* stories are true and justified; *their* stories are biased, hateful, and unjustified.

Dialogical narrative analysis prescribes no ethical criteria, yet it also resists moral relativism. The recognitions that there are always more stories and that any story enacts a particular perspective need not lead to the nihilism of believing any story is as good as any other story. This chapter has suggested some fairly obvious qualities of less-dangerous stories, including openness to more stories; depiction of characters who acknowledge mistakes and work to set things right; making heroes of characters who cooperate; and giving antagonists names, faces, and purposes that cannot be immediately dismissed. Less-dangerous stories make the world and actions *more* complicated.

Stories are Janus-faced: at first stories simplify complexity for humans living in a world that can overwhelm us with perceptual possibilities, but then stories turn around and complicate reality. Translating reality into story underscores reality's openness to multiple interpretations and its inherent morality. Less-dangerous stories and less-dangerous storytelling occasions instigate questions about what to simplify and what effects different simplifications will have. Those who raise such questions are like the weaver of oriental carpets who realizes it would offend the gods not to leave a slight flaw. Stories are less dangerous when they contain an opening to their own unraveling.

Humans' dignity depends on our stories continuing to show us characters working in specific circumstances, finding ways to be better in all the folktale virtues: bravery, wit, faithfulness, perseverance, companionship, love, discernment. Humans' calamity begins with stories that project unrecognized fears onto others; stories that imagine others only as threats; stories that, to paraphrase Hyde, are so convinced of containing no moral ambiguity that they lead to unconscious cruelty. Some threats are real and some fights worth fighting. Stories are good when they are rich in details about when and where to act. In good stories, when heroes do fight, they do so only after initial reluctance, or else they learn from the error of insufficient reflection. These stories do not present themselves as simple models for action. They do not direct action directly but conduct it by indirection. Characters in good stories do not exemplify what anyone anywhere must do; they are doing what they have to do, where and when they find themselves. Their doing does reflect virtues that are good, but how anyone else applies those virtues will be another story.

Dialogical narrative analysis works from within storied lives first to show how people are holding their own, and then to open up the range of stories available to guide their efforts. Life is inherently dangerous, that danger including the companionship of stories. But the enrichment of that companionship outweighs its dangers. If we humans really have no choice but to be companions of stories, we do have all the stories in the world.

Acknowledgments

My thanks first to the hundreds of graduate students and colleagues who have attended my workshops on narrative analysis during the last decade. In 2000 Jan Morse invited me to give my first workshop at a meeting of the International Institute for Qualitative Methodology, and for several years those meetings in Banff, Alberta, were the focus of my narrative work. The geographic scope of workshops broadened first to IIQM affiliate institutions in Korea and South Africa, and then I began to receive invitations that have taken me to New Zealand and Australia, the United Kingdom and Ireland, Japan (particular thanks to Hitoshi Arima as translator and colleague), Sweden, and most recently Norway. For repeated invitations and personal kindness far beyond the conventions of academic hosting, my thanks to Bernie Carter in England, Frances Rapport in Wales, Marilys Guillemin in Australia, and Tatsuya Sato in Japan. Bernie and Marilys, more than anyone, have listened to me talk through multiple versions of this book.

Numerous workshop participants have posed questions that reoriented my thinking. After a Banff workshop, back when my presentation was heavily based on conversation analysis, a participant asked me, "What's the difference between discourse and narrative?" I suddenly realized that I was saying nothing about what made stories worth calling *stories*; this book is an extended response to that question. Many other colleagues have given me similar moments of reorientation; thanks to those I remember and apologies to those whose comments have passed into being ideas I actually believe I thought of first.

Books begin long before they are imagined, and minimal narrative reconstruction is required to tell a story of my academic life that culminates in this book. As an undergraduate at Princeton University, I majored in English within the Program in American Civilization. The interdependence of literature and art, history, and social science was simply taken for granted; literature professors lectured on history, and historians assigned novels. I was fortunate to receive my master's degree at the Annenberg School of Communications, University of Pennsylvania, at a time when the humanists and social scientists were almost evenly balanced and in daily dialogue. The Department of Sociology at Yale, where I completed my doctorate, encouraged me to take philosophy courses, focusing on phenomenology. I had little idea during these years how remarkable any of this was.

If those universities shaped my academic habitus, perhaps I see stories as I do because I enjoyed a childhood defined by them. My grandparents gave me remarkably vivid stories to grow up on. Each was a very different kind of storyteller, but all believed that a family is its stories. Stories that my parents both told and left untold about experiences during World War II were my first lesson in narrative identity: I had the sense of a great story preceding me, and of my life being some yet undefined next part of this story. The few material reminders of the war years that were tucked away in our house fascinated me with what I felt were their untold stories, teaching me the symbiosis of stories and objects. So, as always, I thank my family.

For more than a decade, my participation as a parent in the Calgary Waldorf School allowed me to see stories working in all sorts of ways: as pedagogy, as group affiliation, and as sheer delight. The school also gave me opportunities to practice amateur performance storytelling, which sometimes spills into my workshops. Although the occasions were not research, ten years of coordinating storytelling festivals as a volunteer complemented and enhanced my academic work. To understand how stories work, few observational experiences can match watching children respond (and on occasion, not respond) to storytellers who range from first-time performers to professionals. Whatever I learned from reading about narrative was sifted and tested in those hours of storytelling at the school.

This book like my last one benefited from a Killam Resident Fellowship, a program of the Killam General Endowment Fund. The importance of that award and my appreciation for it cannot be overstated. At the University of Calgary, Tom Langford as head of the Department of Sociology was unfailingly supportive of my work. The Dalla Lana School of Public Health, University of Toronto, was a gracious host during my sabbatical in 2008–9; my particular thanks to Joan Eakin, who initiated my visit. My Toronto students were the first to read a draft of this book, and their enthusiasm and constructive advice were invaluable.

The thoughtful comments of Joseph Davis and Cheryl Mattingly were particularly helpful in revising the post-Toronto manuscript, but that contribution was only part of our ongoing dialogue. At the University of Chicago Press, my thanks once again to my editor, Doug Mitchell, and to Tim McGovern and Mark Heineke. Sandy Hazel, this book's manuscript editor, made numerous improvements to the final version. The friendship of these colleagues is as beneficial as their professionalism.

The rhetoric of acknowledgments includes thanking the author's family for tolerating time taken by writing. Instead, let me thank my wife, Cathie Foote, for having such a consuming job that I had plenty of undisturbed time to work. And I appreciate her eventually coming home, so I could stop.

Notes

PROLOGUE

1. Greg Sarris, *Mabel McKay: Weaving the Dream*, Portraits of American Genius series (Berkeley and Los Angeles: University of California Press, 1994), 5.

2. Susan Sontag, *"Against Interpretation" and Other Essays* (New York: Dell, 1969), 14.

3. Barry Unsworth, *The Songs of the Kings* (New York: Norton, 2003), 192.

4. Alasdair MacIntyre, *After Virtue: A Study of Moral Theory*, 2nd ed. (Notre Dame, IN: University of Notre Dame Press, 1984), 216.

INTRODUCTION: SIX STORIES ABOUT STORIES

1. Eduardo Galeano, *The Book of Embraces* (New York: Norton, 1992), 72.

2. Sharon O'Brien, *The Family Silver: A Memoir of Depression and Inheritance* (Chicago: University of Chicago Press, 2004).

3. Maxine Hong Kingston, *The Warrior Woman: Memoirs of a Girlhood among Ghosts* (New York: Vintage, 1989 [1975]).

4. Leo Tolstoy, *War and Peace*, trans. Anthony Briggs (New York: Viking, 2006).

5. This understanding of emplotment is my own gloss on Cheryl Mattingly's usage in *Healing Dramas and Clinical Plots: The Narrative Structure of Experience* (Cambridge: Cambridge University Press, 1998). Mattingly's research is considered in detail in chapter 5.

6. Words appearing in small capitals are entries in the glossary.

7. Allen Feldman, *Formations of Violence: The Narrative of the Body and Political Terror in Northern Ireland* (Chicago: University of Chicago Press, 1991).

8. Joan Didion, *The White Album* (New York: Farrar, Straus and Giroux, 1990), 11.

9. Frederick Douglass, *Autobiographies* (New York: Library of America, 1994), 367 and 662, original italics. Douglass wrote three versions of his *Autobiography*. The same story is repeated verbatim in the editions of 1855 and 1893. Other stories do change between the two editions, and why Douglass keeps changing them may be explained in part by this story.

10. For historical context of the escaped-slave narrative in the nineteenth century, see Ann Fabian, *The Unvarnished Truth: Personal Narratives in 19th Century America* (Berkeley and Los Angeles: University of California Press, 2000). Fabian emphasizes the problem that Douglass proceeds to discuss, how a former slave needed to establish the credibility of his status and the truth of his stories. As real as Douglass's problem was, and as justified as he was in claiming his status as something original, slavery and captivity stories are found in Homer. Even Douglass was not making up a story without precedent.

11. Recognizable style occurs no less in stories that are artfully constructed to seem to have no style at all. Kathryn Montgomery observes that "physicians' communication about patients strives to be plain and flat and dry." Physicians call their storytelling "case presentation," and she notes that "local variants are minor compared to the fundamental uniformity that has evolved." Kathryn Montgomery Hunter, *Doctors' Stories: The Narrative Structure of Medical Knowledge* (Princeton, NJ: Princeton University Press, 1991), 52.

12. Although I know no other usage of *socio-narratology*, the idea is not original. Tod Chambers's *The Fiction of Bioethics* (New York: Routledge, 1999) applies poststructuralist narratology to the texts of bioethics, with implications for policy and clinical practice; Rita Charon applies literary narratology to clinical storytelling and medical education in *Narrative Medicine: Honoring the Stories of Illness* (New York: Oxford University Press, 2006); Hilde Lindemann Nelson's *Damaged Identities, Narrative Repair* (Ithaca, NY: Cornell University Press, 2001) examines stories that exclude and stigmatize particular groups and identities, as well as counterstories that seek to repair that exclusion; and David Morris's *The Culture of Pain* (Berkeley and Los Angeles: University of California Press, 1993) analyzes a continuum of texts, from clinical reports through fiction, that not only represent pain but construct *pain* as a recognizable and actionable phenomenon. A number of social scientific studies discussed throughout this book translate literary narratology well beyond the literary.

Roland Barthes' *Mythologies* (New York: Hill and Wang, 1972) analyzes the most eclectic range of public narratives, from literary texts to artifacts of popular culture, according to semiotic principles of how signs combine to produce meanings. His analyses may be too semiotic for current taste, but few books bridge literary and social scientific interests in stories so provocatively, and few show narratives to be so omnipresent.

Clearly, however, the founding genius of the socio-narratological impulse is Mikhail Bakhtin (1874–1975). If I cite Bakhtin less in this book, that is because quoting him precipitates discussion of what he might have meant, in his time, at that stage in his work—quoting Bakhtin leads to writing a book about Bakhtin. My earlier book, *The Renewal of Generosity: Illness, Medicine, and How to Live* (Chicago: University of Chicago Press, 2004), introduces Bakhtin and makes use of his work in a manner I now call socio-narratological.

13. David Herman, introduction to *The Cambridge Companion to Narrative*, ed. David Herman (Cambridge: Cambridge University Press, 2007), 14. Herman's emphasis on narrative competence raises the question of what happens to those who lack this competence. For studies of storytelling in conditions of impaired narrative competence, see Lars-Christer Hydén and Jens Brockmeier, eds., *Health, Illness and Culture: Broken Narratives* (London: Routledge, 2008).

14. M. M. Bakhtin and P. M. Medvedev, *The Formal Method in Literary Scholarship: A Critical Introduction to Sociological Poetics* (Baltimore: Johns Hopkins University Press, 1991 [1928]), 134.

15. Brian Boyd claims, and I agree, that jokes are "the commonest of stories,

and the fastest to circulate." *On the Origin of Stories: Evolution, Cognition, and Fiction* (Cambridge, MA: Harvard University Press, Belknap Press, 2009), 392. The rapid circulation of jokes makes it easier and more important for groups to differentiate themselves based on what they find funny or distinctly not funny.

16. Wayne Booth, *The Company We Keep: An Ethics of Fiction* (Berkeley and Los Angeles: University of California Press, 1988), 11.

17. Donna Haraway, *The Companion Species Manifesto: Dogs, People, and Significant Otherness* (Chicago: Prickly Paradigm Press, 2003).

18. Boyd, *On the Origin of Stories*, 384.

19. Claude Levi-Strauss, "Myth and Meaning," in *More Lost Massey Lectures* (Toronto: House of Anansi Press, 2008), 275. I believe it is possible to read Levi-Strauss against the grain of formalist structuralism while still taking very seriously how he conceives the relation between stories and consciousness.

20. I paraphrase Erving Goffman: "Presumably a 'definition of the situation' is almost always to be found, but those who are in the situation ordinarily do not *create* this definition, even though their society often can be said to do so." *Frame Analysis: An Essay on the Social Organization of Experience* (New York: Harper, 1974), 1. Margaret Somers states the issue with respect to stories: "Although social action is only intelligible through the construction, enactment, and appropriation of public narratives, this does not mean that individuals are free to fabricate idiosyncratic narratives at whim; rather, they must 'choose' from a repertoire of stories." "Narrativity, Narrative Identity, and Social Action: Rethinking the English Working-Class Formation," *Social Science History* 16, no. 4 (Winter 1992): 591–630; quotation is from p. 608. Charlotte Linde summarizes the issue: "One's story is not only one's own. It is always told against a background of others' stories." *Working the Past: Narrative and Institutional Memory* (New York: Oxford University Press, 2009), 224.

21. Arthur W. Frank, *The Wounded Storyteller: Body, Illness, and Ethics* (Chicago: University of Chicago Press, 1995), 188n5. For a discussion situating my distinction among the diverse ways that scholars distinguish story, narrative, and event, see Linda C. Garro and Cheryl Mattingly, "Narrative as Construct and Construction," in *Narrative and the Cultural Construction of Illness and Healing*, ed. Cheryl Mattingly and Linda C. Garro (Berkeley and Los Angeles: University of California Press, 2000), 12–16.

22. Anne Harrington, *The Cure Within: A History of Mind-Body Medicine* (New York: Norton, 2008).

23. Booth, *The Company We Keep*, 14–15.

24. Bruno Latour, *Reassembling the Social: An Introduction to Actor-Network-Theory* (New York: Oxford University Press, 2005). Latour, in my reading, depends at least as much as he acknowledges on Harold Garfinkel, *Studies in Ethnomethodology* (Englewood Cliffs, NJ: Prentice Hall, 1967).

25. Margaret Somers also seems to reject understanding *social* as anything substantive: "If we want to be able to capture the narrativity of social life, we need a way of thinking that can substitute relational for totalizing metaphors.

Here I concur with Michael Mann who has written: 'It may seem an odd position for a sociologist to adopt; but if I could, I would abolish the concept of "society" altogether.'" "Narrativity, Narrative Identity, and Social Action," 608; Mann quotation is from Michael Mann, *The Origins of Social Power*, vol. 1, *A History of Power from the Beginning to A.D. 1760* (Cambridge: Cambridge University Press, 1986), 2.

26. Otto Neurath, quoted by David Edmonds and John Eidinow, *Wittgenstein's Poker: The Story of a Ten Minute Argument between Two Great Philosophers* (New York: Ecco, 2002), 163.

27. Booth, *The Company We Keep*, 16.

28. Mikhail Bakhtin, *Problems of Dostoevsky's Poetics* (Minneapolis: University of Minnesota Press, 1984.

29. I emphasize that this book's interest lies in developing a restricted subset of the much larger enterprise of narrative analysis. For a recent and useful overview of different forms of narrative analysis, see Catherine Kohler Riessman, *Narrative Methods for the Human Sciences* (Los Angeles: Sage, 2008).

30. The idea of academic analysis being continuous with everyday analysis derives from Garfinkel, *Studies in Ethnomethodology*. Leisure as the distinguishing feature separating academic work from practical activity is developed by Pierre Bourdieu, *Pascalian Meditations* (Stanford, CA: Stanford University Press, 2000).

31. "Each allows the other to be" is from a personal communication from Annemarie Mol, whose work is considered later. Mol used the phrase while explaining what count as *actors* in Actor-Network-Theory.

32. The most innovative early structuralists, like Todorov and Barthes (n. 12), did not remain structuralists for very long.

33. Julie Cruikshank, *The Social Life of Stories: Narrative and Knowledge in the Yukon Territory* (Lincoln: University of Nebraska Press, 1998), 26, emphases added.

34. Pierre Hadot, *The Present Alone Is Our Happiness: Conversations with Jeannie Carlier and Arnold I. Davidson* (Stanford, CA: Stanford University Press, 2009), 163.

35. My stance is not original. Riessman introduces her work by advising: "Students looking for a set of rules will be disappointed": *Narrative Methods for the Human Sciences*, 53. Later she adds: "I continue to believe . . . that there is no canon, that is formal rules or standardized technical procedure for validation" (186). Jaber F. Gubrium and James A. Holstein also emphasize the flexible and intuitive process of narrative analysis; see *Analyzing Narrative Reality* (Los Angeles: Sage, 2008), 27–28. On both accounts, doing narrative analysis requires not a set of procedures but what Bent Flyvbjerg calls *phronesis*—Aristotle's term most frequently translated as practical wisdom, or wisdom acquired through practice—as the basis of social science research; see *Making Social Science Matter: Why Social Inquiry Fails and How It Can Succeed Again* (Cambridge: Cambridge University Press, 2001).

36. My own past work has often been so concerned to advocate for stories that I have neglected the darker sides of storytelling. See especially Frank, *The Wounded Storyteller*, and "Just Listening: Narrative and Deep Illness," *Families, Systems & Health* 16, no. 3 (Fall 1998): 197–212. Those earlier arguments stand as documents of what sorts of intervention seemed necessary when they were written and still seem useful, but now with some qualification. The politics of the last decade have made the dark side of stories inescapable. Feldman's Irish paramilitary stories anticipate these politics. To find a community that holds its stories closest and is in turn held together by these stories, locate a group of terrorists.

CHAPTER 1. THE CAPACITIES OF STORIES

1. W. J. T. Mitchell, *What Do Pictures Want? The Lives and Loves of Images* (Chicago: University of Chicago Press, 2005), 6.

2. Bruce DeSilva, "Endings," in *Telling True Stories: A Nonfiction Writers' Guide from the Nieman Foundation at Harvard University*, ed. Mark Kramer and Wendy Call (New York; Plume, 2007), 118.

3. For a useful collection of widely disparate definitions of stories and narrative, see H. Porter Abbott, *The Cambridge Introduction to Narrative* (Cambridge: Cambridge University Press, 2008), chapter 2. The considerable disparity of these definitions, each reflecting scholarly expertise and care, is enough to turn a person away from definitional enterprises. Stories, like tools, may be best understood by what they are able to do.

4. Many scholars define *story* as the events that happen and *narrative* as the narration of these events. For an insightful critique of that terminology and way of understanding stories, see Cheryl Mattingly, *Healing Dramas and Clinical Plots: The Narrative Structure of Experience* (Cambridge: Cambridge University Press, 1998), 34.

5. Ibid., 33.

6. Brian Boyd, *On the Origin of Stories: Evolution, Cognition, and Fiction* (Cambridge, MA: Harvard University Press, Belknap Press, 2009), 157.

7. Georges Duby, *William Marshall: The Flower of Chivalry* (New York: Pantheon, 1985), 86.

8. Renato Rosaldo, *Culture and Truth: The Remaking of Social Analysis* (Boston: Beacon Press, 1989), 129.

9. Eric Ormsby, quoted in Alberto Manguel, *The City of Words* (Toronto: House of Anansi Press, 2007), 11.

10. See p. 21 above, quoting Cheryl Mattingly: "Experience is, at best, an enactment of pre-given stories." *Healing Dramas and Clinical Plots*, 33.

11. Jerome Bruner, *Making Stories: Law, Literature, Life* (New York: Farrar, Straus and Giroux, 2002), 34.

12. Mitchell, *What Do Pictures Want?* 6. Compare Alberto Manguel: "This astonishing notion, that words think us into being, that words not only express but create thought, was developed long ago, in the sixth century, by the Indian philosopher Bhartrihari. It deserves close attention." *The City of Words*, 66.

13. Wayne Booth, *The Company We Keep: An Ethics of Fiction* (Berkeley and Los Angeles: University of California Press, 1988), 14.

14. Charlotte Linde, "The Acquisition of a Speaker by a Story: How History Becomes Memory and Identity," *Ethos* 28, no. 4 (2001): 608–32.

15. Charlotte Linde, *Working the Past: Narrative and Institutional Memory* (New York: Oxford University Press, 2009), 222. Linde concludes that her ethnography has been "a story about the adventures of stories in groups of people and the adventures of people in groups of stories" (224). That balance is reflected in all these examples of people speaking of stories as if they were alive.

16. I capitalize *Indigenous* in deference to Archibald's preferred usage. Throughout this book, usage of *indigenous* and *native*, with and without capitals, follows as closely as possible the usage of the author being discussed.

17. Jo-ann Archibald, *Indigenous Storywork: Educating the Heart, Mind, Body, and Spirit* (Vancouver: University of British Columbia Press, 2008), 95.

18. Rita Charon, *Narrative Medicine: Honoring the Stories of Illness* (New York: Oxford University Press, 2006).

19. David Brooks, "The Rush to Therapy." *New York Times*, November 10, 2009.

20. Claude Levi-Strauss, "Myth and Meaning," in *More Lost Massey Lectures* (Toronto: House of Anansi Press, 2008), 275.

21. Archibald, *Indigenous Storywork*, 112.

22. Pierre Bourdieu, *Pascalian Meditations* (Stanford, CA: Stanford University Press, 2000).

23. Margaret Somers presents a more specified statement: "From diverse sources it is possible to identify four features of a reframed narrativity relevant for the social sciences: (1) relationality of parts; (2) causal emplotment; (3) selective appropriation; and (4) temporality, sequence, and place. Above all, narratives are constellations of *relationships* (connected parts) embedded in *time* and *space*, constituted by what I call *causal emplotment*." "Narrativity, Narrative Identity, and Social Action: Rethinking the English Working-Class Formation," *Social Science History* 16, no. 4 (Winter 1992): 601.

24. Frank Kermode, *The Sense of an Ending: Studies in the Theory of Fiction* (New York: Oxford University Press, 1973).

25. Harvey Sacks, "On the Analysability of Stories by Children," in *Ethnomethodology*, ed. Roy Turner (Middlesex UK: Penguin, 1974), 216–32. Reprinted in Sacks, *Lectures on Conversation*, vol. 1, ed. Gail Jefferson (London: Blackwell, 1995).

26. William Labov and Joshua Waletzky, "Narrative Analysis: Oral Versions of Personal Experience," *Journal of Narrative and Life History* 7 (1997): 3–38. See also William Labov, "Some Further Steps in Narrative Analysis," *Journal of Narrative and Life History* 7 (1997): 395–415.

27. Boyd, *On the Origin of Stories*, 392. Boyd also writes: "But works of art need to attract and arouse audiences before they can 'mean'" (232).

28. Ben-Ami Scharfstein, *Art without Borders: A Philosophical Exploration of Art and Humanity* (Chicago: University of Chicago Press, 2009), 17. Scharfstein devel-

ops his argument, which draws extensively on psychological and neuroscientific studies, with particular emphasis on human speech: "The utilitarian aspect of speech is as a rule so hard to divide from its aesthetic aspect because speech is constantly improvised art by whose means we react to and control our everyday life . . . We don't notice that speech is such a great skill because we use it all the time" (13). Stories are, first and foremost, told in speech; throughout this book I write of people *listening* to stories, even though people are reading this book and its stories.

29. The metaphor of stories as *equipment* recurs among several theorists whose work leads to socio-narratology; for example, Kenneth Burke's essay title, "Literature as Equipment for Living," in Burke's *The Philosophy of Literary Form* (New York: Vintage, 1957). My discussion of capacities asks how stories are equipped, those stories then becoming part of humans' equipment for living. Equipment, however, is more than tools for carrying out purposes that preexist; instead, equipment endows any sense of purpose.

30. Bruner, *Making Stories*, 17.

31. Maxine Hong Kingston, *The Warrior Woman: Memoirs of a Girlhood among Ghosts* (New York: Vintage, 1989 [1975]), 5.

32. The concept of *technical account* is developed by Charles Tilly in *Why? What Happens When People Give Reasons . . . and Why* (Princeton, NJ: Princeton University Press, 2006). Technical accounts are, like stories, "cause-effect accounts," but Tilly distinguishes them from stories, because technical accounts reach their conclusions "by widely accepted professional procedures . . . Whole professions and organized bodies of professional knowledge stand behind them" (19). Moreover, as discussed in the next capacity of stories, technical accounts are not driven by character. Their characters tend to be nonhuman and lack either reflective purpose or moral responsibility.

33. Ibid.

34. I do intend to echo Heidegger but cautiously, attempting to stay on the more descriptive side of his existential phenomenology. Martin Heidegger, *Being and Time* (New York: Oxford University Press, 1962). Or, staying on the side of Heidegger most influenced by Kierkegaard.

35. Frederick Douglass, *Autobiographies* (New York: Library of America, 1994), 336. Quoted in the introduction to the present text.

36. The idea of typical motivational schemes as cultural resources is developed by Alfred Schutz, *Collected Papers*, vol. 2: *Studies in Social Theory*, ed. and introduced by Arvid Brodersen (The Hague: Martinus Nijhoff, 1964).

37. The classic sociological work in this regard is C. W. Mills, "Situated Actions and Vocabularies of Motives," *American Sociological Review* 5, no. 6 (December 1940): 904–13. A recent major work is Judith Butler, *Giving an Account of Oneself* (New York: Fordham University Press, 2005).

38. Gubrium and Holstein's narrative analysis equates stories with accounts: "Throughout the book, we use the terms *narrative, story,* and *account* interchangeably to refer to spates of talk that are taken to describe or explain matters

of concern to participants." Jaber A. Gubrium and James F. Holstein, *Analyzing Narrative Reality* (Los Angeles: Sage, 2008), xviii. This usage follows their interest in the collaborative production of talk describing events. Tilly discusses stories in the context of a book about accounts, hence his subtitle: *What Happens When People Give Reasons . . . and Why*. His death leaves us unable to ask him, but my understanding is that he recognizes stories as able to do much more than give reasons, useful as stories are as one form of account. Tilly, *Why?*

39. Philip Smith, *Why War? The Cultural Logic of Iraq, the Gulf War, and Suez* (Chicago: University of Chicago Press, 2005), to be discussed in chapter 5.

40. See the introduction, n. 31, for my appreciation to Annemarie Mol for this way of formulating what an actor is.

41. Boyd, *On the Origin of Stories*, 197.

42. Cheryl Mattingly, "Emergent Narratives," in *Narrative and the Cultural Construction of Illness and Healing*, ed. Cheryl Mattingly and Linda Garro (Berkeley and Los Angeles: University of California Press, 2000), 205.

43. Homer, *The Odyssey*, trans. Robert Fagles (New York: Penguin, 1996). Tiresias gives Odysseus this task in book 11, lines 136–52. Odysseus tells Penelope what he must do in book 23, lines 305–20. *The Odyssey* ends with book 24. Thus, the ending of Homer's telling is not what the story has told us will eventually happen last, which shows how complex endings are.

44. Edmond Wright calls these objects "the ambiguous element" and develops a fascinating narratology around them, using principles of Gestalt psychology. His work is the most definitive treatise on why stories are necessarily open to changing interpretations. *Narrative, Perception, Language, and Faith* (New York: Palgrave Macmillan, 2005).

45. This example is used recurrently in Lewis Hyde, *Trickster Makes This World: Mischief, Myth, and Art* (New York: North Point Press, 1998). Although I knew many of Hyde's exemplary stories before I read them, he changed my sense of everything he discusses, and citations are wholly inadequate to acknowledge my debt to his writing.

46. Thomas King, *The Truth about Stories: A Native Narrative* (Toronto: House of Anansi Press, 2003), 29.

47. *Fantasia*, Walt Disney Productions, 1940. "The Sorcerer's Apprentice" is based on Goethe's poem *Der Zauberlehrling*.

48. The pun and the emphasis on response are both from Mikhail Bakhtin (1895–1975). See especially his *Problems of Dostoevsky's Poetics* (Minneapolis: University of Minnesota Press, 1984).

49. King, *The Truth about Stories*, 92.

50. Northrop Frye, *The Great Code: The Bible and Literature* (New York: Harvest, 2002).

51. Pierre Bayard, *How to Talk about Books You Haven't Read* (New York: Bloomsbury, 2007), 73.

52. Joan Didion, *The White Album* (New York: Farrar, Straus and Giroux, 1990).

53. Keith H. Basso, *Wisdom Sits in Places: Landscape and Language among the Western Apache* (Albuquerque: University of New Mexico Press, 1996), 61.

54. Greg Sarris, *Mabel McKay: Weaving the Dream*, Portraits of American Genius series (Berkeley and Los Angeles: University of California Press, 1994), 115. Ellipses added.

55. Archibald, *Indigenous Storywork*, 97. Ellipses in original.

56. Basso, *Wisdom Sits in Places*, 61.

57. The crucial philosophic source is J. L. Austin, *How to Do Things with Words* (New York: Oxford University Press, 1976 [1955]). Language is performative when some act is performed through the speaking of certain words. Making a promise, placing a bet, performing a marriage, and christening a ship are among Austin's examples. Reading Austin today necessarily invokes more recent work, including Judith Butler's understanding of sexual identity as performance in *Gender Trouble: Feminism and the Subversion of Identity* (New York: Routledge, 1990).

58. Quoted earlier under the "symbiotic" capacity of stories. See n. 54.

59. An extensive literature considers this particularity. One foundational work is Donald Spense, *Narrative Truth and Historical Truth: Meaning and Interpretation in Psychoanalysis* (New York: Norton, 1984).

60. For different versions of this argument, see Mattingly, *Healing Dramas and Clinical Plots*, and also Joseph E. Davis's editorial introduction to *Stories of Change: Narrative and Social Movements* (Albany: State University of New York Press, 2002).

61. Manguel, *The City of Words*, 115.

62. Mattingly, *Healing Dramas and Clinical Plots*, 154. Quoted above, n. 42.

63. Donna Haraway, *The Haraway Reader* (New York: Routledge, 2004), 21.

64. John Law, "On the Subject of the Object: Narrative, Technology, and Interpellation." *Configurations* 8 (2000): 2.

65. Whoever said this, it appears on page 40 of his or her book or article. My apologies to the author, who I hope will read this book and correct me.

66. Donna Haraway, *The Companion Species Manifesto: Dogs, People, and Significant Others* (Chicago: Prickly Paradigm Press, 2003). Elaborated in Haraway, *When Species Meet* (Minneapolis: University of Minnesota Press, 2008).

67. Donna Haraway: "Animals have been active in their relations to humans, not just the reverse . . . Although an unequal relationship, domestication is a two-way matter." *The Haraway Reader*, 142. See also page 330 for elaboration.

68. Scharfstein, *Art Without Borders*, 60.

69. Donna Haraway, *How Like a Leaf: An Interview with Donna Haraway* (New York: Routledge, 1999), 107.

CHAPTER 2. STORIES AT WORK

1. This question can be answered in a multitude of ways; for example, Brian Boyd argues that stories confer an evolutionary advantage. *On the Origin of Stories: Evolution, Cognition, and Fiction* (Cambridge, MA: Harvard University Press, 2009).

2. Lewis Hyde, *Trickster Makes This World* (New York: North Point Press, 1998), 267.

3. Frank Kermode, *The Sense of an Ending: Studies in the Theory of Fiction* (New York: Oxford University Press, 1973).

4. William James, *The Principles of Psychology* (Cambridge, MA: Harvard University Press, 1981 [1890]), 462. James's younger contemporary, George Herbert Mead, expresses the issue more prosaically but with necessary detail: "Our whole intelligent process seems to lie in the attention which is selective of certain types of stimuli. Other stimuli which are bombarding the system are in some fashion shunted off. We give out attention to one particular thing. Not only do we open the door to certain stimuli and close it to others, but our attention is an organizing process as well as a selective process . . . Here we have the organism as acting and determining its environment." *Mind, Self, and Society: From the Standpoint of a Social Behaviorist* (Chicago: University of Chicago Press, 1970 [1934]), 25. In my argument, stories affect what we "open the door to," but stories are also part of the stimuli "bombarding the system" that require selection.

5. Again, nothing said about stories can be original. After I had taught the selection and evaluation work of stories in workshops for years, I found Margaret Somers writing how stories provide "evaluative criteria" and require "selective appropriation," albeit not using the terms in quite the same way I am. Somers, "Narrativity, Narrative Identity, and Social Action: Rethinking English Working-Class Formation," *Social Science History* 16, no. 4 (Winter 1992): 602. My ideas of selection and evaluation also restate Pierre Bourdieu's emphasis on "vision and division," frequently invoked in his *Pascalian Meditations* (Stanford, CA: Stanford University Press, 2000).

6. Julie Cruikshank, *The Social Life of Stories: Narrative and Knowledge in the Yukon Territory* (Lincoln: University of Nebraska Press, 1998), 43. Cruikshank discusses thinking with stories on pp. 39, 43.

7. Donna Haraway, *The Companion Species Manifesto: Dogs, People, and Significant Others* (Chicago: Prickly Paradigm Press, 2003) and *When Species Meet* (Minneapolis: University of Minnesota Press, 2008).

8. John Law, "On the Subject of the Object: Narrative, Technology, and Interpellation." *Configurations* 8 (2000): 1–29; quotation is from p. 2.

9. Paul Radin, quoted by Hyde, *Trickster Makes This World*, 158. Longer quotation occurs earlier in this chapter.

10. An alternative would be to write about the *functions* of stories. That usage would suck the breath out of stories, relegating them to things people use. In contrast to the imagery of functions, work is suspenseful: a number of endings are possible, and none can be predicted in advance

11. Thomas King, *The Truth about Stories: A Native Narrative* (Toronto: House of Anansi Press, 2003), 92. Quoted in the preceding chapter.

12. If pride of place is given to any sources as fundamental to narrative identity, my choices would be Jerome Bruner, for a series of books beginning with *Actual Minds, Possible Worlds* (Cambridge, MA: Harvard University Press, 1987), and

Alasdair MacIntyre, *After Virtue*, 2nd ed. (Notre Dame, IN: University of Notre Dame Press, 1984).

13. Louis Althusser, *"Lenin and Philosophy" and Other Essays*, trans. Ben Brewster (New York: Monthly Review Press, 2001 [1971]).

14. Howard Waitzkin, *The Politics of Medical Encounters: How Patients and Doctors Deal with Social Problems* (New Haven, CT: Yale University Press, 1991).

15. I learned "Coyote and the Shadow People" from Hyde, who includes Archie Phinney's 1934 translation in *Trickster Makes This World*, 83–87. Hyde returns to the story throughout his book. Unable to find my own edition of the Phinney translation, I referred to Deward E. Walker Jr., *Nez Perce Coyote Tales: The Myth Cycle* (Norman: University of Oklahoma Press, 1998), which clearly is based on Phinney, including the "inveterate doer" usage.

16. Hyde, *Trickster Makes This World*, 86.

17. Michel Foucault, who referred to Althusser less often than Althusser claimed him as his student, uses the term *subjectivation* for the process of becoming a subject. An excellent discussion is Paul Rabinow and Nikolas Rose, "Introduction: Foucault Today" in *The Essential Foucault*, ed. Rabinow and Rose (New York: New Press, 1994). Stories subjectify. I discuss *subjectification* as how stories create particular types of subject in A. W. Frank, "Health Stories as Connectors and Subjectifiers," *health: an interdisciplinary journal* 10, no. 4 (2006): 421–40.

18. And this humanity, which is the story's deep sadness, is one reason why the story is an exception within the corpus of Coyote stories, as Hyde notes. *Trickster Makes This World*, 130. In most trickster stories, the trickster "knows how to slip the trap of culture" (204). In "Coyote and the Shadow People," the trap seems inescapable.

19. Charlotte Linde describes "how members are both constrained into particular subject positions by the existing category system, and at the same time move creatively both within and outside the cultural system to establish a position that is not entirely determined by others." *Working the Past: Narrative and Institutional Memory* (New York: Oxford University Press, 2009), 116.

20. Bourdieu, *Pascalian Meditations*.

21. For a collection of Bourdieu's various definitions of *habitus*, see David Swartz, *Culture and Power: The Sociology of Pierre Bourdieu* (Chicago: University of Chicago Press, 1998). For an excellent overview, see Karl Maton, "Habitus," in *Bourdieu: Key Concepts*, ed. Michael Grenfell (London: Acumen, 2008).

22. Leo Tolstoy, *War and Peace*, trans. Anthony Briggs (New York: Viking, 2006), 187.

23. Jo-ann Archibald, *Indigenous Storywork: Educating the Heart, Mind, Body, and Spirit* (Vancouver: University of British Columbia Press, 2008), 93.

24. Barry Lopez, *Crow and Weasel* (New York: Farrar, Straus and Giroux, 1998), 60.

25. Pierre Bayard, *How to Talk about Books You Haven't Read* (New York: Bloomsbury, 2007), 30–31.

26. Kingston plays with this discrepancy of locations. As readers read *The Warrior Woman*, the significance of the opening story changes. In Bayard's terms, as *The Warrior Woman* expands readers' inner libraries, the pregnant-aunt story is relocated to different sections, having a different significance in each section. The effect can be called hermeneutic, insofar as the reader's horizons merge increasingly with Kingston's—or that is the apparent intention. This understanding of hermeneutics is developed in chapter 4.

27. Linda C. Garro and Cheryl Mattingly, "Narrative as Construct and Construction," in *Narrative and the Cultural Construction of Illness and Healing*, ed. Mattingly and Garro (Berkeley and Los Angeles: University of California Press, 2000), 2.

28. Pumla Gobodo-Madikizela, *A Human Being Died That Night* (Boston: Houghton Mifflin, 2003).

29. Mikhail Bakhtin, *Problems of Dostoevsky's Poetics* (Minneapolis: University of Minnesota Press, 1984).

30. Charlotte Linde, "The Acquisition of a Speaker by a Story: How History Becomes Memory and Identity," *Ethos* 28, no. 4 (2001): 608–32.

31. Linde argues that this fragmented telling-in-pieces distinguishes Mid-West's paradigmatic story of Mr. McBee from myths or folktales (ibid., 621), which is true to the extent that many Indigenous stories certainly are told as whole stories. But part of what Archibald means by her title, *Storywork*, is the constant work that living Indigenous communities must do to keep fragments assembled into whole stories, or to reassemble fragments when the whole story has been lost to memory (Archibald, *Indigenous Storywork*, 80). As Coyote stories are experienced among Indigenous groups, each particular story is a piece of a larger whole, and those intertextual connections are how the stories are understood differently within the community than by readers like me, who encounter the stories collected in books. But even within Indigenous groups, as in MidWest, different members will align differently with respect to the story.

32. Hyde, *Trickster Makes This World*, chapter 4, with other discussion inter alia. Hyde's interpretation of Loki would have been less of a surprise to me if I had remembered Milton. Frank Kermode quotes *Areopagitica* (1643): "Good and evil we know in the field of this world grow up together almost inseparably; and the knowledge of good is so involved and interwoven with the knowledge of evil, and in so many cunning resemblances hardly to be discerned, that those confused seeds which were imposed on Psyche as an incessant labour to cull out, and sort asunder, were not more intermixed." Kermode, "Heroic Milton: Happy Birthday," *New York Review* 56, no. 3 (February 26, 2009), 28.

33. Paul Radin, quoted by Hyde, *Trickster Makes This World*, 12.

34. David Grossman, *Lion's Honey* (Edinburgh: Canongate, 2006).

35. On stories of exclusion, see David Gordon White, *Myths of the Dog-Man* (Chicago: University of Chicago Press, 1991). Alberto Manguel concludes his insightful discussion of Dogman stories, which he traces back to Gilgamesh: "So prevalent is this theme that literature can be read as a continuous chronicle of

the resolution and restatement of a defining opposition, since every time a new identity is created, a new exclusion is simultaneously defined." *The City of Words* (Toronto: House of Anansi Press, 2007), 42.

36. Cruikshank, *The Social Life of Stories*, 44. See also Cruikshank, *Life Lived Like a Story: Life Stories of Three Yukon Native Elders* (Lincoln: University of Nebraska Press, 1992).

37. Hyde, *Trickster Makes This World*, Radin quotation from p. 12; trickster quotation from p. 267.

38. King, *The Truth about Stories*.

CHAPTER 3. DIALOGICAL NARRATIVE ANALYSIS AS A METHOD OF QUESTIONING

1. Mikhail Bakhtin, *The Bakhtin Reader: Selected Writings of Bakhtin, Medvedev, and Voloshinov*, ed. Pam Morris (London: E. Arnold, 1994), 159. The quotation is from M. M. Bakhtin and P. M. Medvedev, *The Formal Method in Literary Scholarship: A Critical Introduction to Sociological Poetics* (Baltimore: Johns Hopkins University Press, 1991 [1928]).

2. See the introduction, n. 35.

3. C. Wright Mills, *The Sociological Imagination* (New York: Oxford University Press, 1959).

4. "When you talk to one of the founders you are always dealing with a mind. But once a young man has spent three or four years at this sort of thing, you cannot really talk to him about the problems of studying modern society. His position and career, his ambition and his very self-esteem, are based in large part on this one perspective, this one vocabulary, this one set of techniques. In truth, he does not know anything else." Ibid., 105–6.

5. Mills's argument echoes Max Weber's case for a blending of specialization and "enthusiasm," the latter being "a prerequisite for the 'inspiration' which is decisive." Criticizing what he saw as a contemporary "notion that science has become a problem in calculation," Weber argues: "Some idea has to occur in someone's mind, and it has to be a correct idea, if one is to accomplish anything worthwhile. And such intuition cannot be forced. It has nothing to do with cold calculation." Weber certainly values calculation, just not *cold* calculation, uninformed by inspiration. "Science as a Vocation" [1919], in *From Max Weber: Essays in Sociology*, ed. and trans. H. H. Gerth and C. W. Mills (New York: Oxford University Press, 1958), 135.

6. Paul Rabinow and Nikolas Rose, "Introduction: Foucault Today," in *The Essential Foucault*, ed. Rabinow and Rose (New York: New Press, 1994), xv.

7. James Gordon Finlayson parses out several of the claims that give *critical* its force in critical theory: first, "A critical theory reflect[s] on the social context that gave rise to it, on its own function within that society, and on the purposes and interest of its practitioners." Second, critical theory is practical, having as its aim "to create social and political conditions more conducive to human flourishing than the present ones." Finlayson identifies two aspects of this practical intent:

"diagnostic and remedial." *Habermas: A Very Short Introduction* (Oxford: Oxford University Press, 2005), 3–4.

8. Harold Garfinkel's criticism of theories that formulate people as "cultural dopes" is one prominent example of this reaction against nineteenth-century suspicion and its twentieth-century variations. *Studies in Ethnomethodology* (Englewood Cliffs, NJ: Prentice Hall, 1967). Dorothy Smith represents one of the many social theorists influenced by Garfinkel. Smith emphasizes that actors are skilled and knowledgeable, even when they miss the extensive implications of their actions. *Texts, Facts, Femininity: Exploring the Relations of Ruling* (London: Routledge, 1993).

9. Adapted (with apologies) from Thomas King, *The Truth about Stories: A Native Narrative* (Toronto: House of Anansi Press, 2003).

10. Michael Bérubé, *Life as We Know It: A Father, A Family, and an Exceptional Child* (Boston: Houghton Mifflin, 1996).

11. See Hilde Lindemann Nelson, *Damaged Identities, Narrative Repair* (Ithaca, NY: Cornell University Press, 2001).

12. Paul John Eakin, *How Our Lives Become Stories: Making Selves* (Ithaca, NY: Cornell University Press, 1999).

13. Among numerous studies that could be cited, see Shari Stone-Mediatore, *Reading across Borders: Storytelling and Knowledge of Resistance* (New York: Palgrave Macmillan, 2003).

14. Philip Smith, *Why War? The Cultural Logic of Iraq, the Gulf War, and Suez* (Chicago: University of Chicago Press, 2005). Smith's approach to narrative analysis is discussed in chapter 5.

15. Hillis Miller, quoted by James Childress, "Narrative(s) versus Norm(s): A Misplaced Debate in Bioethics," in *Stories and Their Limits: Narrative Approaches to Bioethics*, ed. Hilde Lindemann Nelson (New York: Routledge, 1997), 263–64.

16. David Grossman, *Lion's Honey* (Edinburgh: Canongate, 2006). Grossman's analysis is considered in detail in chapter 2.

17. Julie Cruikshank, *The Social Life of Stories: Narrative and Knowledge in the Yukon Territory* (Lincoln: University of Nebraska Press, 2000).

18. Recall chapter 2, in which Pierre Bayard retells the story about an anthropologist telling the Tiv the story of Hamlet. The Tiv's inability to hear a story that failed to conform to certain parameters of life as they knew it, and their need to reshape that story to make it fit, echoes throughout Cruikshank's Yukon story. Bayard, *How to Talk about Books You Haven't Read* (New York: Bloomsbury, 2007), 83.

19. Rabinow and Rose, *The Essential Foucault*, 104.

20. Among numerous editions, my favorite is *Beowulf: An Illustrated Edition*, trans. Seamus Heaney (New York: Norton, 2008). Many of the illustrations are photographs of period artifacts, giving the story a material sense of time and place. The poem was composed circa 800 CE.

21. See Arthur W. Frank, "Asking the Right Question about Pain: Narrative and *Phronesis*," *Literature and Medicine* 23, no. 2 (Fall 2004): 209–25.

22. Wolfram von Eschenbach, *"Parzival" and "Titurel,"* trans. Cyril Edwards (New York: Oxford University Press, 2006).

23. Lewis Hyde, *Trickster Makes This World: Mischief, Myth, and Art* (New York: North Point Press, 1998), 141.

24. *Beowulf*, 2007, Robert Zemeckis, director; screenplay by Neil Gaiman and Roger Avary.

25. Bruno Latour, *Reassembling the Social: An Introduction to Actor-Network-Theory* (New York: Oxford University Press, 2005). Reassembling by means of what Latour calls *fabrication mechanisms* is discussed in chapter 5.

26. Norbert Elias, *The Society of Individuals* (New York: Continuum, 1991).

27. Bakhtin, *The Bakhtin Reader*, 42. On the dispute over authorship of this quotation, see Katerina Clark and Michael Holquist, *Mikhail Bakhtin* (Cambridge, MA: Harvard University Press, 1984), 146.

28. Brian Boyd, *On the Origin of Stories: Evolution, Cognition, and Fiction* (Cambridge, MA: Harvard University Press, Belknap Press, 2009), 153.

29. Edward O. Wilson, *Naturalist* (Washington, DC: Island Press, 1994), 16.

CHAPTER 4. DIALOGICAL INTERPRETATION AND STORIES' PARTICULAR TRUTH

1. Brian Boyd, *On the Origin of Stories: Evolution, Cognition, and Fiction* (Cambridge MA: Harvard University Press, Belknap Press, 2009), 382, italics in the original.

2. Cheryl Mattingly, in writing still in press, uses the term *narrative mind reading*, which I find more descriptive than *theory of mind*. *The Politics of Hope: Narrative Constructions of a Clinical Borderland* (Berkeley and Los Angeles: University of California Press, forthcoming).

3. Robert Matthew, quoted in Jo-ann Archibald, *Indigenous Storywork: Educating the Heart, Mind, Body, and Spirit* (Vancouver: University of British Columbia Press, 2008), 139.

4. See, in particular, Cheryl Mattingly's systematic discussion in *Healing Dramas and Clinical Plots: The Narrative Structure of Experience* (Cambridge: Cambridge University Press, 1998). Significant discussions of the limits of mimetic understandings are also found in Julie Cruikshank, *The Social Life of Stories: Narrative and Knowledge in the Yukon Territory* (Lincoln: University of Nebraska Press, 1998); Don Cupitt, *What Is a Story?* (Philadelphia: Trinity Press International, 1991); Joseph Davis, "Narrative and Social Movements" in Davis, ed., *Stories of Change: Narrative and Social Movements* (Albany: State University of New York Press, 2002); Catherine Kohler Riessman, *Narrative Methods for the Human Sciences* (Los Angeles: Sage, 2008); and Hayden White, *Metahistory: The Historical Imagination of Nineteenth-Century Europe* (Baltimore: Johns Hopkins University Press, 1973). Given the extent of this literature, it is possible to characterize recent social scientific work on narrative as *the anti-mimetic turn*, at least at the level of theory. Yet many if not most scholarly journal articles that claim to be doing narrative analysis still depend on mimetic assumptions.

5. "Words, and the relationships between words, thoughts and the irony of thoughts, their divergence—these are the content of art. Art, if it can be compared to a window at all, is only a sketched window." Viktor Shklovsky, *Zoo, or Letters Not about Love* (Ithaca, NY: Cornell University Press, 1971 [1923]), 80. I quote Shklovsky more than a bit out of the context of his formalism, which anticipates a non-socio narratology, focused on the relationships between constituent parts of the narrative.

6. National Gallery of Art, Washington, DC. The painting can be viewed online at multiple Web sites or directly on Google, at least as this book is being written.

7. See also Michel Foucault's essay on Magritte, *This Is Not a Pipe* (Berkeley and Los Angeles: University of California Press, 2008).

8. The journalist Jill Lepore, a trustworthy storyteller, describes a nonmimetic approach when she writes that period newspapers "aren't reliable sources of factual information." As primary documents: "Their value lies in reporting people's understanding of the events, not in describing the events themselves." "Writing about History," in *Telling True Stories: A Nonfiction Writers' Guide from the Nieman Foundation at Harvard University* ed. Mark Kramer and Wendy Call (New York: Plume, 2007), 87.

9. Alessandro Portelli, *The Battle of Valle Guilia: Oral History and the Art of Dialogue* (Madison: University of Wisconsin Press, 1997), 42.

10. Portelli adds that, already having worked on the basis of this understanding, he later discovered the Russian semiotician Jurig Lotman, who wrote how "forgetting is also part of remembering" (ibid., 45). Charlotte Linde's research parallels Portelli's. Like Portelli, Linde recognizes the importance of verifying certain stories—her example is the need to refute Holocaust deniers—but her concern is not verification. Rather, Linde studies how stories as they are told at present affect the present: "how an account of the past is worked in the present, what is remembered, what stories are told, by whom they are told, how they are told, and how they are used for present purposes." *Working the Past: Narrative and Institutional Memory* (New York: Oxford University Press, 2009), 95. See also p. 122.

11. In the sociological literature, the canonical source for this argument is Elliot Mishler, *Research Interviewing: Context and Narrative* (Cambridge: Harvard University Press, 1986).

12. Not only narrative analysts but storytellers themselves want and need the truth of what actually happened; they fear that imagination and memory have distorted their sense of the real. The anguished protagonist of Sandor Marai's novel *Embers* asks, not rhetorically but without hope of an answer: "And indeed, what *had* happened? Am I not just imagining all this? Is the whole thing not just a figment of my imagination? If I tell it to anyone, he or she will probably laugh in my face. I have nothing, no proof, in my hand . . . All I have is a voice inside me, stronger than any proof, crying out unmistakably, incontrovertibly, beyond

all doubt, that I am not deceived, and that I know the truth." Marai, *Embers* (New York: Vintage, 2002 [1942]), 156. The speaker has destroyed several lives because he was certain his wife and his best friend had an affair, yet his evidence is entirely circumstantial. The story he tells of their affair and his friend's plan to murder him fits in every detail, but it can never be more than a story, and the justification for how he has lived requires not the truth of a telling but the telling of a truth. His tragedy is that certainty can never be.

13. Alessandro Portelli, *The Order Has Been Carried Out: History, Memory and Meaning of a Nazi Massacre in Rome* (New York: Palgrave Macmillan, 2003), 16.

14. Eduardo Galeano, "Christmas Eve," in *The Book of Embraces* (New York: Norton, 1992).

15. The quintessential magical realist, Gabriel Garcia Marquez, has consistently insisted: "There is not a single line in any of my books that I can't connect to a real life experience. There is always a reference to a concrete reality." Quoted in Bert Archer, "The Autumn of a Literary Patriarch," *The Globe and Mail* (Toronto), January 31, 2009. See also Garcia Marquez's memoir, *Living to Tell the Tale* (New York: Vintage, 2004). This hardly suggests that his stories reflect concrete reality as they are told; his key-word seems to be *connect*. My point is that more stories than are generally conceded belong to Portelli's hybrid-genre category.

16. For a useful meditation on the multiple senses of *meaning*, see Terry Eagleton, *The Meaning of Life* (Oxford: Oxford University Press, 2007).

17. Portelli, *The Battle of Valle Guilia*, 43.

18. Among the many scholars who make this point, an especially useful example is offered by Joanne Bornat, "Oral History," in *Qualitative Research Practice*, ed. Clive Seale, Giampietro Gobo, Jaber F. Gubrium, and David Silverman (London: Sage, 2007).

19. Susan Sontag, *"Against Interpretation" and Other Essays* (New York: Dell, 1969), 23.

20. Josef Bleicher, *Contemporary Hermeneutics: Hermeneutics as Method, Philosophy, and Critique* (London: Routledge & Kegan Paul, 1980), 136.

21. Hans-Georg Gadamer, *Truth and Method* (New York: Continuum, 2005). Gadamer used the word *prejudice* provocatively, to reclaim its original sense of *prejudgment*. Prejudice is closely aligned with the idea of *tradition* as parameters for what is recognizable and knowable. In Laura Bohannan's example cited by Bayard (chapter 2), the Tiv hear *Hamlet* within a different tradition than a Western listener, so they interpret it differently.

22. Boyd, *On the Origin of Stories*, 134.

23. I explore this balance with respect to Bakhtin, in *The Renewal of Generosity: Illness, Medicine, and How to Live* (Chicago: University of Chicago Press, 2004). The subtle but real divergence between Gadamer and Bakhtin is nicely stated by Carolyn M. Shields: "In contrast to Gadamer's concept of dialogue in which horizons tend to merge even if full fusion is impossible, Bakhtin's horizons never merge . . . Unlike Gadamer's sense that confirmation may be achieved by things

themselves, for Bakhtin there are no fixed meanings or confirmations." *Bakhtin Primer* (New York: Peter Lang. 2007), 71. My prejudices lie on the Bakhtin side of these differences.

24. *Atanarjuat: The Fast Runner*, Canadian, 2001, directed by an Inuit, Zacharias Kunuk; screenplay by Paul Apak Angilirq.

25. Alberto Manguel, *The City of Words* (Toronto: House of Anansi Press, 2007), 73. Manguel compares *Atanarjuat* to Robert Flaherty's 1921 documentary, *Nanook of the North*. While acknowledging the "remarkable achievement" that filming *Nanook* was, his critique is that "in essence it remained a preconception" (ibid.). In hermeneutic terms, *Nanook* adjusted Inuit life to make it recognizable within non-Inuit horizons, rather than providing an opening to seeing that life from within Inuit horizons.

26. Sharon O'Brien, *The Family Silver: A Memoir of Depression and Inheritance* (Chicago: University of Chicago Press, 2004).

27. The mixed silver is an equally good example of Bakhtin's idea of *polyphony* (see the glossary in the present text). Gadamer's fusion emphasizes the harmonic merging of voices. Polyphony emphasizes that harmonized voices retain their individual particularity. Mikhail Bakhtin, *Problems of Dostoevsky's Poetics* (Minneapolis: University of Minnesota Press, 1984), 30.

28. Ibid., 58.

29. Portelli, *The Battle of Valle Guilia*, 3.

30. Bruno Latour, *Reassembling the Social: An Introduction to Actor-Network-Theory* (New York: Oxford University Press, 2005).

31. Bakhtin, *Problems of Dostoevsky's Poetics*, 63. Original emphases.

32. Mitchell Duneier, *Sidewalk* (New York: Farrar, Straus and Giroux, 1999).

33. For exactly how difficult this checking was, see Duneier's description (ibid., 347–52). The point is worth emphasizing that Duneier is not doing what is sometimes called "participant verification," in the sense of giving participants the last word. Rather, he is continuing the dialogue with them, and thus demonstrating to readers of *Sidewalk* that there can be no last word, either about these men or by them.

34. Portelli, *The Battle of Valle Guilia*, 58.

35. Bakhtin, *Problems of Dostoevsky's Poetics*, 63, quoted in full earlier in this chapter.

36. Archibald, *Indigenous Storywork*, 80.

37. Portelli, *The Battle of Valle Guilia*, 51, emphasis in original.

38. Barry Unsworth, *Morality Play* (New York: Penguin, 1996).

39. Manguel, *The City of Words*, 73. Quoted earlier in this chapter.

40. David Grossman, *Lion's Honey* (Edinburgh: Canongate, 2006), 10.

41. Archibald, *Indigenous Storywork*, 134.

42. Grossman, *Lion's Honey*, 12.

43. A recurring technique of recent fiction has been to retell a familiar story from the perspective of a marginalized character; examples include John Gardner, *Grendel* (New York: Knopf, 1971), and Tom Stoppard, *Rozenkrantz and Gilden-*

stern Are Dead (New York: Grove, 1968). The works are both interpretations and stories—further examples of hybrid genres.

44. Grossman, *Lion's Honey*, 11.

45. Portelli, *The Battle of Valle Guilia*, 52.

46. Archibald, *Indigenous Storywork*, 26.

47. Portelli, *The Battle of Valle Guilia*, 10.

48. Michael White and David Epston, *Narrative Means to Therapeutic Ends* (New York: Norton, 1990), and more recently, Michael White, *Maps of Narrative Practice* (New York: Norton, 2007). For an extensive and accessible guide to therapeutic letters, see Lorraine Wright, Wendy L. Watson, and Janice M. Bell, *Beliefs: The Heart of Healing in Families and Illness* (New York: Basic Books, 1996).

49. Archibald, *Indigenous Storywork*, 27.

50. Alfred Doblin, quoted by Manguel, *The City of Words*, 20.

CHAPTER 5. EXEMPLARS OF DIALOGICAL NARRATIVE ANALYSES

1. Bent Flyvbjerg, "Five Misunderstandings about Case-Study Research," in *Qualitative Research Practice*, ed. Clive Seale, Giampetro Gobo, Jaber F. Gubrium, and David Silverman (London: Sage, 2007), 397. That Flyvbjerg's statement occurs in a chapter from a mainstream teaching textbook hardly means that the views expressed in this statement or the quotation from him that follows are mainstream; what he says would be contested, or at least given a highly qualified interpretation, by many social scientists. But Flyvbjerg's views, which express my own perspective, are by no means eccentric.

2. Alessandro Portelli, *The Battle of Valle Guilia* (Madison: University of Wisconsin Press, 1997), 81.

3. Flyvbjerg, "Five Misunderstandings about Case-Study Research," 395.

4. Portelli, *The Battle of Valle Guilia*, 58. Quoted earlier, this chapter.

5. Gareth Williams, "The Genesis of Chronic Illness: Narrative Re-construction," *Sociology of Health and Illness* 6, no. 2 (1984): 175–200.

6. For an example of an autobiographical account of rheumatoid arthritis that shows little interest in the genesis of the disease, see Mary Felstiner, "Casing the Joints: A Story of Arthritis," in *Stories of Illness and Healing*, ed. Sayantani Das-Gupta and Marsha Hurst (Kent, OH: Kent State University Press, 2007).

7. Mike Bury, "Chronic Illness as Biographical Disruption," *Sociology of Health and Illness* 4, no. 2 (1982): 167–82. Williams also cites the influence of Claudine Herzlich, *Health and Illness: A Socio-Psychological Approach* (London: Academic Press, 1979).

8. Williams, "The Genesis of Chronic Illness," 178.

9. Portelli, *The Battle of Valle Guilia*, 6.

10. Cheryl Mattingly, *Healing Dramas and Clinical Plots: The Narrative Structure of Experience* (Cambridge: Cambridge University Press, 1998), 154. Discussed in chapter 1.

11. Arthur W. Frank, *The Wounded Storyteller: Body, Illness, and Ethics* (Chicago: University of Chicago Press, 1995).

12. Claiming that stage theories are not narrative analyses is in no sense a criticism; I simply observe a difference. A stage theory that produces considerable insights while sustaining the highest respect for those whom it discusses is David Karp's study of depression, *Speaking of Sadness: Depression, Disconnection, and the Meaning of Illness* (New York: Oxford University Press, 1997). On my reading, Karp's recurring autobiographical references to his own depression hold the book's narrative together. Read as the work of someone living with depression, the book has a reflexive force that denies the finalization risked by dividing experience into sequential segments describing a category of persons. By showing there is more to himself than either his depression or any theory of that experience, Karp expands the possibilities of anyone living with depression. Writing the book shows that there can always be another stage in any career, thus rendering the stage theory dialogical.

13. At the risk of belaboring too fine a point, I prefer to refer to typologies as *references* or *resources* rather than the often-used term *frameworks*. Frameworks contain, which is on the way toward finalizing. The typologies that dominated sociological theorizing when I was in graduate school in the 1970s sought to encompass all possibilities in mutually exclusive categories. A dialogical ambition is to call attention to the ever-present possibility of more possibilities and the overlapping nature of any categories. In other words, things just aren't that simple, and it does no one a favor to pretend that reality can be so neatly divided and circumscribed. In the 1970s a knockdown seminar question was to ask someone who proposed a typology why it required exactly that number of types. Now, the sensible reply would be to invite the questioner to add more. There is no necessity, except to leave things open.

14. Arthur W. Frank, *At the Will of the Body: Reflections on Illness* (Boston: Houghton Mifflin, 1991; new ed., 2002).

15. As one example, the idea of "normal" is invoked repeatedly in Myra Bluebond-Langer, *In the Shadow of Illness: Parents and Siblings of the Chronically Ill* (Princeton, NJ: Princeton University Press, 2000).

16. Anne Harrington, *The Cure Within: A History of Mind-Body Medicine* (New York: Norton, 2008). Harrington's distinction between narrative and story was discussed in this book's introduction.

17. My usage of *field* follows Pierre Bourdieu; among many works discussing this, see Bourdieu and Loic Wacquant, *An Invitation to Reflexive Sociology* (Chicago: University of Chicago Press, 1992). At minimum, a field circumscribes possibilities for action, based especially on dominant forms of capital and competition for capital. In Native societies, the authority to tell particular traditional stories is very much a form of capital; for a story of the contest that occurred when an emerging storyteller claimed this capital, see Julie Cruikshank, *The Social Life of Stories: Narrative and Knowledge in the Yukon Territory* (Lincoln: University of Nebraska Press, 1998), 28ff. One aspect of my idea of narrative habitus is that the ability to perform what a group perceives as correct telling of certain stories is a

significant form of capital. Failing to respond appropriately to a story is negative capital; not perceiving the humor in a joke is a prime example.

18. Kai Erikson, *Everything in Its Path: Destruction of Community in the Buffalo Creek Flood* (New York: Simon and Schuster, 1976), 28.

19. Paul Draus, *Consumed in the City: Observing Tuberculosis at Century's End* (Philadelphia: Temple University Press, 2004). I contrast Erikson and Draus in part because the situations of their research were so different. Erikson was already a senior scholar and was well funded through the firm that hired him. Draus collected his materials while he held a fairly low-level job, before he even entered a doctoral program. In doing research, resources certainly help. But also, absence of resources is no alibi.

20. Mikhail Bakhtin, *The Bakhtin Reader: Selected Writings of Bakhtin, Medvedev, and Voloshinov*, ed. Pam Morris (London: E. Arnold, 1994).

21. Mikhail Bakhtin, *Problems of Dostoevsky's Poetics* (Minneapolis: University of Minnesota Press, 1984), 5.

22. Joseph E. David, ed., *Stories of Change: Narrative and Social Movements* (Albany: State University of New York Press, 2002).

23. Bruno Latour, *Reassembling the Social: An Introduction to Actor-Network-Theory* (New York: Oxford University Press, 2005).

24. Francesca Polletta, *It Was Like a Fever: Storytelling and Protest in Politics* (Chicago: University of Chicago Press, 2006).

25. While this book was being written, but after Polletta's book was published, Claudette Colvin collaborated in the telling of her story: Phillip Hoose, *Claudette Colvin: Twice toward Justice* (New York: Farrar, Straus and Giroux, 2009).

26. Recall the anthropologist Renato Rosaldo's observation, quoted in chapter 1, that Hlongot huntsmen "seek out experiences that can be told as stories." Polletta ascribes much the same process to social movements. Chapter 1, n. 8.

27. James A. Holstein and Jaber F. Gubrium, "Context: Working It Up, Down, and Across," in *Qualitative Research Practice*, ed. Clive Seale, Giampetro Gobo, Jaber F. Gubrium, and David Silverman (London: Sage, 2007), 277.

28. Alcoholics Anonymous and its recovery narrative have been the subject of numerous if not innumerable studies. The earliest and, to my thinking, foundational reference is Gregory Bateson, "The Cybernetics of Self: A Theory of Alcoholism," in *Steps to an Ecology of Mind: Collected Essays in Anthropology, Psychiatry, Evolution, and Epistemology* (Chicago: University of Chicago Press, 2000 [reissue]).

29. Leslie Irvine, *Codependent Forevermore: The Invention of Self in a Twelve Step Group* (Chicago: University of Chicago Press, 1999), 49.

30. Charlotte Linde observes the same distinction. She refers to "open and closed canons" of group stories; the former "may be added to," but the latter is "fixed." Linde also distinguishes among "textual communities" that are "brought together simply by the act of reading (or hearing)." Textual communities can be more or less "strong" depending on the openness of their canon and their terms

of "allegiance" to that canon. *Working the Past: Narrative and Institutional Memory* (New York: Oxford University Press, 2009), at 87 and 170.

31. Mattingly, *Healing Dramas and Clinical Plots*, 46.

32. For extensive examples of the conversational co-construction of stories, see Jaber F. Gubrium and James A. Holstein, *Analyzing Narrative Reality* (Los Angeles: Sage, 2008). My quibble is whether many of these conversational co-constructions exhibit enough capacities of stories to be recognizable as stories. If one measure of a story is that it can be retold, their examples often fail. Gubrium and Holstein intentionally defer any definition of stories until the end of their book and then say very little, on my reading. Their interest is elsewhere, in conversational co-construction, which they are masters at depicting.

33. Polletta, *It Was Like a Fever*, 20.

34. Philip Smith, *Why War? The Cultural Logic of Iraq, the Gulf War, and Suez* (Chicago: University of Chicago Press, 2005).

35. Smith draws on and augments the genre types proposed by the literary critic Northrop Frye, principally *Anatomy of Criticism* (Princeton, NJ: Princeton University Press: 1957).

36. Mattingly, *Healing Dramas and Clinical Plots*, 60, quoted earlier in this chapter.

37. Smith, *Why War?*, 28.

38. Here the logic of Smith's argument coincides with Alasdair MacIntyre's statement that is discussed in this book's prologue: "I can only answer the question 'What am I to do?' if I can answer the prior question 'Of what story or stories do I find myself a part?'" *After Virtue*, 2nd ed. (Notre Dame, IN: University of Notre Dame Press, 1984), 216. For Smith, knowing what story one is part of depends on a genre guess. He does not cite MacIntyre, an absence that exemplifies the footnote game I described in this book's introduction.

39. Smith, *Why War?*, 28.

40. Simon Critchley, *Continental Philosophy: A Very Short Introduction* (Oxford: Oxford University Press, 2001), 72.

41. Maxine Hong Kingston, *The Warrior Woman: Memoirs of a Girlhood among Ghosts* (New York: Vintage, 1989 [1975]), 48.

CHAPTER 6. HOW STORIES CAN BE GOOD COMPANIONS

1. In Kevin Crossley-Holland, *The Norse Myths* (Middlesex: Penguin, 1980), 70–74; quotation is from p. 71.

2. Jean Améry, quoted in Lawrence Langer, *Holocaust Testimonies: The Ruins of Memory* (New Haven, CT: Yale University Press, 1993), 89.

3. For development of the relation between stories and embodiment, see Arthur W. Frank, "The Force of Embodiment: Bodies, Dispositions and Culture," in *The Oxford Handbook of Cultural Sociology*, ed. Jeffrey C. Alexander et al. (New York: Oxford University Press, forthcoming).

4. Alberto Manguel, *The City of Words* (Toronto: House of Anansi Press, 2007), 118.

5. Donna Haraway, *The Haraway Reader* (New York: Routledge, 2004), 68.

6. Jacqui Banaszynski, "Stories Matter," in *Telling True Stories: A Nonfiction Writers' Guide from the Nieman Foundation at Harvard University*, ed. Mark Kramer and Wendy Call (New York: Plume, 2007), 3.

7. Thomas King, *The Truth about Stories: A Native Narrative* (Toronto: House of Anansi Press, 2003), 10.

8. Philip Smith, *Why War? The Cultural Logic of Iraq, the Gulf War, and Suez* (Chicago: University of Chicago Press, 2005), 209.

9. Tzvetan Todorov, "Exposures," review of Susan Sontag, *Regarding the Pain of Others*, *New Republic*, April 21 and 28, 2003, pp. 28–31; quotation is from p. 28.

10. Susan Sontag, *Regarding the Pain of Others* (New York: Farrar, Straus and Giroux, 2003), 46.

11. Eric Ormsby, quoted in Manguel, *The City of Words*, 11.

12. Todorov, "Exposures," 28, quoted in full earlier.

13. Victor Hugo is among the notable exceptions. Graham Robb, reviewing Julie Rose's translation of *Les Misérables*, describes "Hugo's dizzyingly detailed chapter, 'L'Année 1817,' in which the 'physiognomy' of the period is constructed out of a hundred or so seemingly miscellaneous facts," which have no apparent relevance to the plot, or do they, somehow? On the significance of this chapter, Robb asks: "Who can say what matters and what doesn't? A storyteller's business is precisely to say, but Hugo shows what lurks behind that business. Few storytellers are willing to be so reflexive." Graham Robb, "The Mountains of Les Misérables," *Times Literary Supplement*, TimesOnLine, September 24, 2008. http://entertainment.timesonline.co.uk/tol/arts_entertainment/the_tls/article4816401.ece. Accessed February 10, 2009.

14. Todorov, "Exposures," 28.

15. The exhibition took place in 1994, showing the work of the English photojournalist Paul Lowe. Sontag writes: "Lowe thought the matter was a simple one. He was a professional photographer, and these were two bodies of work of which he was proud. For the Sarajevans, it was also simple. To set their suffering along the sufferings of another people was to compare them (which hell was worse?), demoting Sarajevo's martyrdom to a mere instance . . . It is intolerable to have one's own suffering twinned with anybody else's." *Regarding the Pain of Others*, 113. In terms used earlier in this book, the Sarajevans felt Devushkinized by being presented as "a mere instance"—which from a social scientific perspective, all lives and actions are, all the time.

16. Haraway, *The Haraway Reader*, 246.

17. In this context, the most fitting citation for Blake's comment is Philip Pullman's reference to him in Pullman's introduction to his edition of Milton's *Paradise Lost* (New York: Oxford University Press, 2005), 8. Pullman continues the cycle of story and counterstory, retelling the Garden story in *His Dark Materials*. *His Dark Materials* comprises Pullman's three novels, *The Golden Compass*, *The Subtle Knife*, and *The Amber Spyglass* (all in various editions), each title suggesting how humans can do what they do only through companionship with vital objects

that allow those humans not only possibilities of action but also *to be* who they are. Humans have no dominion over nonhumans in these books, whether those nonhumans are animals or objects.

18. King, *The Truth about Stories*, 10–20.

19. A recent telling of Genesis that undercuts King's claim is the graphic novel version, *The Book of Genesis Illustrated by R. Crumb* (New York: Norton, 2009). Crumb's text is Robert Alter's scholarly translation, but when the words are paired with his images, the telling is anything but the kind of verbatim rendering that King finds typical of biblical readings.

20. My favorite edition of this vast literature is Louis Ginzberg, *Legends of the Bible* (Philadelphia: Jewish Publication Society, 1992), originally in seven volumes. "Lilith was first given to Adam as wife. Like him she had been created out of the dust of the ground. But she remained with him only a short time, because she insisted on enjoying full equality with her husband" (35). Lilith flies away, is found by pursuing angels, defies them, and the story continues. My point is only to show that the biblical story of Genesis is not a closed text, but rather an ongoing storytelling tradition.

21. And dialogue is certainly what Todorov has in mind; see his *Mikhail Bakhtin: The Dialogical Principle* (Minneapolis: University of Minnesota Press, 1984).

22. References are to discussions in chapter 5.

23. Bioethics is one venue where one version of the story must be acted on, and the sooner the better. Statements of objection to relying on stories include John D. Arras, "Nice Story But So What? Narrative Justification in Ethics," pp. 65–88, and Tom Tomlinson, "Perplexed about Narrative Ethics," pp. 123–33, in *Stories and Their Limits: Narrative Approaches to Bioethics*, ed. Hilde Lindemann Nelson (New York: Routledge, 1997). For a general philosophical objection to narrative identity, see Galen Strawson, "Against Narrativity," *Ratio* 27, no. 4 (2004): 428–52.

24. For example, Janik and Toulmin write about Kierkegaard: "The problem of life, the meaning of human existence, is the sole object of his contemplation; yet it is impossible for reason, his own tool, to find any solution to the resulting paradoxes of life. Reason can only lead Kierkegaard to paradox; faith is needed to overcome it." And they write about Karl Kraus, taking up Kierkegaard: "Only the good man knows what values are, and only he can communicate them. No amount of scientific knowledge can ever make a man good." This line of thinking is presented as informing Wittgenstein's views. Allan Janik and Stephen Toulmin, *Wittgenstein's Vienna* (Chicago: Ivan R. Dee, 1996 [1973]), quotations at 178 and 179, respectively.

25. The assertion that people make ethical decisions very quickly and fill in reasons later finds increasing support from experimental studies that, in their methods, have little in common with dialogical commitments or with narrative. See Anthony Appiah, *Experiments in Ethics* (Cambridge, MA: Harvard University Press, 2008). On my limited understanding, these studies have little to say, nor

can they say much, about what people base their quick and unreasoned decisions on, and that leaves stories as a candidate.

26. For a wonderfully lucid account of this symbiosis, written by an ethicist deeply committed to principles, see James F. Childress, "Narrative(s) Versus Norm(s): A Misplaced Debate in Bioethics," in *Stories and Their Limits: Narrative Approaches to Bioethics*, ed. Hilde Lindemann Nelson (New York: Routledge, 1997), 252–71. For an equally lucid philosophical critique of the project of reason separated from experience (and its stories), see Barry Hoffmaster and Cliff Hooker, "How Experience Confronts Ethics," *Bioethics* 23, no. 4 (2009): 214–25.

27. Smith, *Why War?*, 17.

28. Lewis Hyde, *Trickster Makes This World: Mischief, Myth, and Art* (New York: North Point Press, 1998), 10–11.

29. A great narrative description of dumb luck in storytelling is Jerzy Kosinski's 1971 novel *Being There* (New York: Grove Press, 1999). The protagonist, Chauncey Gardiner (born as Chance, the gardener), does not so much tell stories as he begins what could be a story and lets others interrupt and tell the story they want to hear. As Kosinski tells the story of Chance's rise to eminence, he depicts a world where dumb luck rules. Laugh as I do at *Being There*, readers will now realize that my preference is for the reverse plot in which the hero starts out dumb lucky but learns to be smart, like *Parzival*, discussed in chapter 3. Wolfram von Eschenbach, *"Parzival" and "Titurel,"* trans. Cyril Edwards (New York: Oxford University Press, 2006).

GLOSSARY

1. Lewis Carroll, *Through the Looking Glass*, in *The Annotated Alice*, ed. Martin Gardner (London: Penguin, 1970), 269.

2. Charles Tilly, *Why? What Happens When People Give Reasons . . . and Why* (Princeton, NJ: Princeton University Press, 2006), 15.

3. For example, Jaber F. Gubrium and James A. Holstein, *Analyzing Narrative Reality* (Los Angeles: Sage, 2009).

4. A. J. Greimas and J. Courtés, *Semiotics and Language: An Analytical Dictionary* (Bloomington: Indiana University Press, 1982), 5.

5. Charles Taylor, *The Ethics of Authenticity* (Cambridge, MA: Harvard University Press, 1992).

6. Charles Taylor, *The Malaise of Modernity* (Toronto: House of Anansi Press, 1991; original edition of *The Ethics of Authenticity*), 26.

7. Wayne C. Booth, introduction to Mikhail Bakhtin, *Problems of Dostoevsky's Poetics* (Minneapolis: University of Minnesota Press, 1984), xxv.

8. Katerina Clark and Michael Holquist, *Mikhail Bakhtin* (Cambridge, MA: Harvard University Press, 1984).

9. Cheryl Mattingly, *Healing Dramas and Clinical Plots: The Narrative Structure of Experience* (Cambridge: Cambridge University Press, 1998).

10. Brian Boyd, *On the Origin of Stories: Evolution, Cognition, and Fiction* (Cambridge, MA: Harvard University Press, Belknap Press, 2009), 188.

11. Bruno Latour, *Reassembling the Social: An Introduction to Actor-Network-Theory* (New York: Oxford University Press, 2007), especially 31.

12. David Morris, "Voice, Genre, and Moral Community," in *Social Suffering*, ed. Arthur Kleinman, Veena Das, and Margaret Lock (Berkeley and Los Angeles: University of California Press, 1997), 33.

13. Pierre Bourdieu, *The Logic of Practice* (Stanford, CA: Stanford University Press, 1990), 53. The definition of *habitus* referenced here is not the only one Bourdieu proposes, but it is perhaps the most useful.

14. Pierre Bourdieu, *Pascalian Meditations* (Stanford CA: Stanford University Press, 2000), 143.

15. Pierre Bourdieu, *Sketch for a Self-Analysis* (Chicago: University of Chicago Press, 2007).

16. Hans-Georg Gadamer, *Truth and Method* (New York: Seabury Press, 1975), 146. Cheryl Mattingly glosses Gadamer's usage of text "as a trope for all human creation—the works of history" (personal communication).

17. Hans-George Gadamer, "The Hermeneutics of Suspicion," in *Hermeneutics: Questions and Prospects*, ed. Gary Shapiro and Alan Sica (Amherst: University of Massachusetts Press, 1984), 54.

18. Alfred Schutz, *Collected Papers*, vol. 1, *The Problem of Social Reality*, edited and introduced by Maurice Natanson (The Hague: Martinus Nijhoff, 1970), 136.

19. Gadamer, *Truth and Method*, 272.

20. Louis Althusser, *"Lenin and Philosophy" and Other Essays*, trans. Ben Brewster (New York: Monthly Review Press, 2001 [1971]), 174.

21. Charlotte Linde, *Working the Past: Narrative and Institutional Memory* (New York: Oxford University Press, 2009), 168.

22. Terence Hawkes, *Structuralism and Semiotics* (London: Methuen & Co., 1977), 144.

23. Uri Margolin, "Character," in *The Cambridge Companion to Narrative*, ed. David Herman (Cambridge: Cambridge University Press, 2007), 77.

24. H. Porter Abbott, *The Cambridge Introduction to Narrative* (Cambridge: Cambridge University Press, 2008), 193.

25. Hans-Georg Gadamer, *"The Relevance of the Beautiful" and Other Essays* (Cambridge: Cambridge University Press, 1986), 121.

26. Alasdair MacIntyre, *After Virtue: A Study of Moral Theory*, 2nd ed. (Notre Dame, IN: University of Notre Dame Press, 1984), 217.

27. Karl Marx, "Manifesto of the Communist Party," in *The Portable Karl Marx*, ed. Eugene Kamenka (New York Viking Penguin, 1983), 203.

28. Gerald Prince, "Narratology," in *The Johns Hopkins Guide to Literary Theory and Criticism* (Baltimore: Johns Hopkins University Press, 1994), 526.

29. J. L. Austin, *How To Do Things with Words* (New York: Oxford University Press, 1976 [1955]).

30. Wayne C. Booth, *The Rhetoric of Fiction* (Chicago: University of Chicago Press, 1961), 164.

31. Mikhail Bakhtin, *Problems of Dostoevsky's Poetics* (Minneapolis: University of Minnesota Press, 1984), 6, original emphases omitted in this and the following quotations.

32. Booth, introduction to Bakhtin, *Problems of Dostoevsky's Poetics*, xxi.

33. Northrop Frye, *The Great Code: The Bible and Literature* (Toronto: Academic Press Canada, 1982), 217.

34. Ferdinand de Saussure, *Course in General Linguistics* (La Salle, IL: Open Court Press, 1983).

35. Rahib Alameddine, *The Storyteller, or The Hakawati* (New York: Picador, 2008), 450.

36. Vladimir Propp, *Morphology of the Folktale* (Austin: University of Texas Press, 1968), 79.

37. Hilde Lindemann Nelson, *Damaged Identities, Narrative Repair* (Ithaca, NY: Cornell University Press, 2001), 6.

38. Jerome Bruner, *Making Stories: Law, Literature, Life* (New York: Farrar, Straus and Giroux, 2002), 34.

39. Leon Golden, "Aristotle," in *The Johns Hopkins Guide to Literary Theory and Criticism*, ed. Michael Groden and Martin Kreiswirth (Baltimore: Johns Hopkins University Press, 1994), 41.

Glossary

GLOSSARY NOTES ARE ON PP. 187–89.
Unlike many glossaries, this one seeks to expand, not simplify, how key terms are presented in the main text. This glossary provides not definitions but sources of socio-narratology. In a multidisciplinary undertaking, and especially in writing that seeks to be dialogical, no finality can be claimed for how words are used. My presupposition is that an intellectual activity develops through *contests* over the meaning and usage of the words that are its basic vocabulary. Unlike Humpty Dumpty in *Through the Looking Glass* who asserts his use of a word means "just what I choose it to mean—neither more nor less,"[1] when the dialogical thinker uses a word, she or he is aware of all the other possible ways of using it and welcomes those usages.

This glossary can also be read as mapping the influences that shape my version of socio-narratology and as offering resources for other versions.

accounts: The reasons that people offer for why they have acted as they have. Accounts depend on the conventional acceptability of certain reasons, as well as commonsense expectations for what form of explanation fits the circumstances. Most often, the person offering the account appeals to a shared sense of what a typical actor would do in that type of situation (for example: panic, become angry, run away, or other acts that require excuse or justification).

Charles Tilly argues that there are four overlapping forms of accounts: (1) *stories* as "explanatory narratives incorporating cause-effect accounts of unfamiliar phenomena or exceptional events";[2] (2) *codes*, which align the behavior in question with a set of rules, "such as legal judgment, religious penance, or awards of medals" (15); (3) *conventions*, which "involve no pretense of providing adequate causal accounts" but appeal to "conventionally accepted reasons," including fortune and luck; and (4) *technical accounts* that explain outcomes according to specialized, professional knowledge, including science and engineering.

Some sociologists equate stories with accounts, understanding accounting as the primary work of stories.[3]

actant: Whatever acts in a story, but not necessarily a human actor. In semiotic narratology: "The concept of actant has the advantage of replacing . . . the term of character as well as that of 'dramatis persona' . . . , since it applies not only to human beings but also to animals, objects, or concepts."[4] This expansion to include nonhuman actors is especially useful to those who study settings in which machines, equipment, microorganisms, and accepted theories definitely act; science and technology studies benefit from a word reminding readers that the actor is not necessarily human. However, recent studies break from the earlier semiotic understanding of an actant "as that which accomplishes or undergoes an act independently of all other determinations" (5). On the contrary, the focus of contemporary studies is how every actant operates under various degrees of determination and support from other actants.

authenticity: Socio-narratology both respects and critiques the commonsense idea that a story reveals the inner self and unique experience of the storyteller, as in the phrase "our *own* stories." Following the philosopher Charles Taylor, socio-narratology understands authenticity not as *intra*personal but rather as negotiated *between* persons.[5] Taylor points out that authenticity is historically modern as a way of understanding humans: "This is part of the massive subjective turn of modern culture, a new form of inwardness, in which we come to think of ourselves as beings with inner depths."[6] However people think of themselves, any individual's authenticity depends on both cultural resources acquired through group participation and recognition by others. Authenticity is thus understood as a claim, an account, and almost always a negotiation that can become a contest. "Authenticity is not the enemy of demands that emanate from beyond the self," Taylor concludes; "it supposes such demands" (41). Taylor also underscores the "profoundly moral ideal at work" in claims of personal identity (15).

The implication for socio-narratology is that no matter how fervently people may claim their stories as *their own*, anyone's story presupposes both other stories and the recognition of other people. People's stories are their own, but people exist only in dialogical relationships, and stories also express a relation. (See POLYPHONY)

Bakhtin, Mikhail: Russian literary critic, philosopher, and social theorist, 1895–1975. Bakhtin wrote in spite of his circumstances, holding a regular academic position only during his last years. Photographs often show him in bed as a result of osteomyelitis, from which he suffered throughout his life. He was part of a vibrant intellectual circle at the time of the Bolshevik Revolution; in the 1930s his political and possibly religious affiliations led to being exiled in Kazakhstan. Scholars debate the extent to which Bakhtin wrote in the idiom of literary criticism in order to evade censorship; his ideas about dialogue have definite political overtones but are phrased as interpretations of Dostoevsky and Rabelais. Wayne Booth offers one of the finest summaries: "Bakhtin's ultimate value—full acknowledgement of and participation in a Great Dialogue—is thus not to be addressed as just one more piece of 'literary criticism'; even less is it a study of fictional technique or form . . . It is a philosophical inquiry into our limited ways of mirroring—and improving—our lives."[7] That statement also expresses the intentions of what I am calling socio-narratology.

Bakhtin achieved international recognition at the end of his surprisingly long life. His dialogical philosophy has broad influence in literary criticism, philosophy, social sciences, and even theology. (See DIALOGUE, FINALIZATION, MONOLOGICAL, and POLYPHONY) dialogue: Bakhtin's biographers Katerina Clark and Michael Holquist write: "Dialogue is more comprehensively conceived as the extensive set of conditions that are immediately modeled in any actual exchange between two persons but are not exhausted in such an exchange. Ultimately, dialogue means communication between simultaneous differences."[8] If reference to a "set of conditions" makes dialogue sound like a sociolinguistic concept—which it is, on one level—that can be balanced against Clark and Holquist's evocative phrase that Bakhtin's work is about "the mystery of the one and the many" (1). Dialogue includes not only those who are addressing each other in some form of conversation, but also the other voices that speech necessarily and endlessly evokes. Dialogue implies an ethical demand for openness to the difference of the other, both recognizing what is different and also respecting the need to sustain that difference, not assimilate or finalize it. (See FINALIZATION, GENRE, HORIZON, and MONOLOGICAL)

emplotment: In the most general sense, emplotment means shaping events to fit a plot structure: focusing attention on some things and leaving out others; attributing an origin to events and showing how they lead to an ending; making the point of view of particular characters central to how events are understood; and so on. In the active sense developed especially by Cheryl Mattingly, emplotment means proposing a plot that will affect how future events are anticipated and how events are understood as they unfold.[9] The presupposition of emplotment is that life has an interpretive plasticity: what happens can be understood in diverse ways, and anticipations of what will happen become self-fulfilling prophecies, affecting what does happen. Brian Boyd underscores the evolutionary advantage of emplotting future possibilities: "Stories help us to explore possibility as well as actuality, effortlessly and even playfully, and that capacity makes all the difference."[10]

fabrication mechanism: Bruno Latour's term for whatever brings about the assembling of groups. Latour's principal example is the *spokesperson* who fabricates the group—figuratively knitting together its disparate strands—by presenting a common voice that is understood to be speaking the collective judgment and purpose of the group. Following Latour's understanding of groups as perpetually in the process of formation, fabrication mechanisms both accomplish that forming or assembling, and make it appear as if the group's existence was required by some immanent principle of resemblance, rather than being achieved by the efforts of particular persons.[11] Socio-narratology proposes that stories are potent fabrication mechanisms within collectives, from families to nations.

finalize, finalization: From the writing of Bakhtin, to finalize is to claim to speak the last word, especially about who another person can be. Finalization terminates dialogue, because the other is left with nothing to say; the other can be nothing more than what the finalization states he or she is. (See DIALOGUE, MONOLOGICAL) genre: In literary terms, the general types of stories, principally comedy, tragedy, romance, and satire. Nonliterary genres include jokes, journalism, court testimony, and personal anecdotes. Listeners' recognition of a story's genre shapes their expectations for what will happen and how to respond. A character falling down is funny in a comedy, not so in a melodrama. To misunderstand the genre is to miss the point of the story.

Summarizing Bakhtin's idea of *speech genres*, David Morris writes: "Speech genres denote all the formal and informal—pure or mixed—codes that allow us to understand and to construct individual utterances, from legal briefs and government documents to jokes, postcards, papal bulls, football cheers, and letters of recommendation . . . Like texts, voices communicate only by means of genres that impose loose or strict demands on speakers. Speech genres depend, moreover, on the existence of specific discourse communities. A football cheer is meaningless in a culture without sport."[12] Morris adds that speech genres "assure that there is never simply a voice speaking" (33), by which he means a *single* voice.

Because virtually every story is told in recognizable genres, any single voice participates in the multiple voices that have shaped the expectations those genres carry. Most important, genres are not simply conventions that simplify the reciprocal tasks of composing stories and understanding them. Genres "shape the substance of what is said," Morris writes (33). This shaping is often contested, as in the "genre wars" discussed in chapter 5, with reference to Philip Smith's analysis of stories that precipitate entry into war. Which genre best represents certain events is a principal issue of narrative contest.

habitus: A term used by philosophers and social theorists throughout the twentieth century (the same word is both singular and plural), but most fully developed in the sociology of Pierre Bourdieu. Central features of Bourdieu's various definitions of habitus are that (a) habitus refers to tastes and *predispositions*; what people are predisposed to not only like but feel appropriate eating, wearing, or doing; what affirms being the kind of people they believe themselves to be; (b) habitus is embodied early in life and persists; thus Bourdieu refers to it as *durable*; (c) habitus is *transposable*, meaning that an individual will be guided by the same habitus despite being in situations that are far removed from the conditions of original habitus formation and that may reward different predispositions; (d) habitus is a tacit resource that structures how life is experienced; Bourdieu calls it a *structuring structure*; (e) habitus is the basis of intentions but does not presuppose "a conscious aiming at ends or an express mastery of the operations necessary in order to attain them";[13] habitus thus predisposes a volition toward certain ends but is not a conscious strategy; (f) just as habitus can be goal oriented without being consciously strategic, it is both objective—acquired from and most successful within specific social locations—and subjective, *felt* by persons as embodied predispositions.

Bourdieu describes how habitus is embodied as predisposition: "He knows [the world], in a sense, too well, without objectifying distance, takes it for granted, precisely because he is caught up in it, bound up with it; he inhabits it like a garment [*un habit*] or a familiar habitat. He feels at home in the world because the world is also in him."[14] But the dark side of a person knowing the world "too well" is how habitus can be a precondition for inequality within ostensibly merit-based social systems: "In what might be called the Don Quixote effect, dispositions are out of line with the field and with the 'collective expectations' which are constitutive of its normality" (160). Achievement-oriented systems practice symbolic violence when they attribute the failures of those whose habitus is "out of line with the field" to those persons as individually responsible selves—which every human is, but only within the structuring structures of his or her habitus.

However durable habitus is— and Bourdieu argues that a lifetime of sociological research affirmed its durability is robust—this durability *never equates to necessity* or predetermination: "Dispositions do not lead in a determinate way to a determinate action" (149). Habitus is constantly changing, albeit slowly, and changes in habitus can be willed. One great plot of the nineteenth-century novel is the protagonist, typically but not necessarily a young man, who changes his habitus with more or less intention and success; for example, Pip in Charles Dickens's *Great Expectations*. Bourdieu was unwilling to make too much of his own biography, but his own career exemplifies the malleability of habitus.[15]

The idea of *narrative habitus*, developed in chapter 2, is my own adaptation of Bourdieu's concept of habitus. The core elements of narrative habitus are knowing a corpus of stories; feeling comfortable telling and hearing certain stories (and not others); and sharing with others a sense of where events in a story are likely to lead. The issue is not only expectations for how plots develop in stories, but also expectations for how people ought to emplot their lives. (See EMPLOTMENT)

hermeneutics: Most simply, the philosophical study of interpretation. Hans-Georg Gadamer (1900–2002) defined *hermeneutics* as "the art of understanding texts," with *texts* comprising aesthetic objects including visual arts, other persons, and written texts, especially historical documents.[16] For Gadamer, to encounter a text is necessarily to interpret: "Everything written is, in fact, in a special way the object of hermeneutics" (356). But hermeneutics has multiple versions.

Nineteenth-century hermeneutics sought interpretive certainty, especially with respect to biblical texts. Twentieth-century hermeneutics emphasizes *suspicion* of any interpretive certainty, recognizing that an interpreter can never stand outside a tradition and its prejudgments, or as Gadamer provocatively calls them, prejudices. Gadamer summarizes: "This radical suspicion was inaugurated by Nietzsche and had its most striking instances in the critique of ideology on the one hand and of psychoanalysis on the other. Now it is necessary to examine the relationship between traditional hermeneutics [seeking and claiming interpretive certainty] and this radical form of inter-

pretation, which is almost at the opposite end of the spectrum of interpretation—because it challenges the claims to validity of ideas and ideologies."[17]

The problem of suspicion, in my words, is that interpretation is obscured
either way: if the object is within the interpreter's horizons, then interpretation is blurred by familiarity; interpretation takes too much for granted.
If the object is outside the interpreter's horizons, then distance blurs interpretation; the object depends on presuppositions that the interpreter cannot
grasp. However real these issues, interpretation proceeds both within and
across horizons, in part because horizons are never fixed. (See HORIZON)

horizon: In phenomenological usage, the background against which anything is
known, including how it is first recognized as knowable. Alfred Schutz pairs
"horizons of interest" with "perspective of relevance," both affecting what sort
of interest a person takes in an object.[18] In Hans-Georg Gadamer's hermeneutics, the problem becomes the possibility of mutual understanding between
two—often a person and a text, but also two persons—that have different
horizons. The contentious point is how close those separate horizons can or
should move to what Gadamer calls *fusion*.

Understanding, on Gadamer's account, is first determined by *prejudices*:
"They constitute, then, the horizon of a particular present, for they represent that beyond which it is impossible to see."[19] Yet seeing beyond one's own
horizon is not entirely impossible, because while the horizon "embraces us
as the questioners who have responded to the word that has been handed
down," we questioners also experience what Gadamer calls "the openness of
its questionableness" in which a tradition opens to question (337). "A horizon
is not a rigid frontier," Gadamer emphasizes, "but something that moves with
one and invites one to advance further" (217). His imagination of the horizon
moving with the interpreter, as interpretation progresses, and of the horizon
inviting further movement suggest that hermeneutics is not some specialized
activity for academics, but the human calling of mutual understanding.

Hermeneutic inquiry moves toward seeing beyond the original horizon
(see 269). Gadamer's metaphor describing the result is religious, even mystical: "To reach an understanding with one's partner in a dialogue is not merely
a matter of total self-expression and the successful assertion of one's own
point of view, but a transformation into a communion, in which *we do not
remain what we were*" (341, emphases added). *Horizon*, then, is reconstituted
through the active process of hermeneutic interpretation: "The horizon of
understanding cannot be limited either by what the writer had originally in
mind, or by the horizon of the person to whom the text was originally addressed" (356).

Horizon seems to be as much the telos of hermeneutics—the end state
to which interpretation aspires that is always immanent in the interpretive
encounter—as it is the precondition of consciousness caught in its initial
prejudices but invited to movement. Gadamer describes this telos: "This placing of ourselves is not the empathy of one individual for another, nor is it the

application to another person of our own criteria, but it always involves the attainment of a higher universality that overcomes, not only our own particularity, but also that of the other . . . To acquire a horizon means that one learns to look beyond what is close at hand—not in order to look away from it, but to see it better within a larger whole and in truer proportion" (272).

interpellation: The process in which people are called to be particular kinds of *subjects*: that is, students, patients, soldiers, felons, or leaders. For the Marxist philosopher Louis Althusser, who coined this term, interpellation expresses and enacts ideology: "I shall then suggest that ideology 'acts' or 'functions' in such a way that it 'recruits' subjects among the individuals (it recruits them all), or 'transforms' the individuals into subjects (it transforms them all) by that very precise operation which I have called *interpellation* or hailing, and which can be imagined along the lines of the most commonplace everyday police (or other) hailing: 'Hey, you there!'"[20]

The subject hears him- or herself designated and cannot resist the hailing; Althusser then asks why. After considerable argument, his core answer is that "the individual is interpellated as a (free) subject in order that he shall submit freely to the commandments of the Subject . . . in order that he shall make gestures and action of his subjection 'all by himself'" (182, original emphases omitted). The patient in a medical waiting room freely responds when his or her name is called, submitting freely to "the Subject," which in that case is medicine in the persona of the physician; or the student answers "Here" when his or her name is called in class. The dilemma, on Althusser's account (which owes much to the psychoanalyst Jacques Lacan), is that a person cannot be a subject in the sense of a free subjectivity without also being subjected to some greater Subject. If a person does not respond to some "Hey, you" interpellations, then who can that person be?

intertextual: Charlotte Linde describes intertextuality as allowing narrative analysis "to investigate the relation of a story to a prior story, particularly a culturally privileged story."[21] Linde continues: "The focus will be on the ways in which speakers take on these prior texts as relevant to their own story and the possible ways in which they can position their own story in relation to it" (169).

Terence Hawkes summarizes the literary understanding of intertextuality: "As Julia Kristeva has pointed out, no 'text' can ever be completely 'free' of other texts. It will be involved in what she has termed the *intertextuality* of all writing."[22] Intertextuality thus implies a never-ending dialogue among texts, each dependent on others to be understandable. Uri Margolin refers to "intertextual echoes and allusions, calling to our minds same-named or similar characters in other literary works."[23]

For socio-narratology, intertextuality includes a reminder that the telling and the comprehension of stories in one genre depend on familiarity with stories in quite different genres. In particular, fictional and nonfiction stories are mutually dependent.

mimesis: Literally, imitation. As developed in aesthetics, the question of mimesis generates a continuum of views about the relationship between reality and its representations, including stories. The Greeks debated how different forms of representation imitate life: "According to Plato, mimesis [imitation by performance] is one of the two ways to convey a *narrative*, the other being *diegesis* or the representation of an action by telling. By this distinction, plays are mimetic and epic poems are diegetic. Aristotle . . . used the term 'mimesis' as simply the imitation of an action and included in it both modes of narrative representation."[24]

Hans-Georg Gadamer (see HERMENEUTICS) shifts the terms of understanding mimesis: "If we renew the original meaning of mimesis, we can free ourselves from the restrictions that the classicist aesthetic of imitation has imposed upon our thought."[25] And, for socio-narratology, free ourselves from assumptions that people's stories about their lives are transparent imitations of those lives. Gadamer continues: "Mimesis does not imply a reference to an original as something other than itself, but means that something meaningful is there as itself" (121).

Gadamer argues, contrary to classical Greek thought, that an act of mimesis can be accurately called a creation (*Gebilde*). "For the word *Gebilde* implies that the manifestation in question has in a strange way transcended the process in which it originated . . . It is set forth in its own appearance as a self-sufficient creation" (126). Thus stories are never pure imitation of life, but always transcend the original events they depict.

Socio-narratology understands stories as more than representations that imitate life; in Gadamer's phrase, "something meaningful is there as itself" (121).

monological: Speech that is single voiced, as opposed to *dialogical* or multivoiced. Monological speech closes itself from response by the other; it asserts rather than engages. A judge delivering a sentence speaks monologically; or, in biblical terms, the Ten Commandments are monological, as is prophecy. In Bakhtin's usage, monological fiction involves authorial intrusions into the consciousness of characters, claiming to know innermost thoughts and motives of which the characters themselves are unaware. The issue is not the validity of what is said about the characters. Rather, the ethical issue is how authorial intrusions model a form of relationship that finalizes the other. The monological author claims authority over the characters, or in my terms, does not allow them to breathe. (See DIALOGUE, FINALIZATION)

narrative habitus: See HABITUS.

narrative identity or selfhood: Alasdair MacIntyre's philosophical account is classic, although it is only one among many differently nuanced versions of narrative identity, reflecting different academic disciplines. Narrative selfhood is twofold, MacIntyre writes. "On the one hand, I am what I may justifiably be taken by others to be in the course of living out a story that runs from my birth to my death."[26] Being known as living out a story means that this story is open to questions, and these questions generate specific stories about one's life: "It is . . . to be open to being asked to give a certain kind of account of what one did or what happened to one or what one witnessed at any earlier point in one's life" (217). Thus for MacIntyre, narrative identity or selfhood implies "the unity of the character which the unity of a narrative requires. Without such unity there would not be subjects of whom stories could be told" (218). Which is true as MacIntyre writes it, but stories would not be very interesting if subjects always already were and remained unified.

The second, complementary aspect of narrative identity is dialogical: "The narrative of any one life is part of an interlocking set of narratives" (218). MacIntyre argues that the self's narrative is knowable only against the background of the stories that a culture makes available (see AUTHENTICITY). From this follows his famous statement that for moral decision-making, the essential question is, "Of what story or stories do I find myself a part?" (216). MacIntyre is clear that we learn through stories not only which identities are available; more fundamentally, we learn what an identity *is*: "It is through hearing stories about wicked step-mothers, lost children, good but misguided kings, wolves that suckle twin boys, youngest sons who receive no inheritance but must make their own way in the world and eldest sons who waste their inheritance on riotous living and go into exile with the swine, that children learn or mislearn both what a child and what a parent is, what the cast of characters may be in the drama into which they have been born and what the ways of the world are . . . Hence there is no way to give us an understanding of any society, including our own, except through the stock of stories which constitute its initial dramatic resources" (ibid.). Narrative identity is as collective as it is personal. (See HABITUS)

narrative/story distinction: As one example, when Karl Marx writes: "The history of all hitherto existing society is the history of class struggles,"[27] that sets in place a narrative. Marx's narrative of class conflict emplots any number of stories about struggles that become understood to be rooted in class. A narrative encompasses any number of times, places, and persons in its sphere of reference. A story of class struggle begins with a character in a specific situation: an oppressed gladiator in ancient Rome, or a medieval peasant in Germany, or a Paris factory worker in 1848. A story develops using the capacities elaborated in chapter 1: suspense, point of view, and so on. None of these capacities are found in Marx's narrative, and therein lies the narrative/story distinction. Marx's statement is *not in itself a story*; as a narrative, it *generates* stories and it marks a similarity between certain stories.

A *narrative* includes multiple stories featuring characters who share some problem or developmental trajectory. The same narrative can generate stories in multiple genres; narratives of class conflict can be tragedies—the ruthless suppression of the Paris commune—or comedies, like Mozart's *Marriage of*

Figaro. A narrative sets parameters within which predictable kinds of things happen for similar reasons. Thus, a narrative might also be described as an immanent principle of causality; for example, classes by Marx's definition inevitably conflict with each other. Narratives make no mention of individual persons; stories depend on characters. *Stories* are about particular people living lives animated by some principle of causality: class conflict, or the tension between fathers and sons, or the human need for true love. Characters fall victim to this immanent principle (tragedy) or triumph over it (comedy).

That said, the words *narrative* and *story* overlap so frequently that sustaining this distinction in consistent usage proves impossible. The important points are that the statement of a narrative, as in Marx, is not in itself a story, and stories can be collected into types of narratives. Chapter 5 provides examples of narrative types from my own work on illness and Anne Harrington's research on mind-body medicine.

narratology: Gerald Prince attributes the original usage of *narratology* (from the French *narratologie*) to Tzvetan Todorov, writing in 1969 as a structuralist critic concerned with the formal elements of literary texts. "Just as linguists aim to establish the grammar of language," Prince writes of early narratology, "narratologists aim to establish the grammar of narrative."[28] Todorov's career progresses from this grammatical interest in narrative to more *socio* issues of history and political ethics. Narratologists also take particular interest in the *competence* required both to tell stories and to receive them. One minimal competence is the capacity for sequencing events. Knowledge of genre and ability to generate suspense are advanced competences.

performative: Any usage of language or other signs that in itself performs an action; that is, words that *do* something. The philosopher J. L. Austin's examples of performative sentences include promises, bets (as in wagers), vows (as in marriages), and christenings (as in naming a ship).[29] In such uses of language, the action is enacted solely by the words, although these words may require particular contextual conditions, such as having a marriage license. The issue for socio-narratology is that stories do not simply represent; their performative capacity brings something original into being. Moreover, stories are *actors.* (See MIMESIS)

point of view: How storytelling positions a listener or viewer to understand the unfolding of events from the perspective of a particular character in the story. Point of view usually, but not always, creates a sympathetic identification of the listener with the character from whose point of view the story is told. Stories can shift the point of view, and narrative tension often depends on differences between points of view. In a classic work of literary analysis, Wayne Booth writes: "In dealing with point of view the novelist must always deal with the individual work: which particular character shall tell this particular story, or part of a story, with what precise degree of reliability, privilege, freedom to comment, and so on. Shall he be given dramatic vividness? Even if the novelist has decided on a narrator who will fit one of the critic's classifications—

'omniscient,' 'first-person,' 'limited omniscient,' 'objective,' 'roving,' 'effaced,' or whatever—his troubles have just begun."[30]

Narrative analysis in social science is too often concerned exclusively with the reliability of what is told, while ignoring the art of the storyteller to employ the different modes of narration that Booth describes. What Booth calls an unreliable narrator is not at all a bad storyteller—that mode of narration solves some problem. Socio-narratological interest is in why a particular mode of narration is chosen, although not necessarily as a conscious strategy, because everyday storytellers are less self-conscious about their art than novelists are, although everyday storytellers often learn from novelists. The socio-narratological question, to paraphrase Booth, is: what kind of troubles is the storyteller responding to by telling the story from the point of view or multiple points of view that are chosen? And complementary to that: How does the storyteller's narrative habitus render the mode of narration, including choices about point of view, an unchosen choice? (See HABITUS) How do the stories that someone knows impose the point of view from which that person lives his or her life?

polyphony: The dialogical capacity of voices to join in a whole, without each sacrificing its distinctiveness. Bakhtin writes: "A plurality of independent and unmerged voices and consciousnesses, a genuine polyphony of fully valid voices is in fact the chief characteristic of Dostoevsky's novels."[31] He further specifies the quality of polyphony as "a plurality of consciousnesses, with equal rights and each with its own world, [that] combine but are not merged in the unity of the event" (6). Polyphony is not, however, always harmonious in the sense of being in agreement. Bakhtin writes of voices as "an eternal harmony of unmerged voices or as their unceasing and irreconcilable quarrel" (30). In such an "unceasing quarrel," the quality of polyphony is the dependence of each voice on the others. An example, detailed in this book's introduction, is Allen Feldman's dual origin stories told by conflicting paramilitary groups in Ireland, each of which requires its counterpart or antagonist, if it is to be a forceful telling.

Polyphony and dialogue are complementary expressions of the human condition for Bakhtin. Wayne Booth describes why humans are creatures of polyphony, and also the ethical ideal embedded in that term: "We come into consciousness speaking a language already permeated with many voices—a social, not a private language. From the beginning we are 'polyglot,' already in process of mastering a variety of social dialects derived from parents, clan, class, religion, and country. We grow in consciousness by taking in more voices . . . Finally we achieve, if we are lucky, a kind of individuality, but it is never a private or autonomous individuality in the western sense; except when we maim ourselves arbitrarily to monologue, we always speak in a chorus of languages. Anyone who has not been maimed . . . respects the fact that each of us is a 'we,' not an 'I.' Polyphony, the miracle of our 'dialogical' lives together, is thus both a fact of life and, in its higher reaches, a value to be pursued endlessly."[32]

resonance: "Through resonance a particular statement in a particular context acquires a universal significance," writes Northrop Frye.[33] "Thus the tremendous vision of a blood-soaked deity treading through the winepress alone in Isaiah 63 is one that has haunted us ever since with its terrible beauty; through 'The Battle Hymn of the Republic' it entered the American consciousness, and a title such as 'The Grapes of Wrath' testifies to its continuing power" (217). Frye concludes: "Such power would be impossible without, first, an original context, and, second, a power of expanding away from that context" (218). Exactly what animates this power of expanding away from the original context remains one of the great mysteries of human consciousness, however carefully Frye elaborates examples of that power at work.

semiotics: The study of signs and how they convey meaning. Much of semiotics involves the classification of different kinds of signs; for example, *icons* are signs that have an analogical relationship to what they signify, such as a stick figure of a person slipping on ice. Debate concerns the relationship between signs and their *referents*, that is, the actual things in the world that the sign refers to. The radical break of Ferdinand de Saussure (1857–1913) was to argue that signs mean by virtue of their relationship to each other; or, a sign's meaning is its difference from other signs, not its relation to a referent in the world.[34]

Later semiotic studies inquire how signs combine to produce meaning, and how combining signs can fabricate a sense that the referents of those signs are actually related to each other in life. An advertisement shows a pristine wilderness, a car, and the word *freedom*, thus exploiting the narrative predisposition of consciousness to create stories that combine those signs. Creating causal connections that are not inherent in the signs themselves can be the genius of storytelling—or its folly.

socio-narratology: Adapting Wayne Booth, socio-narratology is "inquiry into our limited ways of mirroring—and improving—our lives" (see BAKHTIN). Stories mirror lives not only retrospectively, reporting and revising understanding of what has already happened, but also prospectively: stories emplot what may yet happen. Stories are limited by the narrative resources available to the storyteller, especially the limits associated with narrative habitus (see HABITUS). Socio-narratology reflects on those limits in order to expand them. Its objective is not only descriptive but also normative; as Booth says, improving our lives—specifically, improving lives by enhancing human companionship with stories.

Socio-narratology prefers to turn matters of theory over to storytellers, so here is how a trustworthy storyteller, Rahib Alameddine, expresses it: "Uncle Jihad used to say that what happens is of little significance compared with the stories we tell ourselves about what happens. Events matter little, only stories of those events affect us. My father and I may have shared numerous experiences, but, as I was constantly finding out, we rarely shared their stories; we didn't know how to listen to one another."[35] Alameddine's first two sentences express the presuppositions of socio-narratology. Another of Alameddine's characters puts it slightly differently: "Reality never meets our wants, and adjusting both is why we tell stories" (434). But the point of describing a world in which stories of events are what affect people is to enhance the human capacity to share stories so that we can listen to each other—and that kind of *listening* requires more than sharing only experiences.

subject position: In the classic work of Vladimir Propp (1985–1970), each character type has a particular function or "sphere of action" in the story; for example, the *villain* opposes the *hero*; the *donor* or provider gives the hero "a magical agent" necessary to complete the quest; and so forth.[36] Each character is thus positioned by what the story requires. To be a character is to occupy a subject position, which is both a possibility of acting and a restriction to a specific sphere of action.

Contemporary usage of *subject position* reflects interest in how a character in a story is positioned particularly with respect to power—the entitlements or subjugation that attend being that kind of person, as established by pervasive stories. Characters can be positioned as heroic and trustworthy, as victimized, as villainous, and all positions in between. Speaking of a person or a character as a *subject* emphasizes the primacy of how that person is positioned. Poststructuralists emphasize positioning within *discourses*; for example, the discourse of medicine positions subjects as patients and physicians, and it allocates power between them.

The important linkage for socio-narratology is that just as characters are positioned in stories, so people are known in lives made intelligible by those stories. Hilde Lindemann shows a contemporary concern with subject position when she writes: "Master narratives are often archetypal, consisting of stock plots and readily recognizable character types, and we use them not only to make sense of our experience but also to justify what we do."[37] Lindemann's interest is in how some master narratives impute damaging identities to certain "recognizable character types," and how people who have been thus characterized tell counterstories to resist and repair these identities. The subject of the counterstory claims a different subject position from that asserted by the original narrative. (See INTERPELLATION)

symbiosis: A relation of mutual benefit between two organisms. At the extreme, the existence of one or both depends on the other. Its Greek root word is *sumbios*, which can be translated as "companion."

trouble: What gets a plot moving; not necessarily the first thing told in a story, but what precipitates the action. Jerome Bruner writes: "Kenneth Burke proposed more than a half century ago that, at a minimum, a story (fictional or actual) requires an Agent who performs an Action to achieve a Goal in a recognizable Setting by the use of certain Means—his dramatistic Pentad, as he called his grammar. What drives a story is a misfit between the elements of the Pentad: Trouble."[38] Bruner's example is Agamemnon returning home from the Trojan War to his wife Clytemnestra, "after he had sacrificed their daughter Iphigenia" (34). Their reunion is a definite misfit; nothing but Trouble can ensue. Burke's emphasis on Trouble goes back to Aristotle's concept of *peripeteia*, translated as "reversal of fortune."[39] There stories begin.

Index

accounts (accounting for action), 30, 169n38, 191

actant, 191–92

Alcoholics Anonymous, 135, 183n28. *See also* recovery narrative

Almaddine, Rahib (*The Storyteller*, or *The Hakawati*), 202–3

Althusser, Louis. *See* interpellation

Améry, Jean, 146

Archibald, Jo-ann, 23–25, 39, 52–53, 86–87, 102–3, 106, 108–11, 174n31

Aristotle: *peripeteia* (reversal of fortune), 204; *phronesis* (practical wisdom), 166n35

Armstrong, Jeannette, 110

Atanarjuat: The Fast Runner, 94–95, 105, 180n25

Austin, J. L., 171n57, 200

authenticity, 11–12, 192

"The baby cried. The mommy picked it up" (Sacks), 26, 33, 38, 49, 82, 109

Bakhtin, Mikhail, 13, 41, 60, 71–72, 83, 97–101, 108, 128–29, 164n12, 179n23, 192–93, 201. *See also* dialogue; polyphony

Banaszynski, Jacqui, 147–48, 150

Barthes, Roland, 164n12, 166n32

Basso, Keith, 38–40

Bayard, Pierre, 37, 49, 54–58, 94, 176n18

Beowulf, 81–82

Bérubé, Michael, 75

Blake, William, 153–54

Bleicher, Josef, 94

Bohannan, Laura, 55, 179n21

Booth, Wayne, 13, 15–16, 23, 192, 200–203

Boyd, Brian, 13, 21–22, 27, 31–32, 82–83, 94, 164n15, 168n27, 171n1, 193; evocriticism, 13; "theory of mind," 86

boundaries, in and of stories, 69–70, 80, 142; as categories, 156

Bourdieu, Pierre, 25, 95, 172n5; on capital and field, 182n17. *See also* habitus

Brooks, David, 24

Bruner, Jerome, 22, 28–29, 47, 172n12, 203–4

Burke, Kenneth, 28, 129, 169n29, 203–4

Bury, Mike, 115

Cervantes (*Don Quixote*), 23

character, 29–31

Chambers, Tod, 164n10

Charon, Rita, 24, 164n12

"Christmas Eve" (Galeano), 4–5, 7, 27–28, 30, 33, 37, 40, 43, 50, 91–93, 146

Colvin, Claudette, 132, 183n25

companion (metaphor), 42–43, 157, 160

Coyote, 64

"Coyote Searching for the Bone Needle," 39

"Coyote and the Shadow People," 49–51, 173n18

Critchley, Simon, 143

critical theory, 175n7

Crow and Weasel (Barry Lopez), 53

Cruikshank, Julie, 17, 47–48, 69, 78–83, 172n6, 182n17

Crumb, R. (*The Book of Genesis*), 186n19

elements of, 26–28; making narratable, 75, 92; as material semiotic companions, 42–43, 110; as memory, 82–85, 90; morality of, 36–37; openness to interpretation, 34–35, 62, 132–34, 148; out of control, 35–36; as performative, 40, 75, 82, 89, 171n57, 200; as praxis, 143; "process of authorization" (Portelli), 91; as recipient designed, 90; responsive, 134; as selection/evaluation devices, 46; shape-shifting, 39, 49; silences in, 80, 107; suspenseful, 32–33, 117; symbiotic, 37–39, 123, 126, 141, 146; as "symbolic bricolage" (Smith), 139; trickster quality, 87, 107; as witness, 76; work of, 48, 126, 136. *See also* boundaries; point of view; resonance; subject position; truth
subject position, 51, 203
symbiosis, 37–38, 123, 126, 141, 146, 157, 203

Taylor, Charles, 192
technical accounts (Tilly), 169n32, 191
Tilly, Charles, 29, 40, 191; technical accounts, 169n32, 191
tricksters, 45–48, 63, 77; and luck, 158–59. *See also* Coyote stories; Homer; Loki; Samson

Todorov, Tzvetan, 149–52, 156–57, 166n32, 200
Tolstoy, Leo, 8–10, 15, 21–23, 30, 42–43, 47, 50, 52, 56–57, 69, 76–77, 97, 146
Toulmin, Stephen, 157, 186n24
Trouble (capacity of stories), 28–29, 64, 129, 203–4
truth, 40–41, 88–93, 145, 149, 178n8, 178n12
Truth and Reconciliation Commission, 59–60
typologies. *See under* stories

unfinalized, *See* finalization
Unsworth, Barry, 1, 104–5

validation, 110
verification of stories. *See* truth
Virgil (*The Aeneid*), 3
Volosinov, V. N., 83

War and Peace. See Tolstoy, Leo
The Warrior Woman. See Kingston, Maxine Hong
White, Ellen, 25
Williams, Gareth, 114–17
Waletzky, Joshua, 26
Weber, Max, 175n5
White, David Gordon, 174n35
Wilson, Edward O., 83
Wright, Edmond, 170n44